blue
rider
press

But What If We're Wrong?

Also by Chuck Klosterman

Nonfiction

Fargo Rock City: A Heavy Metal Odyssey in Rural Nörth Daköta

Sex, Drugs, and Cocoa Puffs: A Low Culture Manifesto

Killing Yourself to Live: 85% of a True Story

Chuck Klosterman IV: A Decade of Curious People and Dangerous Ideas

Eating the Dinosaur

I Wear the Black Hat: Grappling with Villains (Real and Imagined)

Fiction

Downtown Owl

The Visible Man

This is not a collection of essays.

It might look like a collection of essays, and—
at times—it might feel like a collection of essays.
But that is not the intention.

Obviously, you can read this book however
you choose. I can't demand people read this book
in sequential order, nor can I stop anyone from
skipping around and reading random chapters in
whatever insane pattern they desire. You can read
it backward, if that's your preference. But it will
make more sense if you don't.

This is not a collection of essays.

But What If We're Wrong?

■ *Thinking About the Present As If It Were the Past*

Chuck Klosterman

BLUE RIDER PRESS | *New York*

blue
rider
press

An imprint of Penguin Random House LLC
375 Hudson Street
New York, New York 10014

Copyright © 2016 by Chuck Klosterman
Penguin supports copyright. Copyright fuels creativity, encourages diverse
voices, promotes free speech, and creates a vibrant culture. Thank you for
buying an authorized edition of this book and for complying with copyright
laws by not reproducing, scanning, or distributing any part of it in any
form without permission. You are supporting writers and allowing
Penguin to continue to publish books for every reader.

Blue Rider Press is a registered trademark and its colophon
is a trademark of Penguin Random House LLC

ISBN 9780399184123

Printed in the United States of America
10 9 8 7 6 5 4 3 2 1

BOOK DESIGN BY NICOLE LAROCHE

For Silas and Hope

If what I say now seems to you to be very reasonable,
then I'll have failed completely.

—Arthur C. Clarke, speaking in the year 1964, attempting to
explain what the world might be like in the year 2000

Contents

I've spent most of my life being wrong.

Not about everything. Just about most things.

I mean, sometimes I get stuff right. I married the right person. I've never purchased life insurance as an investment. The first time undrafted free agent Tony Romo led a touchdown drive against the Giants on *Monday Night Football*, I told my roommate, "I think this guy will have a decent career." At a New Year's Eve party in 2008, I predicted Michael Jackson would unexpectedly die within the next twelve months, an anecdote I shall casually recount at every New Year's party I'll ever attend for the rest of my life. But these are the exceptions. It is far, far easier for me to catalog the various things I've been wrong about: My insistence that I would never own a cell phone. The time I wagered $100—against $1—that Barack Obama would never become president (or even receive the Democratic nomination). My three-week obsession over the looming Y2K crisis, prompting me to hide bundles of cash, bottled water, and Oreo cookies throughout my one-bedroom apartment. At this point, my wrongness doesn't even surprise me. I almost anticipate it. Whenever people tell me I'm wrong about something, I might disagree with them in conversation, but—in my mind—I assume their accusation is justified, even when I'm relatively certain they're wrong, too.

Yet these failures are small potatoes.

These micro-moments of wrongness are personal: I assumed the answer to something was "A," but the true answer was "B" or "C" or "D." Reasonable parties can disagree on the unknowable, and the passage of time slowly proves one party to be slightly more reasonable than the other. The stakes are low. If I'm wrong about something specific, it's (usually) my own fault, and someone else is (usually, but not totally) right.

But what about the things we're *all* wrong about?

What about ideas that are so accepted and internalized that we're not even in a position to question their fallibility? These are ideas so ingrained in the collective consciousness that it seems foolhardy to even wonder if they're potentially untrue. Sometimes these seem like questions only a child would ask, since children aren't paralyzed by the pressures of consensus and common sense. It's a dissonance that creates the most unavoidable of intellectual paradoxes: When you ask smart people if they believe there are major ideas currently accepted by the culture at large that will eventually be proven false, they will say, "Well, of course. There must be. That phenomenon has been experienced by every generation who's ever lived, since the dawn of human history." Yet offer those same people a laundry list of contemporary ideas that might fit that description, and they'll be tempted to reject them all.

It is impossible to examine questions we refuse to ask. These are the big potatoes.

Like most people, I like to think of myself as a skeptical person. But I'm pretty much in the tank for gravity. It's the force most recognized as perfunctorily central to everything we understand about everything else. If an otherwise well-executed argument contradicts the principles of gravity, the argument is inevitably altered to make sure that it does not. The fact that I'm not a physicist makes my adherence to gravity especially unyielding, since I don't know anything about gravity that wasn't told to me by someone else. My confidence in gravity is absolute, and I believe this will be true until the day I die (and if someone subsequently throws my dead body out of a window, I believe my corpse's rate of acceleration will be 9.8 m/s^2).

And I'm probably wrong.

Maybe not completely, but partially. And maybe not today, but eventually.

"There is a very, very good chance that our understanding of gravity will not be the same in five hundred years. In fact, that's the one arena where I would think that most of our contemporary evidence is circumstantial, and that the way we think about gravity will be very different." These are the words of Brian Greene, a theoretical physicist at Columbia University who writes books with titles like *Icarus at the Edge of Time*. He's the kind of physicist famous enough to guest star on a CBS sitcom, assuming that sitcom is *The Big Bang Theory*. "For two hundred years, Isaac Newton had gravity down. There was almost no change in our thinking until 1907. And then from 1907 to 1915, Einstein radically changes our understanding of gravity: No longer is gravity just a force, but a warping of space and time. And now we realize quantum mechanics must have an impact on how we describe gravity within very short distances. So there's all this work that really starts to pick up in the 1980s, with all these new ideas about how gravity would work in the microscopic realm. And then string theory comes along, trying to understand how gravity behaves on a small scale, and that gives us a description—which we don't know to be right or wrong—that equates to a quantum theory of gravity. Now, that requires extra dimensions of space. So the understanding of gravity starts to have radical implications for our understanding of reality. And now there are folks, inspired by these findings, who are trying to rethink gravity itself. They suspect gravity might not even be a fundamental force, but an emergent[1] force. So I do think—and I think many would agree—that gravity is the least stable of our ideas, and the most ripe for a major shift."

If that sounds confusing, don't worry—I was confused when Greene explained it to me as I sat in his office (and he explained it to me twice). There are essential components to physics and math that I will never understand in any functional way, no matter what

----

1 This means that gravity might just be a manifestation of other forces—not a force itself, but the peripheral result of something else. Greene's analogy was the idea of temperature: Our skin can sense warmth on a hot day, but "warmth" is not some independent thing that exists on its own. Warmth is just the consequence of invisible atoms moving around very fast, creating the *sensation* of temperature. We feel it, but it's not really there. So if gravity were an emergent force, it would mean that gravity isn't the central power pulling things to the Earth, but the tangential consequence of something else we can't yet explain. We feel it, but it's not there. It would almost make the whole idea of "gravity" a semantic construction.

I read or how much time I invest. A post-gravity world is beyond my comprehension. But the concept of a post-gravity world helps me think about something else: It helps me understand the pre-gravity era. And I don't mean the days before Newton published *Principia* in 1687, or even that period from the late 1500s when Galileo was (allegedly) dropping balls off the Leaning Tower of Pisa and inadvertently inspiring the Indigo Girls. By the time those events occurred, the notion of gravity was already drifting through the scientific ether. Nobody had pinned it down, but the mathematical intelligentsia knew Earth was rotating around the sun in an elliptical orbit (and that *something* was making this happen). That was around four hundred years ago. I'm more fixated on how life was another four hundred years before that. Here was a period when the best understanding of why objects did not spontaneously float was some version of what Aristotle had argued more than a thousand years prior: He believed all objects craved their "natural place," and that this place was the geocentric center of the universe, and that the geocentric center of the universe was Earth. In other words, Aristotle believed that a dropped rock fell to the earth because rocks belonged on earth and wanted to be there.

So let's consider the magnitude of this shift: Aristotle—arguably the greatest philosopher who ever lived—writes the book *Physics* and defines his argument. His view exists unchallenged for almost two thousand years. Newton (history's most meaningful mathematician, even to this day) eventually watches an apocryphal apple fall from an apocryphal tree and inverts the entire human understanding of why the world works as it does. Had this been explained to those people in the fourteenth century with no understanding of science—in other words, pretty much everyone else alive in the fourteenth century—Newton's explanation would have seemed way, way crazier than what they currently believed: Instead of claiming that Earth's existence defined reality and that there was something essentialist about why rocks acted like rocks, Newton was advocating an invisible, imperceptible force field that somehow anchored the moon in place.

We now know ("know") that Newton's concept was correct. Humankind had been collectively, *objectively* wrong for roughly twenty centuries. Which provokes three semi-related questions:

- If mankind could believe something false was objectively true for two thousand years, why do we reflexively assume that our current understanding of gravity—which we've embraced for a mere three hundred fifty years—will somehow exist forever?

- Is it possible that this type of problem has simply been solved? What if Newton's answer really is—more or less— the *final* answer, and the only one we will ever need? Because if that is true, it would mean we're at the end of a process that has defined the experience of being alive. It would mean certain intellectual quests would no longer be necessary.

- Which statement is more reasonable to make: "I believe gravity exists" or "I'm 99.9 percent certain that gravity exists"? Certainly, the second statement is *safer.* But if we're going to acknowledge even the slightest possibility of being wrong about gravity, we're pretty much giving up on the possibility of being right about anything at all.

There's a popular website that sells books (and if you purchased this particular book, consumer research suggests there's a 41 percent chance you ordered it from this particular site). Book sales constitute only about 7 percent of this website's total sales, but books are the principal commodity this enterprise is known for. Part of what makes the site successful is its user-generated content; consumers are given the opportunity to write reviews of their various purchases, even if they never actually consumed the book they're critiquing. Which is amazing, particularly if you want to read negative, one-star reviews of Herman Melville's *Moby-Dick*.

"Pompous, overbearing, self-indulgent, and insufferable. This is the worst book I've ever read," wrote one dissatisfied customer in 2014. "Weak narrative, poor structure, incomplete plot threads, ¾ of the chapters are extraneous, and the author often confuses himself with the protagonist. One chapter is devoted to the fact that whales don't have noses. Another is on the color white." Interestingly, the only other purchase this person elected to review was a Hewlett-Packard printer that can also send faxes, which he awarded two stars.

I can't dispute this person's distaste for *Moby-Dick*. I'm sure he did hate reading it. But his choice to state this opinion in public—almost entirely devoid of critical context, unless you count his take on the HP printer—is more meaningful than the opinion itself. Publicly attacking *Moby-Dick* is shorthand for arguing that what we're socialized to believe about art is fundamentally questionable. Taste is subjective, but some subjective opinions are casually expressed the same way we articulate principles of math or science. There isn't an ongoing cultural debate over the merits of *Moby-Dick*: It's not merely an epic novel, but a transformative literary innovation that helps define how novels are supposed to be viewed. Any discussion about the clichéd concept of "the Great American Novel" begins with this book. The work itself is not above criticism, but no individual criticism has any impact; at this point, attacking *Moby-Dick* only reflects the contrarianism of the critic. We all start from the supposition that *Moby-Dick* is accepted as self-evidently awesome, including (and perhaps especially) those who disagree with that assertion.

So how did this happen?

Melville publishes *Moby-Dick* in 1851, basing his narrative on the real-life 1839 account of a murderous sperm whale nicknamed "Mocha Dick." The initial British edition is around nine hundred pages. Melville, a moderately successful author at the time of the novel's release, assumes this book will immediately be seen as a masterwork. This is his premeditated intention throughout the writing process. But the reviews are mixed, and some are contemptuous ("it repels the reader" is the key takeaway from one of the very first reviews in the London *Spectator*). It sells poorly—at the time of Melville's death, total sales hover below five thousand copies. The failure ruins Melville's life: He becomes an alcoholic and a poet, and eventually a customs inspector. When he dies destitute in 1891, one has to assume his perspective on *Moby-Dick* is something along the lines of "Well, I guess that didn't work. Maybe I should have spent fewer pages explaining how to tie complicated knots." For the next thirty years, nothing about the reception of this book changes. But then World War I happens, and—somehow, and for reasons that can't be totally explained[2]—modernists living in postwar America start to view literature through a different lens. There is a Melville revival. The concept of what a novel is supposed to accomplish shifts in his direction and amplifies with each passing generation, eventually prompting people (like the 2005 director of Columbia University's American studies program) to classify *Moby-Dick* as "the most ambitious book ever conceived by an American writer." Pundits and cranks can disagree with that assertion, but no one cares if they do. Melville's place in history is secure, almost as if he were an explorer or an inventor: When the prehistoric remains of a previously unknown predatory whale were discovered in Peru in 2010, the massive creature was eventually named *Livyatan melvillei*. A century after his death, Melville gets his own extinct super-whale named after him, in tribute to a book that commercially tanked. That's an interesting kind of career.

Now, there's certainly a difference between collective, objective wrongness (e.g., misunderstanding gravity for twenty centuries) and collective, subjective wrongness (e.g., not caring about *Moby-Dick* for seventy-five years). The machinations of the transitions are completely different. Yet both scenarios hint at a practical

---

2 The qualities that spurred this rediscovery can, arguably, be quantified: The isolation and brotherhood the sailors experience mirrors the experience of fighting in a war, and the battle against a faceless evil whale could be seen as a metaphor for the battle against the faceless abstraction of evil Germany. But the fact that these details can be quantified is still not a satisfactory explanation as to why *Moby-Dick* became the specific novel that was selected and elevated. It's not like *Moby-Dick* is the only book that could have served this role.

reality and a modern problem. The practical reality is that any present-tense version of the world is unstable. What we currently consider to be true—both objectively and subjectively—is habitually provisional. But the modern problem is that reevaluating what we consider "true" is becoming increasingly difficult. Superficially, it's become easier for any one person to dispute the status quo: Everyone has a viable platform to criticize *Moby-Dick* (or, I suppose, a mediocre HP printer). If there's a rogue physicist in Winnipeg who doesn't believe in gravity, he can self-publish a book that outlines his argument and potentially attract a larger audience than *Principia* found during its first hundred years of existence. But increasing the capacity for the reconsideration of ideas is not the same as actually changing those ideas (or even *allowing* them to change by their own momentum).

We live in an age where virtually no content is lost and virtually all content is shared. The sheer amount of information about every current idea makes those concepts difficult to contradict, particularly in a framework where public consensus has become the ultimate arbiter of validity. In other words, we're starting to behave as if we've reached the end of human knowledge. And while that notion is undoubtedly false, the sensation of certitude it generates is paralyzing.

In her book *Being Wrong*, author Kathryn Schulz spends a few key pages on the concept of "naïve realism." Schulz notes that while there are few conscious proponents of naïve realism, "that doesn't mean there are no naïve realists." I would go a step further than Schulz; I suspect most conventionally intelligent people are naïve realists, and I think it might be the defining intellectual quality of this era. The straightforward definition of naïve realism doesn't seem that outlandish: It's a theory that suggests the world is exactly as it appears. Obviously, this viewpoint creates a lot of opportunity for colossal wrongness (e.g., "The sun appears to move across the sky, so the sun must be orbiting Earth"). But my personal characterization of naïve realism is wider and more insidious. I think it operates as the manifestation of two ingrained beliefs:

1. "When considering any question, I must be rational and logical, to the point of dismissing any unverifiable data as preposterous," and
2. "When considering any question, I'm going to assume that the information we currently have is all the information that will ever be available."

Here's an extreme example: the possibility of life after death. When considered rationally, there is no justification for believing that anything happens to anyone upon the moment of his or her death. There is no reasonable counter to the prospect of nothingness. Any anecdotal story about "floating toward a white light" or Shirley MacLaine's past life on Atlantis or the details in *Heaven Is for Real* are automatically (and justifiably) dismissed by any secular intellectual. Yet this wholly logical position discounts the overwhelming likelihood that we currently don't know something critical about the experience of life, much less the ultimate conclusion to that experience. There are so many things we don't know about energy, or the way energy is transferred, or why energy (which can't be created or destroyed) exists at all. We can't truly conceive the conditions of a multidimensional reality, even though we're (probably) already living inside one. We have a limited understanding of consciousness. We have a limited understanding of time, and of the perception of time, and of the possibility that all time is happening at once. So while it seems unrealistic to seriously consider the prospect of life after death, it seems equally naïve to assume that our contemporary understanding of this phenomenon is remotely complete. We have no idea what we don't know, or what we'll eventually learn, or what might be true despite our perpetual inability to comprehend what that truth is.

It's impossible to understand the world of today until today has become tomorrow.

This is no brilliant insight, and only a fool would disagree. But it's remarkable how habitually this truth is ignored. We constantly pretend our perception of the present day will not seem ludicrous in retrospect, simply because there doesn't appear to be any other option. Yet there *is* another option, and the option is this: We must start from the premise that—in all likelihood—we are already wrong. And not "wrong" in the sense that we are examining questions and coming to incorrect conclusions, because most of our conclusions are reasoned and coherent. The problem is with the questions themselves.

A Brief Examination as to Why This Book Is Hopeless (and a Briefer Examination as to Why It Might Not Be)

The library in my sixth-grade classroom contained many books that no one ever touched. It did, however, include one book that my entire class touched compulsively: *The Book of Lists*. Published in 1977, *The Book of Lists* was exactly what it purported to be—521 pages of lists, presented by *The People's Almanac* and compiled by three writers (David Wallechinsky, his sister Amy, and their father Irving). This was a book you didn't really *read*, per se; you just thumbed through it at random and tried to memorize information that was both deliberately salacious and generally unencumbered by the fact-checking process (I still recall the book's list of famous homosexuals, which included only three rock musicians—Janis Joplin, Elton John, and David Bowie, the last of whom was married to the same woman for more than twenty years). Sequels to the book were released in 1980 and 1983. What I did not realize, however, was that the creators of *The Book of Lists* also published a similar work titled *The Book of Predictions*, in 1980. (I stumbled across it in the late nineties, in the living room of a friend who liked to buy bizarre out-of-print books to peruse while stoned.) Like its more famous predecessor, *The Book of Predictions* describes itself: It's several hundred pages of futurists and scientists (and—somewhat distractingly—psychics) making unsystematic predictions about life on Earth in the coming fifty years.

On those rare occasions when *The Book of Predictions* is referenced today, the angle is inevitably mocking: The most eye-catching predictions are always the idiotic ones. As it turns out, there has not been a murder in outer space committed by a jealous astronaut, which is what lawyer F. Lee Bailey predicted would occur in 1990 (and evidently struck Bailey as more plausible than the possibility of defending a jealous Hall of Fame running back for an earthbound murder in 1994). According to population expert Dr. Paul Ehrlich, we should currently be experiencing a dystopian dreamscape where "survivors envy the dead," which seems true only when I look at Twitter. Yet some of the book's predictions are the opposite of terrible: Several speculators accurately estimated the world population in 2010 would be around seven billion. A handful of technology experts made remarkably realistic projections about an imminent international computer network. Charlie Gillett, a British musicologist best known for writing the first comprehensive history of rock music (1970's *The Sound of the City*), somehow managed to outline the fall of the music industry in detail without any possible knowledge of MP3s or file sharing.[1] Considering how difficult it is to predict what will

----

1 "The days of buying records are already numbered," Gillett begins. "The current process is inefficient, cumbersome and expensive, with musicians transferring their noises onto tape, somebody else transferring the tape to disc, and the

still be true a year from now, any level of accuracy on a fifty-year guess feels like a win.

Yet what is most instructive about *The Book of Predictions* is not the things that proved true. It's the bad calculations that must have seemed totally justifiable—perhaps even conservative—at the time of publication. And the quality all these reasonable failures share is an inability to accept that the status quo is temporary. *The Book of Predictions* was released in 1980, so this mostly means a failure to imagine a world where the United States and the Soviet Union were not on the cusp of war. Virtually every thought about the future of global politics focuses on either (a) an impending nuclear collision between the two nations, or (b) a terrifying alliance between the USSR and China. As far as I can tell, no one in the entire *Book of Predictions* assumed the friction between the US and Russia could be resolved without the detonation of nuclear weapons. A similar problem is witnessed whenever anyone from 1980 attempts to consider the future of interpersonal communication: Even though widespread cell phone use was right around the corner—there was already a mobile phone network in Japan in '79—it was almost impossible to think this would ever replace traditional landlines for average people. All speculation regarding human interaction is limited by the assumption that landline telephones would always be the best way to communicate. On page 29, there are even escalating predictions about the annual number of long-distance calls that would be made in the US, a problem that's irrelevant in the age of free calling. Yet as recently as twenty years

---

whole complicated mess of distributing and selling records, shipping unwanted returns back to the warehouse . . ."

ago, this question still mattered; as a college student in the early nineties, I knew of several long-term romantic relationships that were severed simply because the involved parties attended different schools and could not afford to make long-distance calls, even once a week. In 1994, the idea of a sixty-minute phone call from Michigan to Texas costing less than mailing a physical letter the same distance was still unimaginable. Which is why no one imagined it in 1980, either.

This brand of retrospective insight presents a rather obvious problem: My argument requires a "successful" futurist to anticipate whatever it is that can't possibly be anticipated. It's akin to demanding someone be spontaneous on command. But there's still a practical lesson here, or at least a practical thought: Even if we can't foresee the unforeseeable, it's possible to project a future reality where the most logical conclusions have no relationship to what actually happens. It feels awkward to think like this, because such thinking accepts irrationality. Of course, irrational trajectories happen all the time. Here's an excerpt from a 1948 issue of *Science Digest*: "Landing and moving around the moon offers so many serious problems for human beings that it may take science another 200 years to lick them." That prediction was off by only 179 years. But the reason *Science Digest* was so wrong was not technological; it was motivational. In 1948, traveling to the moon was a scientific aspiration; the desire for a lunar landing was analogous to the desire to climb a previously unscaled mountain. *Science Digest* assumed this goal would be pursued in the traditional manner of scientific inquiry—a grinding process of formulating theories and testing hypotheses. But when the Soviets launched the Sputnik satellite in 1957, the meaning of the enterprise changed.

Terrified Americans suddenly imagined Khrushchev launching weapons from the lunar surface. The national desire to reach the moon first was now a military concern (with a sociocultural subtext over which country was intellectually and morally superior). That accelerated the process dramatically. By the summer of '69, we were planting flags and collecting moon rocks and generating an entirely new class of conspiracy theorists. So it's not that the 1948 editors of *Science Digest* were illogical; it's that logic doesn't work particularly well when applied to the future.

Any time you talk to police (or lawyers, or journalists) about any kind of inherently unsolvable mystery, you will inevitably find yourself confronted with the concept of Occam's Razor: the philosophical argument that the best hypothesis is the one involving the lowest number of assumptions. If (for example) you're debating the assassination of John F. Kennedy, Occam's Razor supports the idea of Lee Harvey Oswald acting alone—it's the simplest, cleanest conclusion, involving the least number of unverifiable connections. With Occam's Razor is how a serious person considers the past. Unfortunately, it simply doesn't work for the future. When you're gazing into the haze of a distant tomorrow, *everything* is an assumption. Granted, some of those competing assumptions seem (or maybe feel) more reasonable than others. But we live in a starkly unreasonable world. The history of ideas is littered with more failures than successes. Retroactively, we all concede this. So in order to move forward, we're forced to use a very different mind-set. For lack of a better term, we'll just have to call it Klosterman's Razor: the philosophical belief that the best hypothesis is the one that reflexively accepts its potential wrongness to begin with.

A Quaint and Curious Volume of (Destined-to-Be) Forgotten Lore

Let's start with books.

Now, I realize the risk inherent in this decision: By the time the questions I'm about to ask are resolved, it's possible that books won't exist. Some will argue that such an inevitability borders on the probable. But I'm starting with books, anyway, and mainly for two reasons. The first is that *this* is a book, so if all books disappear, there's no way anyone will be able to locate my mistake. The second is that I suspect we will always use the word "book" to signify whatever we incorporate in its place, even if that new thing has almost no relationship to what we consider to be a "book" right now.

Language is more durable than content. Words outlive their definitions. Vinyl represented around 6 percent of music sales in 2015, but people continue to say they listen to "records" and "albums" and (on rare occasions) "LPs" whenever they're describing any collection of music. This is even true for music that was never pressed on vinyl at all. So-called long-playing records weren't introduced to the public until 1948 and didn't matter commercially until the sixties, but the term "record" has come to characterize the entire concept. And since books are way, way older—*The Epic of Gilgamesh* was written somewhere in the vicinity of 2000 BC—it seems impossible that we'll ever stop using that term, even if the future equivalent of a "book" becomes a packet of granulized data that is mechanically injected directly into the cerebral cortex. We also have too many ancillary adjectives connected to books ("He's only book smart," "She's a real bookworm," "The pigs are gonna throw the book at him") to jettison the root word from the lexicon. Many people use physical books as art objects in their homes, and the Library of Congress would need to be hit by a nuclear weapon in order to disappear. It's possible that no one will buy (or read) books in some remote future, but we can (tentatively) assume that people of that era will at least know what "books" are: They are the collected units containing whatever writers write. So even though future writers might not be producing anything resembling present-day books, that's still how society will refer to whatever works they are producing.

[I would love to promise that the rest of this book will not be as pedantic and grinding as the previous two paragraphs. I want to believe I won't spend thousands of words describing why various nouns won't evaporate into the cultural troposphere. But I can't make that promise. It's entirely possible that—two hundred pages from now—I will find myself describing what "food" is, and explaining that food is what we put in our mouths in order to avoid starvation, and arguing that we will always talk about food as something that exists. But take solace in the fact that you can quit at any time. I cannot.]

A few pages back, I cited *Moby-Dick* as the clearest example of a book that people were just flat-out wrong about, at least during the life span of the author. But this doesn't mean that no one thought it was good, because certain people did. That's not the point. This has nothing to do with personal taste. What any singular person thought about *Moby-Dick* in 1851 is as irrelevant as what any singular person thinks about *Moby-Dick* today. What critics in the nineteenth century were profoundly wrong about was not the experience of reading this novel; what they were wrong about was how that experience would be valued *by other people*. Because that's what we're really talking about whenever we analyze the past. And when I refer to "other people," I don't mean the literary sphere of 1851. I mean "other people" throughout the expanse of time, including those readers a critic in 1851 could never fathom. Which forces us to consider the importance—or the lack of importance— of plot mechanics.

Moby-Dick is about a dude hunting a whale. The novel includes autobiographical details from Herman Melville's own tenure on a whaling vessel, so one can conclude that he couldn't have written a novel with such specificity and depth if it had not been something he'd experienced firsthand. But what if the same Mr. Melville had lived a different kind of life: Could he have written a similar nine-hundred-page book about hunting a bear? Or climbing a mountain? Or working as a male prostitute? How much of this novel's transcendent social imprint is related to what it mechanically examines?

The short answer seems to be that the specific substance of a novel matters very little. The difference between a whale and a bear and a mountain is negligible. The larger key is the tone, and particularly the ability of that tone to detach itself from the social moment of its creation.

"It's a terrifying thought," George Saunders tells me, "that all of the things we—that I—take for granted as being essential to good literature might just be *off.* You read a 'good' story from the 1930s and find that somehow the world has passed it by. Its inner workings and emphases are somehow misshapen. It's answering questions in its tone and form that we are no longer asking. And yet the Gaussian curve[1] argues that this is true—that most of us are so habituated to the current moment that what we do will fade and lose its power and just be an historical relic, if that. I've been reading a lot of Civil War history lately, and it is just astonishing how *wrong* nearly everyone was. Wrong—and emphatic. Even the people who were 'right' were off, in their sense of how things would play out . . . The future we are now living in would have been utterly unimaginable to the vast majority of even the most intelligent thinkers and writers of that time."

Saunders is an especially significant character in this discussion, based on the perception of his work within the living present. In January of 2013, *The New York Times Magazine* published a cover story with the earnest headline "George Saunders Has

---

1 This is the traditional bell curve. "Gaussian" refers to the mathematician who came up with it, Carl Friedrich Gauss.

Written the Best Book You'll Read This Year." That book, *Tenth of December*, was a slim, darkly humorous collection of short stories, most of which deal with the quintessence of kindness and the application of empathy. Though no writer can honestly be categorized as universally beloved, Saunders comes closer than any other white American male. He has never published an official novel, which plays to his advantage—the perception of his career does not hinge on the perception of any specific work. He is also viewed (with justification) as being unusually humble and extraordinarily nice to pretty much everyone he encounters.[2] So when *The New York Times Magazine* published that story, and when *Tenth of December* subsequently made the bestseller list, there was a collective assumption that Saunders was—perhaps, maybe, arguably—this nation's greatest living author, and that it was wonderful that the person occupying that space seemed like a legitimately kind person (as opposed to some jerk we simply had to begrudgingly *concede* was better than everyone else). If George Saunders eventually becomes the distant historical figure who defines American writing at the turn of the twenty-first century, it seems like this would be good for everyone involved.

And yet . . . there is something about this notion that feels overwhelmingly impermanent. It doesn't seem plausible that some-

----

2 I once gave a speech at a Midwestern college, and I asked the person who picked me up at the airport what other authors the university had invited to speak in the past. The driver mentioned George Saunders. When I asked what he was like, the driver claimed that Saunders had pre-Googled the name of almost every person involved with his visit—including the driver himself—so that the brief conversations he would inevitably have with those around him would not be one-sided. He wanted to be able to ask them questions about their lives. Part of me finds this story implausible, but maybe that just proves I'm not very thoughtful.

one could do exceptional work, be recognized as exceptional, and then simply remain in that cultural space for the rest of time. Art history almost never works that way. In fact, it often seems like our collective ability to recognize electrifying genius as it occurs paradoxically limits the likelihood of future populations certifying that genius as timeless.

"What ages [poorly], it seems, are ideas that trend to the clever, the new, or the merely personal," Saunders continues. "What gets dated, somehow, is that which is too ego inflected—that hasn't been held up against the old wisdom, maybe, or just against some innate sense of truth, and rigorously, with a kind of self-abnegating fervor. Again and again some yahoo from 1863 can be heard to be strenuously saying the obvious, self-aggrandizing, self-protective, clever, banal thing—and that crap rings so hollow when read against Lincoln or Douglass. It gives me real fear about all of the obvious, self-aggrandizing, self-protective, clever, banal things I've been saying all my life."

Here again, I'd like to imagine that Saunders will be rewarded for his self-deprecation, in the same way I want him to be rewarded for his sheer comedic talent. But I suspect our future reality won't be dictated by either of those qualities. I suspect it will be controlled by the evolving, circuitous criteria for what is supposed to matter about anything. When trying to project which contemporary books will still be relevant once our current population has crumbled into carbon dust and bone fragments, it's hopeless to start by thinking about the quality of the works themselves. Quality will matter at the end of the argument, but not at the beginning. At the beginning, the main thing that matters is what that future world will be like. From there, you work in reverse.

[2] "All I can tell you is that in 100 years I seriously doubt that the list of the 100 best writers from our time is going to be as white, as male, as straight, as monocultural as the lists we currently produce about the 100 best writers of our time." This an e-mail from Junot Díaz, the Dominican-American novelist who won a Pulitzer Prize in 2008 and a MacArthur Fellowship in 2012. "In all frankness, our present-day evaluative criteria are so unfairly weighted towards whiteness, maleness, middle-classness, straightness, monoculturality—so rotted through with white supremacy—as to be utterly useless for really seeing or understanding what's going on in the field, given how little we really see and value of the art we're now producing because of our hegemonic scotoma. Who can doubt that the future will improve on that? No question that today, in the margins of what is considered Real Literature, there are unacknowledged Kafkas toiling away who are more likely women, colored, queer and poor."

Díaz is a bombastic intellectual with a limitless career (his debut novel about an overweight weirdo, *The Brief Wondrous Life of Oscar Wao*, was named the best book of the twenty-first century by a panel of critics commissioned by the BBC). It's unsurprising that this is how he views society, and his argument is essentially bulletproof. It's a worldview that's continually gaining traction: You can't have a macro discussion about literary canons without touching on these specific points. When *The New York Times* released its 2014 "100 Notable Books" list, several readers noticed how there were exactly twenty-five fiction books by men, twenty-five fiction books by women, twenty-five nonfiction books by men, and twenty-five nonfiction books by women. Do I have a problem with this? I have no problem with this. But it does reflect something telling about the modern criteria for quantifying art: Symmetrical representation sits at the center of the process. It's an aesthetic priority. Granted, we're dealing with a meaningless abstraction, anyway—the list is called "notable" (as opposed to "best"), it's politicized by the relationships certain authors have with the list makers, it annually highlights books that instantly prove ephemeral, and the true value of inclusion isn't clear to anyone. Yet in the increasingly collapsible, eternally insular idiom of publishing, the *Times*' "100 Notable" list remains the most visible American standard for collective critical appreciation. This is why the perfect 25:25:25:25 gender split is significant. Does it not seem possible—in fact, probable—that (say) twenty-six of the most notable novels were written by women? Or that perhaps men wrote twenty-seven of the most notable nonfiction works?[3] I suppose it's mathematically possible that an objective, gender-blind judging panel might look at every book released in 2014 and arrive at the same conclusion as *The New York Times*. Perfect statistical symmetry is within the realm of possibility. But no impartial person believes that this is what happened. Every rational person knows this symmetry was conscious, and that this specific result either

----

3 And, in fact, on the 2015 list, this was indeed the case—twenty-six of the books in the fiction and poetry category were by female authors and twenty-seven of the nonfiction works were by male authors (although the second category is complicated by posthumous anthology collections of male writers that were edited or compiled by women). It's not like symmetry is the newspaper's policy. It's just an overwhelming trend, designed to combat an overwhelming disparity: In 2004, the first year *The New York Times* capped the list at one hundred books, only five women made the nonfiction list.

(a) slightly invalidates the tangible value of the list, or (b) slightly elevates the intangible value of the list. (I suppose it's also possible to hold both of those thoughts simultaneously.) In either case, one thing is absolutely clear: This is the direction in which canonical thinking is drifting. Díaz's view, which once felt like an alternative perspective, is becoming the entrenched perspective. And when that happens, certain critical conclusions will no longer be possible.

Let's assume that—in the year 2112—someone is looking back at the turn of the twenty-first century, trying to deduce the era's most significant writers. Let us also assume Díaz's opinion about the present culture has metabolized into the standard view; let's concede that people of the future take for granted that the old evaluative criteria were "unfairly weighted towards whiteness, maleness, middle-class-ness, straightness, [and] monoculturality." When that evolution transpires, here's the one critical conclusion that cannot (and will not) happen: "You know, I've looked at all the candidates, consciously considering all genders and races and income brackets. I've tried to use a methodology that does not privilege the dominant class in any context. But you know what? It turns out that Pynchon, DeLillo, and Franzen *were* the best. The fact that they were white and male and straight is just coincidental." If you prioritize cultural multiplicity above all other factors, you can't make the very peak of the pyramid a reactionary exception, even in the unlikely event that this is what you believe (since such a conclusion would undoubtedly be shaped by social forces you might not recognize). Even more remote is the possibility that the sheer commercial force of a period's most successful writers—in the case of our period, Stephen King and J. K. Rowling—will be viewed as an argument in their historical favor. If you accept that the commercial market was artificially unlevel, colossal success only damages their case.

This is not a criticism of identity politics (even though I know it will be taken that way), nor is it some attempt at diminishing the work of new writers who don't culturally resemble the old writers (because all writing is subjective and all writers are subjectively valid). I'm not saying this progression is unfair, or that the new version of unfairness is remotely equivalent to the old version of unfairness. Such processes are never fair, ever, under any circumstances. This is just realpolitik reality: The reason something becomes retrospectively significant in a far-flung future is detached from the reason it was significant at the time of its creation—and that's almost always due to a recalibration of social ideologies that future generations will accept as normative. With books, these kinds of ideological transfers are difficult to anticipate, especially since there are over two million books published in any given year. But it's a little easier to conjecture how this might unspool in the smaller, more contained idiom of film. Take a movie like *The Matrix*: When *The Matrix* debuted in 1999, it was a huge box-office success. It was also well received by critics, most of whom focused on one of two qualities—the technological (it mainstreamed the digital technique of three-dimensional "bullet time," where the on-screen action would freeze while the camera continued to revolve around the participants) or the philosophical (it served as a trippy entry point for the notion that we already live in a simulated world, directly quoting philosopher Jean Baudrillard's 1981 reality-rejecting book *Simulacra and Simulation*). If you talk about *The Matrix* right now, these are still the two things you likely discuss. But what will still be interesting about this film once the technology becomes ancient and the philosophy becomes standard? I suspect it might be this: *The Matrix* was written and directed by "the Wachowski siblings." In 1999, this designation meant two brothers; as I write today, it means two sisters. In the years following the release of *The Matrix*, the older Wachowski (Larry, now Lana) completed her transition from male to female. The younger Wachowski (Andy, now Lilly) publicly announced her transition in the spring of 2016. These events occurred during a period when the social view of transgender issues radically evolved, more rapidly than any other component of modern society. In 1999, it was almost impossible to find any example of a trans person within any realm of popular culture; by 2014, a TV series devoted exclusively to the notion won the Golden Globe for Best Television Series. In the fifteen-year window from 1999 to 2014, no aspect of interpersonal civilization changed more, to the point where Caitlyn (formerly Bruce) Jenner attracted more Twitter followers than the president (and the importance of this shift will amplify as the decades pass—soon, the notion of a transgender US president will not seem remotely implausible). So think how this might alter the memory of *The Matrix*: In some protracted reality, film historians will reinvestigate an extremely commercial action movie made by people who (unbeknownst to the audience) would eventually transition from male to female. Suddenly, the symbolic meaning of a universe with two worlds—one false and constructed, the other genuine and hidden—takes on an entirely new meaning. The idea of a character choosing between swallowing a blue pill that allows him to remain a false placeholder and a red pill that forces him to confront who he truly is becomes a much different metaphor. Considered from this speculative vantage point, *The Matrix* may seem like a breakthrough of a far different kind. It would feel more reflective than entertaining, which is precisely why certain things get remembered while certain others get lost.

This is how the present must be considered whenever we try to think about it as the past: It must be analyzed through the values of a future that's unwritten. Before we can argue that something we currently appreciate deserves inclusion in the world of tomorrow, we must build that future world within our mind. This is not easy (even with drugs). But it's not even the hardest part. The hardest part is accepting that we're building something with parts that don't yet exist.

[**3**] Historical wrongness is more profound than simply hitting the wrong target. If we project that the writer who will be most remembered is "Person X," but it actually turns out to be his more formally inventive peer "Person Y" . . . well, that barely qualifies as *wrong*. That's like ordering a Budweiser and getting a Coors. It's fun to argue over which contemporary juggernaut will eventually become a freestanding monolith, because that dispute is really just a reframing of every preexisting argument over whose commercial work is worthy of attention. It's a hypothetical grounded in actuality. But there are different possibilities that are harder to parse. There are stranger—yet still plausible— outcomes that require an ability to reject the deceptively sensible. What if the greatest writer of this generation is someone who will die totally unknown? Or—stranger still—what if the greatest writer of this generation *is* a known figure, but a figure taken seriously by no one alive (including, perhaps, the writer in question)?

[**4**] Before explaining how and why these things might happen, I must recognize the dissenting opinion, particularly since my opinion is nowhere near normal. I do this by quoting novelist Jonathan Lethem as he casually quotes someone else from memory: "W. Somerset Maugham had a rather dry remark somewhere, which I won't look up, but instead paraphrase: 'Literary posterity may often surprise us in its selections, but it almost exclusively selects[4] from among those known in their day, not the unknown.' And I do think that's basically true."

Lethem is a prolific writer of fiction and criticism, as well as the unofficial curator and public advocate for the catalog of Philip K. Dick (a sci-fi writer who embodies the possibility of seeming more consequential in retrospect than he did as an active artist). Somewhat surprisingly, Lethem's thoughts on my premise skew conservative; he seemed intrigued by the possibility, but unable to ignore the (seemingly) more plausible probability that the future will reliably reflect some version of the present. I've focused on Melville, and Díaz referenced Franz Kafka. But Lethem views both of those examples as high-profile exceptions that inadvertently prove the rule.

"Kafka and Melville are both really weird cases, unlikely to be repeated," Lethem explains. "And it's worth being clear that Melville wasn't some self-published marginal crank. He was a bestselling writer, widely reviewed and acknowledged, up to the point

---

4 In the actual quote, Maugham used the word "selected" instead of "selects." I think we can all agree that this mistake invalidates Lethem's entire career.

where he began to diverge from the reading taste of his time. What's weird is that all his greatest work came after he fell out of fashion, and also that there was such a strong dip in his reputation that he was barely remembered for a while . . . Kafka was conversant with a sophisticated literary conversation, and had, despite the strongly self-defeating tendencies to neither finish nor publish his writings, the attention of various alert colleagues. If he'd lived longer, he might very likely have become a prominent writer . . . The most canonical figure in literary history who was essentially a self-published kook would arguably be William Blake."

The arc of Lethem's larger contention boils down to two points. The first is that no one is *really* remembered over the long haul, beyond a few totemic figures—Joyce, Shakespeare, Homer—and that these figures serve as placeholders for the muddled generalization of greatness ("Time is a motherfucker and it's coming for all of us," Lethem notes). The second is that—even if we accept the possibility that there *is* a literary canon—we're really discussing multiple canons and multiple posterities. We are discussing what Lethem calls "rival claims": in essence, the idea that the only reason we need a canon is so that other people can disagree with it. The work of the writers who get included becomes almost secondary, since they now exist only for the purposes of contradiction.

"Let me try to generate an example of a very slapdash guess about the present situation," Lethem writes me in an e-mail (and since it's an especially interesting e-mail, I'm going to leave in his unorthodox parentheses and capitalizations). "The VERY most famous novelists alive (or just-dead) right now might be destined to be thought about for a good long time. Even if little read. You could see Wallace-Franzen-King as having some probable long-term viability, in the sense that when we talk about the French novel from a certain period, everyone's sure to know that Stendhal-Balzac-and-Victor-Hugo existed (and yes, I do intend the comparison of the reputations of the six people in those two categories, in the order I put them in). But how many people do you know who have read them, apart from a school assignment of Balzac, possibly? [So] here's where I get back to 'rival claims'—for everyone who nods their heads solemnly at the idea that French literature of the not-too-medieval-past consists of those guys, there'll be some wise guy who'll say: 'Fuck those boring novelists, the action in Paris at that time was Baudelaire and Verlaine!' Or someone else who'll say, 'Did you know that Anatole France outsold all of those guys, and was pretty amazing, even if we don't read him anymore?' (Which might be like saying, 'Jane Smiley was the key American novelist of the turn of the millennium.') And someone else who'll say, 'I'm much more interested in Guy de Maupassant' (which might be comparable to advancing a claim for, I dunno, George Saunders or Lorrie Moore). Meanwhile, we live in a time where the numbers of creators of literature has just exploded—and that plenitude *is* the field, and the context for the tiny, tiny number of things that get celebrated in the present, let alone recalled ten or twenty years later, let alone by the 22nd century. And it is all absolutely without any mercy destined to evaporate into the memory hole—irretrievably."

Now, I'm not sure if Lethem's final claim here is daring or anodyne. I certainly understand the mentality behind forwarding the possibility that *nothing* from this era will be remembered, simply due to volume. There are also those who contend we no longer need to "remember" anything at all, since the Internet has unlimited storage and ebooks never go out of print (and that there's no longer any point in classifying any one creative person as more consequential than another, since we'll all have equal and immediate access to both of their catalogs). Both thoughts share a curious combination of optimism, pessimism, and pragmatism. But they both overlook something else: human nature. Society enjoys this process, even if the job is superfluous and the field is too large to manage. Practicality is not part of the strategy. People will always look backward in an attempt to re-remember what they want to be true, just as I currently look ahead in an attempt to anticipate how that reverse engineering will work. Certain things will not evaporate, even if they deserve to.

I try to be rational (or at least my imaginary facsimile of what rationality is supposed to be). I try to look at the available data objectively (fully aware that this is impossible). I try to extrapolate what *may* be happening now into what *will* be happening later. And this, of course, is where naïve realism punches me in the throat. There's simply no way around the limited ceiling of my own mind. It's flat-out impossible to speculate on the future without (a) consciously focusing on the most obvious aspects of what we already know, and (b) unconsciously excluding all the things we don't have the intellectual potential to grasp. I can't describe what will happen in one hundred years if my central thesis insists that the best guess is always the worst guess. I can't *reasonably argue* that the most important writer of this era is (for example) a yet-to-be-identified Irish-Asian skoliosexual from Juárez, Mexico, who writes brilliantly about migrant cannibalism from an anti-union perspective. That's not even an argument, really. It's just a series of adjectives. It's a Mad Lib. I can't list every possible variety of person who might emerge from the ether and eventually become mega-important, based on the premise that the best answer to this question must be whatever answer no one else has ever conceived. That would be insane.

Yet that insanity is (probably) closer to what will transpire. For an assortment of reasons, I suspect that whoever gets arbitrarily selected to represent turn-of-the-twenty-first-century literary greatness is—at the moment—either totally unknown or widely disrespected.

So here's where we try to answer the question that can't be answered: Who would this person be?

[**5**] Just for a moment, let's return to Kafka. Lethem notes that he had the "attention" of various peers (most notably his friend Max Brod, who ultimately published Kafka's work posthumously, against the dead writer's expressed wishes). Kafka delivered a few readings of his work to small local crowds, and these performances were rumored to be hilarious. Some of his shorter stories were published in small German-language literary journals, and he released two complete collections of those stories before he died. This guy was not exactly living in a cave and drinking his own urine. But Kafka did not have any semblance of a normal literary career, unless you assume "a normal literary career" constitutes dying poor and hating everything about yourself. He represents the Platonic ideal of the tortured genius who dies virtually unknown: He was paralyzed by both a hatred of his own writing and a buried arrogance over his intellectual superiority. He never got over his relationship with his tyrannical father; he was obsessed

with (and insecure about) sex; his Jewishness quietly informed everything he wrote. He died in 1924, at age forty, in a sanatorium outside Vienna. Nobody cared (including Kafka, who supposedly saw no value in fame). Some estimates suggest he burned 90 percent of what he wrote. Yet the 10 percent that survived is the apotheosis of dreamlike fiction, to the point where his surname has become the adjective describing that quality. His novel *The Trial* defined a narrative condition that will exist in perpetuity, crossing all genres, from *The Twilight Zone* to *Eyes Wide Shut* to *Sleep No More*. Jonathan Franzen classifies *The Metamorphosis* as "the most autobiographical novella ever written," a story so ingrained in mainstream consciousness that it was turned into a short film and broadcast on MTV throughout the early nineties. Kafka is the easiest example of a canonical writer whose life ended in anonymity, and (as Lethem notes) the uniqueness of his trajectory might be too sublime to happen again. But I am not so sure. I think it's quite possible that no writer from this era will be remembered at all—yet if someone *is* embraced by the currently unborn, it will likely be a Kafka-like character. It will be someone we're not currently aware of, which will allow this person to feel fresh to the generation that adopts him.

So who might this person be?

The superficial, seemingly obvious answer is, "Some person on the Internet." That, however, misses the crux of the comparison. The conventional Internet is the ideal vessel for the acquisition of temporary fame; unpublished writers who actively amass substantial social media followings are inevitably trying to leverage those followings into a book or TV deal, on the basis of the premise that they are already relatively famous. If you are heavily involved with normal Internet culture, you are partially involved with branding (even if you're trying to be weird and obtuse on purpose). Internet writing is, by definition, public writing. Which means our Contemporary Kafka must be doing something slightly different. Contemporary Kafka must be working in a medium that is either (a) extremely traditional, and therefore unpopular, or (b) extremely new, and therefore unseen by almost everyone else. One radical pole of this continuum would be a hermit typing his thoughts onto eight-and-a-half-by-eleven paper on a manual typewriter and storing them in a trunk, a vision almost too insane to even consider. But the opposite pole seems significantly more plausible: the so-called Deep Web.

Beyond the Internet, there is another Internet (invisible to search engines and impracticable for 99 percent of the populace). You need to download a special proxy browser to get there, and everything is encrypted and difficult to navigate. It is "an idea more than a place," writes Jamie Bartlett, author of *The Dark Net*. "Internet underworlds set apart yet connected to the Internet we inhabit, [a world] of freedom and anonymity, where users do and say what they like, often uncensored, unregulated, and outside of society's norms." It is, at the moment, used almost exclusively for criminal transactions: drugs, guns, prostitution, mercenary hackers, and—most problematically—child pornography (some estimates suggest 80 percent of Deep Web visits are tied to pedophilia, although that statistic seems apocryphal). The best-known extension of the Deep Web was a drug marketplace called Silk Road, which the FBI shut down in 2014. This is not a cyber realm the average person surfs; to the best of my knowledge, I don't know anyone whose personal experience with the Deep Web extends beyond journalistic curiosity. But it presents a zone where a certain kind of faceless artist could flourish, completely detached from a mainstream society that might not accept or appreciate the work.

Look: It's not like any (honest) writer wants *no one* to see what he's writing. If he did, he'd just sit in a dark room and imagine that he wrote it already. Even the self-loathing Kafka sent Brod a copy of *The Trial*, insisting that Brod destroy it, likely aware that Brod never would. No matter what they may claim, even the most transgressive of writers don't want to work in a total vacuum; they simply want to control the composition of their audience. If you operate in the regular world, this is almost impossible. But it could work on the Deep Web.[5] An unknown genius could create a space where his or her work is seen very selectively, only by those who are like-minded and similarly invested, and without any relationship to the rest of society (and without any risk of the content going viral). Behind an invisible digital wall, our Contemporary Kafka could interact with a Contemporary Brod, and virtually no one else would know this exchange was even happening. The work itself might not emerge for decades, sitting stagnant until the Deep Web is (eventually) explored by technological archaeologists. And that social separation is the critical detail. For this exaltation to happen, our writer *needs* to be unknown to all the established kingmakers who will eventually embrace the work. That compo-

---

5 Now, the easy counter to this suggestion is, "That's crazy. Nobody uses the Deep Web for *artistic* purposes, and nobody ever would. That's like saying the next great movie director might currently be involved with the production of snuff films." But this response is already false. The British electronica artist Aphex Twin released the title and track listing for his 2014 album *Syro* on the hidden Deep Web service Tor. The reason this was done remains unclear—but that's part of the value here. Clarity is not required.

nent is more essential than anything else. There's no question that what we know about Kafka's life is part of what makes him "great," and no present-day person reading his novels is unaware that he died in total obscurity. The confusion experienced by his character K is not received as a creative construct, but as a way to lock into the depressing alienation within any simple, private, painful life. The fact that *we know* that Kafka's brilliance was not recognized during his time on earth magnifies his existential despair in a way that words alone never could. And we believe his voice can be trusted, because he (seemingly) had no ulterior motive. He was just typing into the abyss. Which is pretty much the definition of writing on a version of the Internet nobody sees.

So this is the venue. This is where our candidate lives.

But who will that person be, and what will that person write about?

[6] Here's where we encounter our first collision with the hammer of overthinking, which—according to a 2013 neuroscience study at UC Santa Barbara—actually impedes mental performance. There's real potential for diminishing returns. But I guess I'll have to take that risk, since overthinking is the only way to figure out the opposite of something that hasn't actually happened. That argument Junot Díaz made four thousand words ago? His assertion that our future literary canon will be populated with the types of people who currently tend to be excluded from it? That *will* happen. Such an evolution *will* occur. And the inevitability of that evolution makes deducing the profile of our hypothetical outlier that much harder.

For most of the twentieth century, there was an ever-growing realization (at least among intellectuals) that the only way to understand the deeper truth about anything complicated was through "shadow histories": those underreported, countercultural chronicles that had been hidden by the conformist monoculture and emerge only in retrospect. Things that seem obvious now— the conscious racism of Nixon's "Southern Strategy," the role the CIA played in the destabilization of Iran, how payola controlled what was on FM radio, the explanation behind America's reliance on privately owned cars instead of public transportation, et al.— were all discussed while they were happening . . . but only on the marginalized periphery. They were not taken that seriously. Over time, these shadow ideas—or at least the ones that proved factually irrefutable—slowly became the mainstream view. Howard Zinn's 1980 depiction of how America was built in *A People's History of the United States* is no longer a counterbalance to a conventional high school history text; in many cases, it *is* the text. This kind of transition has become a normal part of learning about anything. In literature, there were the established (white, male) classics that everyone was forced to identify as a senior in high school. But once you went to college—and especially if you went to an expensive school—you learned about the equally important works that were mostly hidden (and usually for nonliterary reasons). That was the secret history of literature.

But this process is fading (and while it's too easy to say it's all because of the Internet, that's inarguably the main explanation). The reason shadow histories remained in the shadows lay in the centralization of information: If an idea wasn't discussed on one of three major networks or on the pages of a major daily newspaper or national magazine, it was almost impossible for that idea to gain traction with anyone who wasn't consciously searching for alternative perspectives. That era is now over. There is no centralized information, so every idea has the same potential for distribution and acceptance. Researching the events of the 9/11 attack on the World Trade Center is no harder or easier than absorbing the avalanche of arguments from those who believe 9/11 was orchestrated by the US government. There will be no shadow history of the 2008 financial crisis or the 2014 New England Patriots' "Deflategate" scandal, because every possible narrative and motive was discussed in public, in real time, across a mass audience, as the events transpired. Competing modes of discourse no longer "compete." They coexist. And the same thing is happening in the arts. The diverse literary canon Díaz imagines is not something that will be reengineered retroactively. We won't have to go back and reinsert marginalized writers who were ignored by the establishment, because the establishment is now a multisphere collective; those marginalized writers will be recognized as they emerge, and their marginalized status will serve as a canonical advantage.

So what does that tell us about our Contemporary Kafka?

It tells us that Contemporary Kafka will need to be a person so profoundly marginalized that almost no one currently views his or her marginalization as a viable talking point.

Take, for example, the plight of Native Americans. What American subculture has suffered more irrevocably? Prior to Columbus's landing in the New World, the Native American population approached one hundred million. Now it's a little over three million, two-thirds of whom are relegated to fifty delineated reservations on mostly undesirable land. Still, that equates to roughly

1 percent of the total US population. Yet Native Americans are essentially voiceless, even in conversations that specifically decry the lack of minority representation. Who is the most prominent Native American media figure or politician? Sherman Alexie? Louise Erdrich? Tom Cole or Markwayne Mullin, both of whom are from the same state? Who, for that matter, is the most famous Native American athlete, or rapper, or reality star? Maybe Sam Bradford? Maybe Sacheen Littlefeather, who's been virtually invisible since the seventies? When the Academy Awards committee next announces the nominations for Best Picture, how many complaints will focus on the lack of films reflecting the Native American experience? Outside the anguish expressed over the use of the term "Redskin" by the Washington football franchise, it's hard to find conversation about the biases facing Native Americans; outside the TV show *Fargo*, you almost never see it reflected in the popular culture. Everyone concedes it exists, but it's not a *popular* prejudice (at least not among the mostly white liberals who drive these conversations). Their marginalization is ignored, thus creating a fertile factory for the kind of brilliant outsider who won't be recognized until that artist is dead and gone. So this is one possibility—a Navajo Kafka.

But here's where we taste the insecure blood from Klosterman's Razor: The mere fact that I can imagine this scenario forces me to assume that it won't happen. It's a reasonable conclusion to draw from the facts that presently exist, but the future is a teenage crackhead who makes shit up as he goes along. The uncomfortable, omnipresent reality within any conversation about representation is that the most underrepresented subcultures are the ones that don't even enter into the conversation. They are, by definition, impossible to quantify. They are groups of people whom—right now, in the present tense—it is still acceptable to dislike or discount or ignore. They are groups who are not seen as *needing* protection or support, which makes them vulnerable to ridicule and attack. Who are they? As already stated in this paragraph, I am in no position to say. If I try, I can only be wrong. Any argument in their favor is an argument against my premise.

Still, the history of ideas tells us that there are many collections of current humans we do not currently humanize. They exist. So find them right now, inside your own head: Imagine a certain kind of person or a political faction or a religious sect or a sexual orientation or a social group you have no ethical problem disliking, to the point where you could safely ridicule it in public without fear of censure.

Whatever you imagined is the potential identity of the Contemporary Kafka. And if your fabricated answer seems especially improbable, it just means you might actually be close.

[7] So what will this impossible-to-visualize person write about? Or—more accurately—what will this person *have written* about, since the comprehension of its consequence won't occur until he (or she) has already vamoosed? The first clue can be extrapolated from a single line in Kurt Vonnegut's *A Man Without a Country*: "I think that novels that leave out technology misrepresent life as badly as Victorians misrepresented life by leaving out sex." In the context of day-to-day publishing, that sentiment is 100 percent true. But when you're trying to isolate unique transcendence, it's not quite that simple.

The reason Vonnegut's writing advice remains (mostly) correct has to do with the myth of universal timeliness. There is a misguided belief—often promoted by creative writing programs—that producing fiction excessively tied to technology or popular culture cheapens the work and detracts from its value over time. If, for example, you create a plot twist that hinges on the use of an iPad, that story will (allegedly) become irrelevant once iPads are replaced by a new form of technology. If a character in your story is obsessed with watching *Cheers* reruns, the meaning of that obsession will (supposedly) evaporate once *Cheers* disappears from syndication. If your late-nineties novel is consumed with Monica Lewinsky, the rest of the story (purportedly) devolves into period piece. The goal, according to advocates of this philosophy, is to build a narrative that has no irretraceable connection to the temporary world. But that's idiotic, for at least two reasons. The first is that it's impossible to generate deep verisimilitude without specificity.[6] The second is that if you hide the temporary world and the work somehow does beat the odds and become timeless, the temporary world you hid will become the *only* thing anyone cares about.

Vonnegut's reference to the Victorians is the superlative exam-

---

6 When casually talking to like-minded friends, people rarely say, "I saw a movie last night." People more often say things like "I saw *The Hateful Eight* last night" or "I finally saw the new Tarantino last night." We live in a proper-noun culture. Now, is it possible that this specific film will be lost to history? Is it possible that referring to Quentin Tarantino in an offhand manner will be confusing or misleading? Sure. But the two seconds it will take a future reader to figure this out from context is better than directly reminding that reader that this is a fiction that never happened at all.

ple. Jane Austen (as timeless a writer as there will ever be) wrote about courtship and matrimony in an essentially sexless universe. As a result, the unspoken sexual undercurrents are the main gravitational pull for modern readers. "When a character in an Austen novel walks into a room and starts speaking," wrote Victorian scholar Susan Zlotnick, "we understand the words . . . but not always the layers of meaning compressed into those words." Reading *Pride and Prejudice* requires the reader to unpack the sex—and if you love Austen, the unpacking process is a big part of what you love. A book becomes popular because of its text, but it's the subtext that makes it live forever. For the true obsessive, whatever an author doesn't explicitly explain ends up becoming everything that matters most (and since it's inevitably the obsessives who keep art alive, they make the rules). Take *Beowulf*: While there is a limited discussion to have about Grendel and his mother, there's a limitless discussion to be had about ninth-century England, the nature and origin of storytelling, and how early Christians viewed heroism and damnation. Consumed today, *Beowulf* is mostly about what isn't there. And that will be the same for whatever 2016 text survives into 3016.

Now, here's where things get hard.

On the one hand, we must accept Vonnegut's larger argument. We must concede that important writing finds a way to accurately represent life, and that the writing that does so will consciously intermingle with the meaningful culture of the time (impermanent though it may be). What that constitutes in our present culture is debatable, but here's a partial, plausible list . . .

- The psychological impact of the Internet on day-to-day living.
- The prevailing acceptance of nontraditional sexual identities.
- The (seemingly regular) deaths of unarmed black men at the hands of white police officers.
- An unclear definition of privacy.
- An impotent, unspecified hatred of the wealthiest "one percent."
- The artistic elevation of television.
- The cultural recession of rock and the cultural ascension of hip-hop.
- The prolonging of adolescence and the avoidance of adulthood.
- A distrust of objective storytelling.
- The intermittent rebooting of normalcy in the years following 9/11.

I'm not saying an important book must include one of these ideas, or even an idea that would comfortably fit on this list. But it needs to include *something* that taps into what matters about the world *now*. There has to be something at stake that involves modernity. It can't just be well written or smartly plotted; a well-written, smartly plotted book can absolutely be "great," but—within the context of this debate—"great" is not enough. (A list of great books that have been forgotten completely would be exponentially longer than the book you're reading right now.) In order to overcome such impossible odds and defeat the unrelenting ravages of time, the book has to offer more. It has to offer a window into a world that can no longer be accessed, insulated by a sense that this particular work is the best way to do so. It must do what Vonnegut requests—reflect reality. And this is done by writing about the things that matter today, even if they won't necessarily matter tomorrow.

Yet herein lies the paradox: If an author does this *too* directly, it won't work at all.

The aforementioned "unpacking" of literature isn't just something people enjoy. It's an essential part of canonization (and not just in literature, but in every form of art). If the meaning of a book can be deduced from a rudimentary description of its palpable plot, the life span of that text is limited to the time of its release. Historically awesome art always means something different from what it superficially appears to suggest—and if future readers can't convince themselves that the ideas they're consuming are less obvious than whatever simple logic indicates, that book will disappear. The possibility that a cigar is just a cigar doesn't work with literary criticism, and that's amplified by the passage of time. Gary Shteyngart's *Super Sad True Love Story* is literally about media alienation, so it can't *really* be about media alienation. Jonathan Safran Foer's *Extremely Loud and Incredibly Close* is literally about the 9/11 attacks, so it can't *really* be about the 9/11 attacks. When any novel is rediscovered and culturally elevated, part of the process is creative: The adoptive generation needs to be able to decide for themselves what the deeper theme is, and it needs to be something that wasn't widely recognized by the preceding generation. In one hundred years, it's possible that the contemporary novel best illustrating media alienation will be something like

Cormac McCarthy's *The Road*, even though nobody makes that connection now. The defining 9/11 novel may end up being *Infinite Jest*, even though it was written five years before the actual event and has very little to do with New York or terrorism or global politics.[7] The only detail we can all be certain of is that a novel's (eventual) interpretation will (eventually) be different from its surface meaning—and if that doesn't happen, the book won't seem significant enough to retroactively canonize.

So this, it seems, is the key for authors who want to live forever: You need to write about important things without actually writing about them.

I realize this sounds like advice from a fortune cookie. In fact, I suspect my whole line of reasoning reads like a collection of ineffectual riddles: *"The most amazing writer of this generation is someone you've never heard of, representing a subculture we don't even recognize,*

---

7 This is something I think actually *will* happen, in just the way I describe it here. Because of his suicide and specialized type of brilliance, David Foster Wallace will remain historically relevant. *Infinite Jest* will be perceived as his defining work, even though it will rarely be read, simply due to its size and complexity. Since that novel will be both deeply remembered and widely unread, it will become a perfect vessel for radical, obtuse interpretation (in the same way this is currently done with *Moby-Dick*). Two or three centuries from now, the events of September 11, 2001, will be the singular social touchstone for all creative American works that happened within the general vicinity of that date (and if you don't believe me, try to find deep analysis of any American art from the middle nineteenth century that doesn't glancingly reference the Civil War). This is the recipe for how a book about one subject ends up becoming the defining book about something else entirely. Someday, there will be a college literature class connected to the events of 9/11, *Infinite Jest* will be included on the reading list, and there will be an inordinate amount of emphasis on the passages about the militant Quebecois. And when that happens, the professor better give me credit for this prediction. Note me in the syllabus or something. I don't care if the students don't care. I mean, half of them will be cyborgs, anyway.

expressing ideas that don't signify what they appear to mean." It's a little like insisting the best musician in China is someone who's never had the opportunity to learn an instrument—even if that's true, what good is the theory without proof? But that's the wrong way to look at it. My goal is not to contradict conventional answer "X" by replacing it with unconventional answer "Y." My goal is to think about the present in the same way we think about the past, wholly aware that such mass consideration can't happen until we reach a future that no longer includes us. And why do I want to do this? Because this is—or should be—why we invest time into thinking about anything that isn't essential or practical or imperative. The reason so many well-considered ideas appear laughable in retrospect is that people involuntarily assume that whatever we believe and prioritize now will continue to be believed and prioritized later, even though that almost never happens. It's a mistake that never stops being made. So while it's impossible to predict what will matter to future versions of ourselves, we can reasonably presume that whatever they elect to care about (in their own moment) will be equally temporary and ephemeral. Which doesn't necessarily provide us with any *new* answers, but does eliminate some of the wrong ones we typically fail to question.

[**8**] "I would say the likelihood of the greatest writer of this period being totally unknown is twenty percent," says *New Yorker* book critic Kathryn Schulz.[8] "The likelihood that

----

8   In the introduction of this book, I identify Schulz as the author of *Being Wrong*. It's the same person in both instances.

he or she will be known, but not currently appreciated? Higher. That would be more like fifty-fifty."

Schulz gave these answers off the top of her head, having no idea that this was the question I was going to ask. If I'd given her more time to consider the answer, I would not have been surprised if her response had been different (in fact, by the end of our seventy-five-minute conversation, I'd already gotten the sense that she wished she had provided a slightly lower percentage for the first part of the query and a slightly higher percentage for the second). Both figures are offhand guesstimates, impossible to justify in any conversation that doesn't take place inside a tavern. But if you happened to be inside that hypothetical tavern, the second half of the equation is certainly more fun. There is a finite threshold to how much you can debate the possibility that we don't know who somebody is, but there's unlimited bandwidth for speculation over which nondescript contemporary artist is more important than we realize. This practice is central to the entire game of criticism. Here, for example, is a line from the last paragraph of a 2015 *New York Times Book Review* notice for Elisa Albert's novel *After Birth*: "No doubt *After Birth* will be shunted into one of the lesser subcanons of contemporary literature, like 'women's fiction,' but it ought to be as essential as *The Red Badge of Courage*." Now, I have not read *After Birth*, so I can't agree or disagree with this critic's assertion. But I've been a paid critic for enough years to know my profession regularly overrates many, many things by automatically classifying them as potentially underrated. The two terms have become nonsensically interchangeable. My current interest, however, doesn't focus on the overrated or the underrated, or even the properly rated. I'm more concerned with the unrated, and particularly things that are unrated on purpose.

[**9**] Imagine a giant, bottom-heavy, two-dimensional pyramid.[9] Imagine that every living American writer occupies a level within this structure. Imagine that every living writer is a brick.

At the top of this two-dimensional pyramid are the irrefutably elite, proven by both the length of their careers and a consensus about what those careers have meant. These bricks are writers like Philip Roth. Roth has written twenty-seven novels over a span of fifty years, many of which have been successful and all of which have been taken seriously. Someone can certainly dislike Philip Roth's ideas or argue his reputation exceeds his talent, and someone else can dismissively claim no one talks about him anymore. But even those who hate him have to open their attack by conceding his perceived greatness, since that classification is no longer dependent on the subjective opinion of any one person. The nonfiction wing of this level houses elemental tacticians like Robert Caro; someone like William T. Vollmann straddles both lines, fortified by his sublime recklessness. Even the lesser books from these writers are historically important, because—once you're *defined* as great[10]—failures become biographically instructive.

----

9 Which, technically speaking, would be a triangle.

10 This is probably obvious, but—just in case it isn't—I should mention that whenever I call something "great," I'm not arguing that I necessarily consider that particular thing to reflect any greatness to me personally, or even that I like (or fully understand) what that something is. I'm using it more like the editorial "we": There is a general harmonic agreement that this particular thing is

The next tier encompasses those writers who are broadly classified as "great," but who have not worked long enough to prove this
designation as non-transferable. These are the likes of Jennifer Egan
and Dave Eggers and Donna Tartt, plus a host of nonfiction writers
who've produced meaningful, influential journalism in a relatively
short time (Ta-Nehisi Coates, Jon Krakauer, Lawrence Wright, et
al.). If these people continue to produce new work that's comparable
to their old work (or if they happen to die young), they will creep
into the pyramid's elite tier. But for reasons that are (usually) beyond
their control, this rarely happens. Space at the top is limited.

The third tier houses commercial writers who dependably publish major or minor bestsellers and whose success or failure is generally viewed as a reflection of how much (or how little) those
books sell. These individuals are occasionally viewed as "great *at*
writing," but rarely as great writers. They are envied and dis-
counted at the same time. They are what I call "vocally unrated":
A large amount of critical thought is directed toward explaining how these types of novels are not worth thinking about.
Books purchased exclusively by women tend to get placed in this
category,[11] along with legal thrillers, YA novels marketed toward

---

important and artful, both by people invested in supporting that assertion and
(especially) by people who will accept that designation without really considering
why. My own taste might play a role in the examples I select, and it's certainly
possible that I might misread society's opinion. But it's not part of my
categorization process (at least not in this particular book). I mean, I've never
finished a Faulkner novel. I've never loved a Joni Mitchell record or a Bergman
film. But I still know they're great (or "great"). I don't need to personally agree
with something in order to recognize that it's true.

11 In 1998, three of the year's ten best-selling fiction titles were published by
romance novelist Danielle Steel, who somehow managed to have at least one
book in the commercial top ten from 1983 to 1999. Steel is on pace to sell a

adults, novels that become action movies about dinosaurs, and anything involving weird sex or vampires or weird sex with vampires or detailed descriptions of nuclear submarines.

The fourth tier includes writers who produce good work every two or three years, alongside one glaring outlier—a good book that *becomes* the working equivalency of "great," based on the way it is received by the public. These tend to be expertly plotted novels that tap into something universal and underserved; they sell like crazy and are inevitably converted into major motion pictures[12] that supplant the novels in the mind of the public. In 1996, this occurred twice (Alex Garland's *The Beach* and Chuck Palahniuk's *Fight Club*). A more recent example was Gillian Flynn's *Gone Girl* in 2012. The upside to this experience is that the writers become rich enough to write forever, in whatever way they choose. The downside of this experience is that the rest of those writers' careers are viewed through the prism of their singular supersuccess.

The fifth tier comprises authors who write decent books that are well reviewed, but *only* well reviewed. Such writers might even be described as "brilliant" in high-profile places. But the books make no impact and sell less than fifteen thousand copies. Any perceived success is mostly a media illusion. Among their limited fan base (and often in their own minds), these authors are considered criminally underrated, even if the passage of time tends to prove the opposite. They share this tier with the handful of cult

---

billion books in her lifetime. Yet many of these novels don't have Wikipedia entries. They are not even critically appraised by non-critics.

12 Or, in the case of George R. R. Martin's *A Song of Ice and Fire*, a TV series.

writers[13] who can make a semi-decent living writing exclusively for a small, specific audience. These are the novelists working in genre fiction, six or seven poets, and nonfiction autodidacts who tend to focus on drugs and arts criticism and conspiracy theories and actual cults.

Which brings us to the final tier: the "quietly unrated." This is the level encompassing the vast majority of American writers. The reality of publishing is that most books just *come out*. They are written, edited, marketed, and publicized—but nothing else happens. They are nominally reviewed by the trade publications that specialize in reviewing everything, and that's as far as it goes (if they receive any attention beyond that, it likely skews positive, but only because there's no point in criticizing a book nobody else has heard of). I could easily give you examples of these books, but I don't need to—just look at your own bookshelf and note any book that you wouldn't even know existed if you didn't somehow happen to possess a copy. The bulk of fantasy fiction lives in this category, along with the lesser vampire novels and self-published memoirs and self-help books that don't go viral and non-salacious unauthorized biographies and dense literary fiction that appealed only to the lone acquisition editor who got fired for acquiring it. Which is not to suggest that these books are necessarily bad, because that kind of subjective deliberation isn't even on the table. *These books are just books.* They were produced in a factory, they were made available in multiple bookstores, and (even in the worst-case sce-

---

13 Here is how cult writer Dennis Cooper described the term "cult writer" to *The Paris Review*: "It's a weird term because it's complimentary but condescending at the same time."

nario) at least five hundred strangers took them home or downloaded them in exchange for money. If you put the author's name and the exact title into a search engine, it will be the first entry. The books can be found in public libraries, but not all public libraries. Their technical, physical similarities to *Goodbye, Columbus* are greater than the differences, but the key difference is that no one cared about them at the time of their release. Which will make them that much greater if someone eventually does.

So that's the pyramid.

Now, if the world were logical, certain predictions could be made about what bricks from that pyramid will have the greatest likelihood of remaining intact after centuries of erosion. Devoid of all other information, a betting man would have to select a level-one writer like Roth, just as any betting man would take the Yankees if forced to wager on who will win the World Series one hundred seasons from now. If you don't know what the weather will be like tomorrow, assume it will be pretty much the same as today. But this would require an astonishing cultural stasis. It would not simply mean that the way we presently consume and consider Roth will be the way Roth is consumed and considered forevermore; it would mean that the manner in which we value and assess *all novels* will remain unchanged. It also means Roth must survive his inevitable post-life reevaluation by the first generation of academics who weren't born until he was already gone, a scenario where there will be no room for advancement and plenty of room for diminishing perceptions (no future contrarian can provocatively claim, "Roth is actually better than everyone thought at the time," because—at the time—everyone accepted that he was viewed as remarkable). He is the safest bet, but still not a safe bet. Which is why I find myself fixated on the third and sixth tiers of my imaginary triangle: "the unrated." As specific examples, they all face immeasurable odds. But as a class, they share certain perverse advantages. One is that they are insulated against the shifting perception of commercial success.[14] Another is the narrative potential of the unsung, unappreciated hero. But the advantage that matters most is the one that's also most obvious: Unrated books are a neutral charge. The weight of history is not there. They have the ability to embody whatever people want, without the complication of reinvention.

I am, against my better judgment, making a prediction: I am predicting that the future world will be fundamentally unlike our present world. And this prediction can be seen as either risky or safe, depending on how far you extend the timeline. Ask anyone reading *Anna Karenina* in the present day what they think of the story, and they will often mention how surprisingly contemporary it seems. That would suggest the 1877 age of Tolstoy is essentially similar to the age of today, and that the only antiquated details are the details that don't matter. Part of me would like to believe this will always be true. But the part of me who's writing this book is more skeptical. I think the social difference between 2016 and 2155 will be significantly more profound than the social difference between 1877 and 2016, in the same way that the 139-year gap

---

14 It's easy to imagine a future where commercial success matters much more than it currently does (since that has been the overall trend for the past two hundred fifty years). But it's equally possible to imagine a future where the only culture is niche culture, and commercial success becomes irrelevant (or maybe even an anchor).

between the publication of *Anna Karenina* and today is much vaster than the 139-year gap between 1877 and 1738. This acceleration is real, and it will be harder and harder for future generations to relate to "old" books in the way they were originally intended. In as little as fifty years, the language and themes of *The Corrections* will seem as weird and primordial as *Robinson Crusoe* feels to the consumer of today: It will still be readable, but that reading experience won't reflect the human experience it describes (because the experience of being human will be something totally different).

This is where the unrated book holds its contradictory advantage. We know what *The Corrections* is supposed to be about, and the public record of that knowledge will remain as static as the novel's content. Now, could some future person reinterpret and recast its meaning to make it more pliable to her era? Yes. But it would be far more effective—and considerably more inventive—to enact that same process with a text *that has no preexisting meaning*. A book that is "just a book": the forgotten airport bestseller no one took seriously or the utterly unknown memoir that can be re-framed as brilliant and ultra-prescient. Instead of fitting the present (past) into the future, we will jam the present (future) into the present (past).[15] And it won't be the first time this has been done.

Am I certain this will happen? I am not certain. I'm the opposite of certain, for motives that are even more convoluted than the

---

15 Yeah, I know: This sentence is fucking confusing. But it's more straightforward than it seems: Our present time will eventually become the past, hence the designation "present (past)." Our future will eventually become the present, hence "present (future)." It's kind of like the prologue to *Star Wars*, where we are told that the following events happened "a long time ago, in a galaxy far, far away." But the people in *Star Wars* shoot laser guns and travel at the speed of light, so we are forced to conclude that their past is our future.

ones I just expressed (more on that later). But this possibility strikes me as plausible, primarily for a reason that must never be ignored: History is a creative process (or as Napoleon Bonaparte once said, "a set of lies agreed upon"). The world happens as it happens, but we construct what we remember and what we forget. And people will eventually do that to us, too.

But That's the Way
I Like It, Baby.
I Don't Want to Live Forever.

First, there was rock and roll.

Actually, that's not true. First, there was absolutely everything else that ever existed, and *then* there was rock and roll, spawned sometime in the vicinity of 1950. It was named after a 1934 song by a female harmony trio known as the Boswell Sisters, although this might be more of a coincidence than a causal relationship; the term was popularized by the Cleveland radio DJ Alan Freed, a man who played black music for white audiences and unwittingly caused the Rock and Roll Hall of Fame to be built on the shores of Lake Erie, the artistic equivalent of naming North America after the first guy who happened to draw a map of it. "Rock and roll" is a technical term that denotes a specific kind of music—you can (almost) always dance to it, it (quite often) involves a piano, and it has not flourished in any meaningful way for well over fifty years, except as a novelty. This is because "rock and roll" soon morphed into "rock 'n' roll," a mid-sixties derivative of the same music now packaged with an ingrained mission statement: Here is art made exclusively for teenagers, self-consciously reflecting what is assumed to be their non-musical mores and values. (This period exists inside a small chronological window, beginning the night the Beatles first performed on *The Ed Sullivan Show* and ending with the December 1967 release of Jimi Hendrix's *Axis: Bold as Love*.) By the dawn of 1968, "rock 'n' roll" had evolved and expanded into "rock," which is *only* a cultural designation—but a designation encompassing all popular music that has roots in "rock and roll," including the preexisting artists who invented it.[1] Almost anything can be labeled "rock"—Metallica, ABBA, Mannheim Steamroller, a haircut, a muffler. If you're a successful tax attorney who owns a hot tub, clients will refer to you as a "rock star CPA" when describing your business to their less hip neighbors. The metaphysical conception of "rock" cuts such a wide swath that it even includes subgenres that can be applied with equal ubiquity, like *punk* and *metal* and (until the mid-nineties) *hip-hop*. The defining

----

1 Here's a simple way to parse this not-so-simple description: Play the song "Rock and Roll" by Led Zeppelin. Based on a traditional twelve-bar blues progression, "Rock and Roll" is the only song in the Zeppelin catalog that is literally *rock and roll music*, unless you count "Hot Dog" and "Boogie with Stu." Every other Zeppelin song is a sophisticated iteration of "rock," even when the drums are reggae. Jerry Lee Lewis played rock and roll. Jerry Garcia played rock. The song "Rock Around the Clock" is a full-on rock and roll number, but the Moody Blues' "I'm Just a Singer (in a Rock and Roll Band)," Rick Derringer's "Rock and Roll, Hoochie Koo," and Bad Company's "Rock 'n' Roll Fantasy" remain inflexibly rock (with no rolling whatsoever). John Lennon's 1975 solo album *Rock 'n' Roll* is actually a self-conscious attempt at rock *and* roll, while Joan Jett's 1982 cover of "I Love Rock 'n' Roll" professes a love for something it technically isn't. The least ambiguous rock and roll song ever recorded is "Tutti Frutti" by Little Richard, closely followed by the Kingsmen's 1963 cover of "Louie Louie." The least ambiguous rock 'n' roll song is "(I Can't Get No) Satisfaction" by the Rolling Stones. The least ambiguous rock song ever recorded is "I Like to Rock" by April Wine.

music of the first half of the twentieth century was jazz; the defining music of the second half of the twentieth century was rock, but with an ideology and saturation far more pervasive. Only television supersedes its influence. And pretty much from the moment it came into being, people who liked "rock" insisted it was dead. The critic Richard Meltzer allegedly claimed that rock was already dead *in 1968*. And he was wrong to the same degree that he was right.

Meltzer's wrongness on this point is obvious and does not require explanation, unless you honestly think *Purple Rain* blows. But his rightness is more complicated: Rock *is* dead, in the sense that its "aliveness" is a subjective assertion based on whatever criteria the listener happens to care about. When someone argued rock was "dead" in 1968 or 1977 or 1994 or 2005, that individual was making an aesthetic argument, grounded in whatever that person assumed to be the compromised motives of the artists of the time (customarily built on the conviction that the current generation of musicians were more careerist in nature, thus detracting from the amount of raw emotion they were allegedly injecting into the music). The popularity of the rock genre is irrelevant to this accusation. People insisted rock was dead in the mid-1980s, the absolute commercial peak for guitar-driven music. Normal consumers declare rock to be dead whenever they personally stop listening to it (or at least to new iterations of it), which typically happens about two years after they graduate from college. This has almost nothing to do with what's actually happening with the artists who make it. There will always be a handful of musicians making new rock music, just as there will always be a handful of musicians making new mariachi music. The entire debate is semantic: Something that's only metaphorically alive can never be literally dead.

But rock can (and will) recede, almost to the level of nihility. And for the purposes of this book, that's the same as dying.

Now, here is the paradox (and you knew a paradox was coming, because that's how this works): The cultural recession of rock is intertwined with its increased cultural absorption, which seems backward. But this is a product of its design. The symbolic value of rock is conflict-based. It emerged as a by-product of the post–World War II invention of the teenager.[2] This was a twenty-five-year period when the gap between generations was utterly real and uncommonly vast. There was virtually no way a man born in 1920 would (or could) share the same musical taste as his son born in 1955, even if they had identical personalities. That inherent dissonance gave rock music a distinctive, non-musical importance for a very long time. But that period is over. Ozzy Osbourne's "Crazy Train" is used in a commercial for a Honda minivan. The Who's "Won't Get Fooled Again" was the opening theme for one of the most popular series in the history of CBS, the network with the oldest average viewership. The music of the Ramones has been converted into lullabies. There are string renditions of Joy Division's "Love Will Tear Us Apart" for lush, sardonic wedding processions. NBC used the Nine Inch Nails track "Something I Can

---

2 Obviously, there have always been living humans between the ages of twelve and twenty. But it wasn't until after World War II that the notion of an "in between" period connecting the experience of childhood with the experience of adulthood became something people recognized as a real demographic. Prior to this, you were a child until you started working or got married; the moment that happened, you became an adult (even if those things happened when you were eleven).

Never Have" as bumper music for the Wimbledon tennis tournament. "Rock" can now signify anything, so it really signifies nothing; it's more present, but less essential. It's also shackled by its own formal limitations: Most rock songs are made with six strings and electricity, four thicker strings and electricity, and drums. The advent of the digital synthesizer opened the window of possibility in the 1980s, but only marginally. By now, it's almost impossible to create a new rock song that doesn't vaguely resemble an old rock song. So what we have is a youth-oriented musical genre that (a) isn't symbolically important, (b) lacks creative potentiality, and (c) has no specific tie to young people. It has completed its historical trajectory. It will always subsist, but only as itself. And if something is *only* itself, it doesn't particularly matter. Rock will recede out of view, just as all great things eventually do.

"For generations, rock music was always there, and it always felt like it would somehow come back, no matter what the current trend happened to be," Eddie Van Halen told me in the summer of 2015. "For whatever reason, it doesn't feel like it's coming back this time."

Mr. Van Halen was sixty when he said this, so some might discount such sentiments as the pessimistic opinion of someone who's given up on new music. His view, however, is shared by rock musicians who were still chewing on pacifiers when Van Halen was already famous. "I've never fully understood the references to me being a good guitarist," thirty-seven-year-old Muse front man Matt Bellamy told *Classic Rock* magazine that same summer. "I think it's a sign that maybe the guitar hasn't been very common in the last decade . . . We live in a time where intelligent people—or creative, clever people—have actually chosen computers to make music. Or they've chosen not to even work in music. They've chosen to work in tech. There's an exhaustion of intelligence which has moved out of the music industry and into other industries." The fantasies of *Fast Times at Ridgemont High* are not the fantasies of now: We've run out of teenagers with the desire (and the potential) to become Eddie Van Halen. As far as the mass culture is concerned, that time is over.

But some people will still care.

Some people will *always* care.

Even in three hundred years, some people will remember that rock happened and that rock mattered.

So what, exactly, will they remember?

[2] The concept of *success* is personal and arbitrary, so classifying someone as the "most successful" at anything tends to reflect more on the source than the subject. So keep that in mind when I make the following statement: John Philip Sousa is the most successful American musician of all time.

Marching music is a maddeningly durable genre, recognizable to pretty much everyone who's lived in the United States for any period of time. It works as a sonic shorthand for any filmmaker hoping to evoke the late nineteenth century and serves as the auditory backdrop for a national holiday, the circus, and major college football. It's not "popular" music, but it's entrenched within the popular experience. It will be no less fashionable in one hundred years than it is today. And this entire musical idiom is defined by one person—John Philip Sousa. Even the most cursory two-sentence description of marching music inevitably cites him by name. I have no data on this, but I'd confidently assert that if we were to spontaneously ask the entire US population to name every composer of marching music they could think of, over 98 percent of the populace would name either one person (Sousa) or no one at all. There's no separation between the awareness of this person and the awareness of this music, and there is no reason to believe this will ever change.

Now, the reason this happened—or at least the explanation we've decided to accept—is that Sousa was simply the best at this art. He composed 136 marches over a span of five decades and is regularly described as the most famous musician of his era. He also possessed some expressly American traits (he was born in Washington, D.C., and served as a member of the Marine Band) that make him an ideal symbol for such archly patriotic music. The story of his career has been shoehorned into the US education curriculum at a fundamental level (I first learned of Sousa in fourth grade, a year before we memorized the state capitals). And this, it seems, is how mainstream musical memory works. As the timeline moves forward, tangential artists in any genre fade from the collective radar, until only one person remains; the significance of that individual is then exaggerated, until the genre and the person become interchangeable. Sometimes this is easy to predict: I have zero doubt that the worldwide memory of Bob Marley will eventually have the same tenacity and familiarity as the worldwide memory of reggae itself.

But envisioning this process with rock is harder.

It's so hard, in fact, that most people I interviewed about this possibility can't comprehend such a reality ever happening. They all seem to think rock will always be defined by a diverse handful of artists—and for the next thirty or forty years, that will be true.

But this is because we're still trapped inside the system. The essential significance of rock remains a plausible thing to debate, as does the relative value of major figures within that system (the Doors, R.E.M., Radiohead). Right now, rock music still projects the illusion of a universe containing multitudes. But it won't seem that way in three hundred years, because nothing in the culture ever does. It will eventually be explained by one artist.

Certainly, there's one response to this hypothetical that feels immediate and sensible: the Beatles. All logic points to their dominance.[3] They were the most popular band in the world during the years they were active and they are only slightly less popular now, five decades later. The Beatles defined the conception of what a "rock group" was supposed to be, so all subsequent rock groups are (consciously or unconsciously) modeled upon the template they embodied naturally. Their aforementioned appearance on *The Ed Sullivan Show* is so regularly cited as the genesis for other bands that the Beatles arguably invented the culture of the 1970s, a decade when they were no longer together. They arguably invented *everything*, including the notion of a band breaking up. The Beatles were the first major band to write their own songs, thus making songwriting a prerequisite for credibility; they also released tracks that unintentionally spawned entire subgenres of

----

3 In fact, it's possible to imagine a fantastically far-flung future where rock music serves as a footnote *to* the Beatles, where rock only matters because it was the medium the Beatles happened to pursue. *Rolling Stone* writer Rob Sheffield has asserted this on multiple occasions, in at least two different bars. And this isn't a solely retrospective opinion, either—people speculated about that possibility from the moment the Beatles broke up. When CBS News covered the group's legal dissolution in 1970, the broadcaster only half-jokingly categorized the split as "an event so momentous that historians may one day view it as a landmark in the decline of the British Empire."

rock, such as heavy metal ("Helter Skelter"), psychedelia ("Tomorrow Never Knows"), and country rock ("I'll Cry Instead"). And though this is obviously subjective, the Beatles wrote the *best* songs (or—at the very least—the greatest number of timeless, familiar singles within the shortest window of time).

"Look, we did a lot of good music," Paul McCartney said in 2004, the kind of statement that would normally seem arrogant but actually scans as self-deprecation, considering the source and the subject. "You look at *Revolver* or *Rubber Soul*. They are decent efforts by any standards. If they're not good, then has anyone ever been any good?"

There are still things about the Beatles that can't be explained, almost to the point of the supernatural—the way their music resonates with toddlers, for example, or the way it resonated with Charles Manson. It's impossible to imagine another rock group where half its members faced assassination attempts. In any reasonable world, the Beatles are the answer to the question "Who will be the Sousa of rock?"

But our world is not reasonable. And the way this question will be asked tomorrow is (probably) not the same way we'd ask it today.

Do I think the Beatles will be remembered in three hundred years? Yes. I believe the Beatles will be the Sousa of Rock (alongside Michael Jackson, the Sousa of Pop[4]). If this were a book of

----

4 This contrast is complicated by those who insist the Beatles were actually a pop band (as opposed to a rock band), based on the contention that the Beatles had no relationship to the blues (which is mostly true—John Lennon once described the track "Yer Blues" as a parody). But I'm not going to worry about this distinction here, since worrying about it might spiral into a debate over "rockism vs. poptimism," an imaginary conflict that resembles how music writers would talk if they were characters on a TV show written by Aaron Sorkin.

predictions, that's the prediction I'd make. But this is not a book about being right. This is a book about being wrong, and my faith in wrongness is greater than my faith in the Beatles' unassailability. What I think will happen is probably not what's going to happen. So I will consider what might happen instead.

[3] Part of what makes this problem thorny is the duality of rock: It is somehow both obvious and indistinct. The central tropes of rock—crunching guitars, 4/4 time signatures, soaring vocals, long hair and leather pants, sex and drugs and unspecific rebellion—seem like a musical caricature that's identifiable to the level of interchangeability. From enough distance, the difference between Foghat and Foreigner and Soundgarden is negligible. But conversations inside music culture fixate on those negligible differences: There is still no consensus, for example, on what the first rock and roll song supposedly was (the most popular answer is 1951's "Rocket 88," but that's nowhere close to definitive). The end result is a broad definition of rock music that everyone roughly agrees upon and a working definition of rock music that is almost entirely individualized.

"I think of rock and roll as something fairly specific," says David Byrne, a gangly bicycle enthusiast best known for fronting the band Talking Heads. "Chuck Berry, early Beatles, the Stones, and a bunch of others. By the late sixties, I think other than a few diehards—many of them very good—it was over. The music was now a glorious, self-aware, arty hybrid mess."

Beyond his work with Talking Heads, Byrne is also the author of an astute book titled *How Music Works*, which is the main reason I wanted to ask him what rock music might live beyond the rock era. I suppose I literally wanted to know "how music works" over the expanse of time. What was surprising was the degree to which he denied himself this authority. As is so often the case with popular music, he ceded his own views to that of a younger person—in this case, his daughter (born in 1989).

"I would not be surprised if my daughter and some of her pals have heard of the Velvet Underground, but not many of the other acts who were having hits back in the late sixties. The Association? The Monkees? ELO? I bet she's never heard of them. Suspect she's heard of the Eagles but maybe only knows 'Hotel California' from the radio. Suspect she's heard of the Grateful Dead but has probably never heard a song."

What Byrne is unconsciously reacting to, I suspect, is an aspect of pop appreciation that latently informs everything else about it: the tyranny of the new. Since rock, pop, and rap are so closely tied to youth culture, there's an undying belief that young people are the only ones who can *really* know what's good. It's the only major art form where the opinion of a random fourteen-year-old is considered more relevant than the analysis of a sixty-four-year-old scholar. (This is why it's so common to see aging music writers championing new acts that will later seem comically overrated—once they hit a certain age, pop critics feel an obligation to question their own taste.) Even someone with Byrne's pedigree feels like he must defer to all those born after him; he graciously expresses confusion over an idiom he understands completely. Which doesn't remotely bother him, considering the role confusion plays in all of this.

"I remember reading in John Carey's book[5] that Shakespeare and Rembrandt both went through periods of being considered not important," Byrne concludes. "Carey's point was that there is no such thing as absolute, timeless, eternal artistic values that will inevitably rise and endure. It just doesn't happen. No matter how timeless and classic I think Hank Williams is, in one hundred years, some obscure recordings by some minister in Lake Charles might come out of nowhere and snatch the crown. It happens all the time. Or it might be that some cranked-out commercial crap gets a cultural reappreciation. We've seen that happen too. For all we know, the classic Greek plays were daytime dramas to the locals. I can see it now—in one hundred years, university students will be analyzing the details of every *Three's Company* episode!"

[4] What Byrne suggests is applicable to almost every topic mentioned in this book. Yet it feels particularly likely with rock music, a haphazard pursuit that's inherently irrational. There is no way to anticipate or understand how Hootie and the Blowfish's *Cracked Rear View* sold sixteen million copies while the Rolling Stones' *Exile on Main Street* was certified platinum only once. It's hard to explain how Nirvana's "Smells Like Teen Spirit" was unable to climb higher than number six on the *Billboard* Hot 100 chart, despite being viewed (almost from its media inception) as the defining song of its era. The prospect of rock's entire history being perversely formalized through a random, middling song is extraordinarily high.

----

5 *What Good Are the Arts?*

That prospect is magnified by rock's role as an ancillary vehicle. Quite often, rock music is used in conjunction with something else that's better suited to stand the test of time, inadvertently elevating a song that would have been otherwise lost. Here's an easy example: television. Three or four generations from now, the present-day entertainment medium most likely to be "studied" by cultural historians will be television, based on the belief that TV finally became a serious, meaningful art form around the turn of the twenty-first century. The first TV show imbued with this new seriousness was *The Sopranos*, so future scholars interested in the evolution of television will always recognize and reexamine that specific series. The most interpretative moment in the history of *The Sopranos* is the last scene of the final episode, set in a diner. It's a long scene with little dialogue, scored by the track "Don't Stop Believin'" by Journey. Whether or not this choice was motivated by irony is beside the point, as is the critical (traditionally negative) or popular (traditionally positive) assessment of this song: "Don't Stop Believin'" will exist as long as *The Sopranos* is considered significant. And let's suppose that future scholarship around *The Sopranos* is tenacious and comprehensive; let's suppose *The Sopranos* gets lumped in with the *Godfather* films and *Goodfellas* and *The Departed* as a means for understanding the social depiction of white organized crime, an essential cog in the history of twentieth-century America. If that happens, every directorial detail will become worth considering. Suddenly, people who don't care about the history of music will have to care about Journey. Their inclusion in this episode of television will need to be explained. And since Journey is so emblematic of the clichés of classic rock, they will become a shorthand model for what rock supposedly was.

"When you're talking about individual artists from any period of time, all those various people exist within a washing machine of chaos," argues musician Ryan Adams, phoning from the backseat of a car while touring through Denmark. Adams is a maniacally prolific songwriter who makes music in multiple genres (he's recorded fifteen albums and eight EPs in a span of fifteen years, along with hundreds of other songs that have never been officially released). He's also a published poet, a dater of celebrities, an oft-stoned goofball, and a legitimately unorthodox thinker. "Someone like Mozart or Bach remains relevant because they either contradict or embody the idea of the hero's journey. Their life—or their death—aligns with whatever it is we value about that music. Maybe the way they live or die draws attention to the work. Or with someone like Beethoven, you're talking about a musician who was deaf. But it's a more complex question with how this would apply to rock 'n' roll. Classical music, which is an extraordinarily sophisticated thing to compose, requires a listener with a lot of attention to detail and a willingness to really think about what they're experiencing. That's culturally different from something like the Sex Pistols, where you're looking at music that stimulates us because it shocks people or awakens people or scares people or electrifies people in a much more immediate way. But that's also the way all culture has progressed. It seems like people have just become more bored with being human."

Adams is asserting that the things people like about rock are less predictable than the things people like about classical music, and that this divergence increases the possibility that rock will matter for non-musical reasons. What people appreciate about rock and pop is less cerebral—the subjective notion of *cool* is the most critical aesthetic factor, and any emotional exchange can trump everything else. This, curiously, is a big part of what makes rock music compelling: There's no consistent criterion for what is (or isn't) good. Sometimes virtuosity is essential; sometimes it's actually viewed as a detriment. This is almost never the case with classical music, where non-negotiable genius is the omnipresent goal. But given enough time, both genres will fold into the same historical space. They will both be represented in totality by an exceedingly small sample of artists.

"When you look at the classical-music repertory, you can't really complain that a bunch of mediocrities have crowded out the composers of real talent," says Alex Ross, the author of *The Rest Is Noise*, a 720-page exploration of modern classical music. As a younger man, Ross was also a top-shelf rock writer (his 2001 article on Radiohead remains the best thing ever written about the group). "If you have Monteverdi representing the late Renaissance and early Baroque, or Haydn and Mozart representing the Classical era, or Beethoven, Schubert, Verdi, Wagner, and Brahms standing in for the nineteenth century, you get to feast on a tremendous body of work. Posterity has been more or less right in its judgments. The problem, though, is that Mozart becomes a brand to sell tickets, and there's an assumption that *any* work of Mozart is worth scrutiny. In fact, he wrote a fair amount of music that doesn't radiate genius in every bar. Meanwhile, there are composers of his era—Luigi Boccherini, for example—who produced many fascinating and beautiful pieces, even if you can't quite claim that they rise to Mozart's level. Ultimately, the repertory operates on a celebrity logic. These happen to be celebrities of thundering genius, but we're still giving in to a winner-takes-all mentality.

There's a basic human reason for this simplification: It's difficult to cope with the infinite variety of the past, and so we apply filters, and we settle on a few famous names."

Yes.

[5] Ryan Adams referenced the idea of "the hero's journey," a contention similar to what you'd hear from mythologist Joseph Campbell: the notion that all stories are essentially the same story. It's a narrative template Campbell called "the monomyth."[6] In Western culture, pretty much everything is understood through the process of storytelling, often to the detriment of reality. When we recount history, we tend to use the life experience of one person—the "journey" of one particular "hero"—as a prism for understanding everything else. In rock, there are two obvious candidates for this purpose: Elvis Presley and Bob Dylan. The Beatles are the most famous musical collective, but Elvis and Dylan are the towering individuals—so eminent that I don't need to use Elvis's last name or Dylan's first.

Now, neither is an ideal manifestation of rock as a sonic concept. It's been said that Presley invented rock and roll, but he actually

---

6 Here's Campbell's description of the monomyth from his book *The Hero with a Thousand Faces*: "A hero ventures forth from the world of common day into a region of supernatural wonder: fabulous forces are there encountered and a decisive victory is won: the hero comes back from this mysterious adventure with the power to bestow boons on his fellow man." This is loosely tied to Carl Jung's idea of the collective unconscious, and a heavy degree of symbolism needs to be applied—"supernatural wonder" can be anything creative or spiritual and the "mysterious adventure" (and its subsequent "boons") can just be a productive, significant livelihood. These kinds of metaphors tie into another of Campbell's core philosophies—the notion that all religions are true, but none are literal.

staged a form of seminal "pre-rock" that barely resembles the post–*Rubber Soul* universe that became the prevailing characterization of what this music is. He also exited rock culture relatively early—he was pretty much out of the game by 1973. Conversely, Dylan's career spans the entirety of rock. Yet he never made an album that "rocked" in any conventional way (the live album *Hard Rain* probably comes closest, or maybe the song "Hurricane").

Still, these people are Rock People. Both are baked into the core of the enterprise and influenced everything we understand about the form (including the Beatles themselves, a group who would not have existed without Elvis and would not have pursued introspection without Dylan). In one hundred or two hundred or five hundred years, the idea of "rock music" being represented by a two-pronged combination of Elvis and Dylan would be equitable and oddly accurate. But the passage of time makes this progressively difficult. It's simply easier for a culture to retain one story instead of two, and the stories of Presley and Dylan barely intersect (they supposedly met only once, in a Las Vegas hotel room). As I write this sentence, the social stature of Elvis and Dylan feels similar—perhaps even identical. But it's entirely possible that one of these people will get dropped as time plods forward. And if that happens, the consequence will be huge. If we concede that the "hero's journey" is the de facto story through which we understand history, the differences between these two heroes would profoundly alter the description of what rock music supposedly was.

If Elvis (minus Dylan) is the definition of rock, then rock is remembered as showbiz. Like Frank Sinatra, Elvis did not write songs; he interpreted songs that were written by other people (and like Sinatra, he did this brilliantly). But removing the essentialism of songwriting from the rock equation radically alters the context of its social value. It becomes a solely performative art form, where the meaning of a song matters less than the person singing it. It becomes *personality music*, and the dominant qualities of Presley's persona—his sexuality, his masculinity, his larger-than-life charisma—become the dominant signifiers of what rock was. His physical decline and reclusive death become an allegory for the entire culture. The reminiscence of the rock genre adopts a tragic hue, punctuated by gluttony, drugs, and the conscious theft of black culture by white opportunists. But if Dylan (minus Elvis) becomes the definition of rock, everything reverses. In this contingency, lyrical authenticity becomes everything: Rock is galvanized as an intellectual craft, interlocked with the folk tradition. It would be remembered as far more political than it actually was, and significantly more political than Dylan himself. The fact that Dylan does not have a conventionally "good" singing voice becomes retrospective proof that rock audiences prioritized substance over style, and the portrait of his seven-decade voyage would align with the most romantic version of how an eclectic collection of fifty autonomous states eventually became a place called "America."

These are the two best versions of this potential process. And both are flawed.

There is, of course, another way to consider how these things might unspool, and it might be closer to the way histories are actually built. I'm creating a binary reality where Elvis and Dylan start the race to posterity as equals, only to have one runner fall and disappear. The one who remains "wins" by default (and maybe that happens). But it might work in reverse. A slightly more plausible scenario is that future people will haphazardly decide how they want to remember rock, and whatever they decide will dictate who is declared as its architect. If the constructed memory is a caricature of big-hair arena rock, the answer is probably Elvis; if it's a buoyant, unrealistic apparition of punk hagiography, the answer is probably Dylan. But both conclusions direct us back to the same recalcitrant question: *What makes us remember the things we remember?*

[6] "Most commercial music disappears when the generation that made it dies," Ted Gioia writes me in an e-mail. "When I was a youngster, many adults could have given me a detailed account of the popular music of the 1920s. They could have told me the names of bands and songs, and why they were popular, and where they were performed. Those fans are all dead now, and only a few specialists understand this music—and even the specialists don't grasp it with the immediacy and 'deep' knowledge our grandparents possessed. After each generation dies, only a few songs and artists enjoy a lingering fame. Louis Armstrong didn't sell as many records as Ben Selvin in the 1920s, but he has retained his fame because he's been championed by critics, historians and later musicians. A few artists succeed on both artistic and commercial rankings (for example, Bing Crosby), but for a reputation to last, the artistry needs to be at the highest rung. Record sales don't matter when the people who bought the records are dead and gone."

Gioia is a historian, best known in academic circles for his authoritative books on jazz and the Delta blues. However, his mainstream profile peaked in 2014, when he published a short essay about the state of music criticism that outraged a sect of perpetually outraged music critics. Gioia's assertion was that twenty-first-century music writing has devolved into a form of lifestyle journalism that willfully ignores the technical details of the music itself. Many critics took this attack personally and accused Gioia of devaluing their vocation.[7] Which is ironic, considering the colossal degree of power Gioia ascribes to record reviewers: He believes specialists are the people who galvanize history. Music critics have almost no impact on what music is popular at any given time, but they're extraordinarily well positioned to dictate what music is reintroduced after its popularity has waned.

"Over time, critics and historians will play a larger role in deciding whose fame endures. Commercial factors will have less impact," he writes. "I don't see why rock and pop will follow any different trajectory from jazz and blues. For example: In 1956, Nelson Riddle and Les Baxter sold better than almost every rock 'n' roll star not named Elvis Presley, but historians and critics don't care about 1950s bachelor pad music. They've constructed

----

7 This controversy was small but still hilarious. Gioia's issue with music writing—that it's become overly obsessed with celebrity and personality—is something music critics had privately discussed among themselves for at least forty years. Gioia just wrote it in public, from the perspective of an uninvolved outsider. But more pressingly, I'm not sure if this categorization (even if true) is remotely troubling. Lifestyle reporting, when done well, informs how art can be understood and received. It aligns with the way most consumers interact with pop music. I don't need to analyze bass tabs in order to recognize how the bass line on "Billie Jean" is a different level of awesome. In what universe is it fun to read about time signatures and chord changes? I want to hear more about the propofol and the Elephant Man bones and the crank calls to Russell Crowe's hotel room. I want to know about the individual who imagined those bass lines in his head.

a historical perspective on the period that emphasizes the rise of rock, and that pushes everything else into the background. In 1957, Tab Hunter's 'Young Love' sold better than anything by Chuck Berry or Jerry Lee Lewis or Fats Domino. Hunter was #1 on the *Billboard* chart for six weeks in a row. But critics and music historians hate sentimental love songs, so these artists and songs struggle to get a place in the history books. Transgressive rockers, in contrast, enjoy lasting fame . . . right now, electronic dance music probably outsells hip-hop. In my opinion, this is identical to the punk-versus-disco trade-off of the 1970s. My prediction: edgy hip-hop music will win the fame game in the long run, while EDM will be seen as another mindless dance craze."

Gioia is touching on a variety of volatile ideas here, particularly the outsized memory of transgressive art. His example is the adversarial divide between punk and disco: 1977 saw the release of both the disco soundtrack to *Saturday Night Fever* and the Sex Pistols' *Never Mind the Bollocks, Here's the Sex Pistols*. The soundtrack to *Saturday Night Fever* has sold over fifteen million copies; it took *Never Mind the Bollocks* fifteen years to go platinum. Yet virtually all pop historiographers elevate the importance of the Sex Pistols above that of the Bee Gees. The same year the Sex Pistols finally sold the one millionth copy of their debut, *SPIN* placed them on a list of the seven greatest bands of all time. *Never Mind the Bollocks* is part of the White House record library, inserted by Amy Carter just before her dad lost to Ronald Reagan. The album's reputation improves by simply existing: In 1985, the British publication *NME* classified it as the thirteenth-greatest album of all time; in 1993, *NME* made a new list and decided it now deserved to be ranked sixth. This has as much to do with its transgressive identity as its musical integrity. The album is *overtly* transgressive (and therefore memorable), while *Saturday Night Fever* has been framed as a pre-fab totem of a facile culture (and thus forgettable). For almost forty years, that's been the overwhelming consensus. But I've noticed—just in the last four or five years—that this consensus is shifting. Why? Because the definition of "transgressive" is shifting. It's no longer appropriate to dismiss disco as superficial. More and more, we recognize how disco latently pushed gay, urban culture into white suburbia, which is a more meaningful transgression than going on a British TV talk show and saying "fuck." So is it *possible* that the punk-disco polarity will eventually flop? Temporarily, yes. It's possible everyone could decide to reverse how we're sup-posed to remember 1977. But there's still another level here, beyond that hypothetical inversion: the level where *everybody* who was around for punk and disco is dead and buried, and no one is left to contradict how that moment felt. When that happens, the debate over transgressions freezes and all that is left is the music. Which means the Sex Pistols win again (or maybe they lose big-ger, depending on the judge).

"There is a pragmatic, justice-driven part of my brain that believes—or needs to believe—that the cream rises to the top, and the best work endures by virtue of its goodness." These are the words of fair-minded music writer Amanda Petrusich. "That music becomes emblematic—it becomes shorthand—because it's the most effective. 'Effective,' of course, is a slippery slope when applied to art, and especially to the feelings art incites. It's a theory that presumes all examples of a given genre are accessible and able to be heard in the same way. But yeah: I think the biggest part of this just has to do with goodness. Maybe that sounds naïve."

Petrusich is the author of three books, most notably *Do Not Sell at Any Price*, a deep dive into the obsessive world of 78 RPM record collectors. The men (and it's pretty much *only* men) Petrusich chronicles are actively constructing the universe of a specific musical realm—they collect the ancient, ultra-rare recordings that were pressed onto defunct ten-inch shellac discs and rotated at the fastest turntable setting. This form of collecting is, in many ways, a technological pursuit. The obscurity of the disc itself is the essential draw. But it is still psychologically grounded in what the collectors consider *musically* essential, and those choices have a completely capricious relationship to whatever was really happening in 1933.

"With a genre like the country-blues, that shit got curated," Petrusich says. "Specific people made specific choices about what would endure. In this particular case, the people making those choices, the ones picking which records would *literally survive*, were the collectors of 78s. And, if you subscribe to the archetype—which I believe to be mostly true—collectors are outliers who feel marginalized by society, and they were personally drawn to music that reflected those feelings. And now, when people think of the Delta blues, they think of players like Skip James—a guy who made terrifying-sounding records that were not remotely popular or relevant in their time, outside of a few oddball fans and acolytes. But collectors heard them, and they recognized something in that dude's extraordinary anguish. So he became an emblem."

There is, certainly, something likable about this process: It's nice to think that the weirdos get to decide what matters about the past, since it's the weirdos who care the most. Within the insular world of pre-Depression 78s, weirdos might be the only ones who care at all. But it will be a very, very long time before the entire category of "rock" becomes that insular and arcane. There is too much preexisting mediated history to easily upend the status quo. The meaning of rock—at least in a broad sense—has already calcified. "As far as what artists get anointed, I suppose it's just whoever or whatever embodies those [central] attributes in the simplest, most direct way," Petrusich concludes. "When I think of rock 'n' roll, and who might survive, I immediately think of the Rolling Stones. They're a band that sounds like what we've all decided rock 'n' roll should sound like—loose and wild. Their story reflects that ethos and sound—loose and wild. And also, they are good."

This is true. The Rolling Stones are good, even when they release records like *Bridges to Babylon*. They've outlived every band who ever competed against them, with career album sales exceeding the present population of Brazil. From a credibility standpoint, the Rolling Stones are beyond reproach, regardless of how they choose to promote themselves: They've performed at the Super Bowl, in a Kellogg's commercial, and on an episode of *Beverly Hills, 90210*. The name of the biggest media property covering rock music was partially inspired by their sheer existence. The group members have faced arrest on multiple continents, headlined the most disastrous concert in California history, and classified themselves (with surprisingly little argument) as "the greatest rock and roll band in the world" since 1969. Working from the premise that the collective memory of rock[8] should dovetail with

----

8 I have a tendency to get fixated on the connotation and definition of specific words, but particularly the word "rock." Sometimes I think the word "rock" is literally the most important characteristic of the entire genre, in the same way

the artist *who most accurately represents what rock music actually was*, the Rolling Stones are a very, very strong answer.

But not the final answer.

[7] NASA sent the unmanned craft *Voyager* into deep space in 1977. It's still out there, forever fleeing Earth's pull. No man-made object has ever traveled farther; it passed Pluto in 1990 and currently tumbles through the interstellar wasteland. The hope was that this vessel would eventually be discovered by intelligent extraterrestrials, so NASA included a compilation album made of gold, along with a rudimentary sketch of how to play it with a stylus. A team led by Carl Sagan curated the album's contents. The record, if played by the aliens, is supposed to reflect the diversity and brilliance of earthling life. This, obviously, presupposes a lot of insane hopes: that the craft will somehow be found, that the craft will somehow be intact, that the aliens who find it will be vaguely human, that these vaguely human aliens will absorb stimuli both visually and sonically, and that these aliens will not still be listening to eight-tracks. The likelihood that anyone in the universe will play this record is only slightly greater than the likelihood that my dad will play a Kendrick Lamar album, and my dad is dead. But it was a charming idea—very optimistic

----

the prefix "rag" seems to be the critical detail within all ragtime music. Perhaps the rock artist who outlives the ravages of time will simply be whichever artist employs the word "rock" most prominently when titling their musical compositions, which would mean the band who'll eventually come to symbolize the entire rock idiom will be AC/DC (who've somehow done this on twenty-three separate occasions throughout their career). Weirdly, this would be a better resolution than almost every other possible scenario.

and Sagan-like—and it guaranteed that one rock song will exist even if the Earth is spontaneously swallowed by the sun: "Johnny B. Goode" by Chuck Berry. The song was selected by Timothy Ferris, a science writer and friend of Sagan's who'd contributed to *Rolling Stone* magazine. Ferris is considered the album's de facto producer. Supposedly, folklorist Alan Lomax was against the selection of Berry and argued that rock music was too childish to represent the highest achievements of the planet (I'm assuming Lomax wasn't too heavily engaged with the debate over the Sex Pistols and *Saturday Night Fever*).

"Johnny B. Goode" is the only rock song on the *Voyager* disc, although a few other tunes were considered. "Here Comes the Sun" was a candidate, and all four Beatles wanted it to be included—but none of them owned the song's copyright, so it was killed for legal reasons.[9] The fact that this happened in 1977 was also relevant: "Johnny B. Goode" was nineteen years old in '77, which seemed almost prehistoric at the time; if such a project was pursued in 2016, the idea of picking a nineteen-year-old song would be unthinkable (unless you find me an astrophysicist who lost her virginity to "MMMBop"). I suspect the main reason "Johnny B. Goode" was chosen is that it seemed like a levelheaded track to select. But it was more than merely reasonable. It was—either consciously or accidentally—the best possible artist for NASA to select. This is because Chuck Berry may very well become the artist *society* selects, when (and if) rock music is retroactively reconsidered by the grandchildren of your grandchildren. We might

---

9 This was probably for the best. NASA would not want the aliens to overestimate the creative role of George Harrison.

be wrong about the Beatles and the Stones; that music might matter only to people who remember it for real.

Two thousand words ago, I speculated on the divergent ways rock would be remembered if Elvis or Dylan became the sole totem for what it was. And that will be true, assuming the idea of celebrity culture dominates history in the same way it dominates modernity. If we pick the person first, that person's function becomes the genre's form. But what if it works the other way? What if all the individual components of rock shatter and dissolve, leaving behind a hazy gestalten residue that categorizes rock 'n' roll as a collection of memorable tropes? If this transpires, historians will reconstitute the genre like a puzzle. They will look at those tropes as a suit and try to decide who fits that suit best. And that theoretical suit was tailored for Chuck Berry's body.

Rock music is simple, direct, rhythm-based music. Chuck Berry made simple, direct, rhythm-based music. Rock music is black music mainstreamed by white musicians, particularly white musicians from England. Chuck Berry is a black man who directly influenced Keith Richards and Jimmy Page.[10] Rock music is grounded in the American South.[11] Chuck Berry is from St. Louis, which certainly feels like the South for most of the year. Rock

----

10 Some might argue that the artist I'm describing here actually sounds more like a description of Jimi Hendrix. But here's the problem: Hendrix's exploratory genius and musical vocabulary were so unique that he ended up being the polar opposite of a "pure distillation." He was too inventive to represent anyone but himself.

11 There's a brilliant moment in the 1995 PBS miniseries *Rock & Roll* when Gregg Allman mocks the term "Southern rock," arguing that all rock music originated in the South: "Saying *Southern* rock is like saying *rock* rock." This was back when Allman still had his original liver.

music is preoccupied with sex. Chuck Berry was a sex addict whose only American number-one single was about playing with his penis. Rock music is lawless. Chuck Berry went to prison twice before he turned forty. Rock music is tied to myth and legend (so much so that the decline of rock's prominence coincides with the rise of the Internet and the destruction of anecdotal storytelling). Chuck Berry is the subject of multiple urban legends, several of which might actually be true (and which often seem to involve cheapness, violence, and sexual defecation). "If you tried to give rock and roll another name," John Lennon famously said, "you might call it *Chuck Berry*." That quote is as close as we come to a full-on Sousa scenario, where the person and the thing are ideologically interchangeable. Chuck Berry's persona is the purest distillation of what we understand rock music to be. The songs he made are essential, but secondary to who he was and why he made them. He is the idea itself.

[8] Not everyone agrees with this, or with me. "I don't think *purest distillation* is how giant fields get replaced by one single figure," novelist Jonathan Lethem contends. "I think the one single figure isn't the inventor or the purest distillation, but the most embracing and mercurial, and often incredibly prolific." Ryan Adams disputes Berry on similar grounds: "If you're looking for a cultural highlight that will still be talked about later, it would be a symptom of the thing that was set in motion—not the inventor itself. We talk about Twitter all the time, but rarely about the person who designed it." Interestingly (or maybe unavoidably), Lethem and Adams both think the better answer is

Bob Dylan. But something tells me that their dual conclusion is too rooted in the world we still inhabit. It seems self-evident only because Dylan still feels culturally present.

I keep imagining a college classroom in five hundred years, where a hipster instructor is leading a tutorial filled with students. These students relate to rock music with the same level of fluency as the music of Mesopotamia: It's a style of music they've learned to recognize, but just barely (and only because they've taken this specific class). Nobody in the room can name more than two rock songs, except the professor. He explains the sonic structure of rock, and its origins, and the way it served as cultural currency, and how it shaped and defined three generations of a global super-power. He attempts to personify the concept of rock through the life of a rock person. He shows the class a photo—or maybe a hologram—of this chosen individual. *This is the guy.* This is the image of what rock was, and what rock is.

Will that image be a Jewish intellectual from Minnesota who never rocked?

I don't think so. And if it is, I don't know if that means things went wrong or right. Both, probably.

"Merit"

Right about now, were I reading this book (as opposed to writing it), I'd probably be asking myself the following reasonable questions: "But what about the *merit* of these things? Shouldn't we emphasize *that*? Isn't merit the most reliable criteria for longevity?" Were I the type of person predisposed toward disagreeing with whatever I was reading, I might suspect the author viewed the actual quality of these various artifacts as tangential to their ultimate value, and that all the author's suppositions inevitably suggest that what things actually are matters less than random social conditions and capricious assessments from people who don't necessarily know what they're talking about.

If that is what you assume, here is my response: You're right. Not totally, but mostly.

[This is not what people want to hear.]

I realize my partial dismissal of "merit" as a vital element of the historical record is problematic (even to me). Part of this problem is philosophical—it's depressing to think quality doesn't necessarily matter. Another part is practical—whenever we consider any specific example, it *does* seem like merit matters, in a way that feels too deep-seated to ignore. William Shakespeare is the most famous playwright who's ever lived, and his plays (or at least the themes and the language of those plays) still seem better than those of his peers. *Citizen Kane* is a clichéd response within any debate about the greatest film of all time, but it's also a legitimate response—it's a groundbreaking movie that can be rewatched and reevaluated dozens of times, somehow improving with every fresh viewing. It doesn't seem arbitrary that we all know who Vincent van Gogh is, or Pablo Picasso, or Andy Warhol. In the broadest possible sense, merit does play a key role: The work has to be good enough to enter the critical conversation, whatever that conversation happens to be. But once something is safely inside the walls of that discussion, the relative merits of its content matters much less. The final analysis is mostly just a process of reverse engineering.

Take architecture: Here we have a creative process of immense functional consequence. It's the backbone of the urban world we inhabit, and it's an art form most people vaguely understand—an architect is a person who designs a structure on paper, and that design emerges as the structure itself. Architects fuse aesthetics with physics and sociology. And there is a deep consensus over who did this best, at least among non-architects: If we walked down the street of any American city and asked people to name the greatest architect of the twentieth century, most would say Frank Lloyd Wright. In fact, if someone provided a different answer, we'd have to assume we've stumbled across an actual working architect, an architectural historian, or a personal friend of Frank Gehry. Of course, most individuals in those subsets would cite Wright, too.

But in order for someone to argue in favor of any architect *except* Wright (or even to be in a position to name three other plausible candidates), that person would almost need to be an expert in architecture. Normal humans don't possess enough information to nominate alternative possibilities. And what emerges from that social condition is an insane kind of logic: Frank Lloyd Wright is indisputably the greatest architect of the twentieth century, and the only people who'd potentially disagree with that assertion are those who legitimately understand the question.

History is defined by people who don't really understand what they are defining.

As a brick-and-mortar visionary, Wright was dazzling. He was also prolific, which matters almost as much. He championed the idea of "organic architecture," which—to someone who doesn't know anything about architecture, such as myself—seems like the condition all architecture should aspire to. But I know these imperative perspectives have no origin in my own brain. The first time I ever heard Frank Lloyd Wright's name, I was being told he was brilliant, which means the first time I looked at a building he designed, I thought either, "That is what brilliance looks like," or "This is what everyone else recognizes as brilliance." I knew he was considered "prolific" long before I ever wondered how many buildings an architect needed to design in order to be considered average, much less productive. I believe all architecture should aspire to be in harmony with its habitat, because (a) it seems like a good line of reasoning, and (b) that was Wright's line of reasoning. Yet I am certain—*certain*—that if I had learned that Wright had instead pioneered the concept of "inorganic architecture," based on a premise that architecture should be an attempt to separate the rational world of man from the uncivilized creep of nature . . . not only would I agree with those thoughts, but I would actively *see* that philosophy, fully alive within his work (even if the buildings he designed were exactly the same as they are now).

I don't believe all art is the same. I wouldn't be a critic if I did. Subjective distinctions can be made, and those distinctions are worth quibbling about. The juice of life is derived from arguments that don't seem obvious. But I don't believe subjective distinctions about quality transcend to anything close to objective truth—and every time somebody tries to prove otherwise, the results are inevitably galvanized by whatever it is they get wrong.[1]

In 1936, a quarterly magazine called *The Colophon* polled its subscribers (of whom there were roughly two thousand, although who knows how many actually voted) about what contemporary writers they believed would be viewed as canonical at the turn of the twenty-first century. The winner was Sinclair Lewis, who had won the Nobel Prize for literature just five years earlier. Others on the list include Willa Cather, Eugene O'Neill, George Santayana, and

---

1 I used to work at the rock magazine *SPIN*, a print publication that existed for twenty-seven years. Like all rock magazines, *SPIN* annually published an "Albums of the Year" list, diligently selected by its editorial board to exemplify how *SPIN* defined artistic achievement during whatever week they happened to be compiling the list. Almost all of these rankings have been completely forgotten. It's become extremely difficult to remember what album was chosen number one from any given year, even for the people who worked there and nominated the selections . . . except for the year 1991. That was the year *SPIN* placed Teenage Fanclub's *Bandwagonesque* above Nirvana's *Nevermind*. This singular misstep is cited more often than the combined total of every other selection made throughout the magazine's other twenty-six years, exacerbated by the fact that *SPIN* ultimately put Kurt Cobain on the cover ten times, seven of which came after he was dead. Because it feels so wrong in retrospect, the 1991 list is the only one that historically matters.

Robert Frost. It's a decent overview of the period. Of course, what's more fascinating is who was left off: James Joyce, F. Scott Fitzgerald, and Ernest Hemingway (although the editors of *The Colophon* did include Hemingway on their own curated list). Now, the predictive time frame we're dealing with—sixty-four years—is not that extreme. It's possible that someone who voted in this poll was still alive when the century turned. I also suspect several of the 1936 writers who still seem like valid picks today will be barely recognizable in another sixty-four years and totally lost in 640. That's just how history works. But the meaningful detail to glean from such a list is the probable motives used by the voters, since that's how we dissect their reasonable mistakes. For example: Edna St. Vincent Millay is fourth on the *Colophon* list, and Stephen Vincent Benét is ninth. Both were known primarily as poets—Millay won the Pulitzer Prize in 1923 and Benét in '29. Benét was something of a Rock Star Poet (at least at the time of the poll) and is retroactively described by the Poetry Foundation as "more widely read than Robert Frost." Yet of the three poets on this list, only Frost remains familiar. Now, the fact that *Colophon* voters went only one-for-three in their poet prognostication is not what matters here; what matters is that they voted *for three poets*. If such a poll were taken today, it's hard to imagine how far down the list one would have to scan before finding the name of even one. A present-day *Colophon* would need to create a separate category exclusively for poetry, lest it not be recognized at all. So what we see with this 1936 list is people selecting artists under the assumption that 1936 is the end of time, and that the temporary tastes and obsessions of 1936 would remain historically universal. The poll operates from the perspective that poetry is roughly half as important as prose, which is how the literary world thought in 1936. These voters were okay at gauging the relative timelessness of the various literary works, but they were terrible at projecting what the literary world would be like in the year 2000 (when the planet's best-selling, highest-profile book of poetry was *A Night Without Armor*, written by Alaskan pop star Jewel). The forces shaping collective memory are so complicated and inconsistent that any belief system dogmatically married to the concept of "merit" ends up being a logical contention that misses the point entirely. It's like arguing that the long-term success of any chain restaurant is a valid reflection of how delicious the food is.

Do you unconsciously believe that Shakespeare was an *objectively* better playwright than his two main rivals, Christopher Marlowe and Ben Jonson? If so, have no fear—as far as the world is concerned, he was. If you want to prove that he was, all you need to do is go through the texts of their respective plays and find the passages that validate the opinion most of the world already accepts. It will not be difficult, and it will feel like the differences you locate are a manifestation of *merit*. But you will actually be enforcing a tautology: Shakespeare is better than Marlowe and Jonson because Shakespeare *is more like Shakespeare*, which is how we delineate greatness within playwriting. All three men were talented. All three had enough merit to become the historical equivalent of Shakespearean, had history unspooled differently. But it didn't. It unspooled the way we understand it, and Shakespeare had almost nothing do with that. He is remembered in a way that Marlowe and Jonson are not, particularly by those who haven't *really* thought about any of these guys, ever.

To matter forever, you need to matter to those who don't care. And if that strikes you as sad, be sad.

Burn Thy Witches

I've written about pop music for over twenty years, productively enough to deliver musicology lectures at universities I could've never attended. I've been identified as an expert in rock documentaries broadcast in countries where I do not speak the language. I've made a lot of money in a profession where many talented peers earn the adult equivalent of birdseed. I've had multiple conversations about the literal meaning of the Big Star single "September Gurls," chiefly focused on who the September girls were, what they allegedly did, and why the word "girls" needed to be misspelled. I own a DVD about the prehistory of Quiet Riot and I've watched it twice. Yet any time I write about popular music—and even if the sentiment I articulate is something as banal and innocuous as "The Beach Boys were pretty great"—many, many people will tell me I don't know *anything* about music, including a few people I classify as friends. Even though every concrete signifier suggests my understanding of rock music is airtight and stable, I live my life with an omnipresent sensation of low-level anxiety about all the things I don't know about music. This is a reflection of how the world works and how my brain works.

So now I'm going to write about fucking physics.

And here are my qualifications for doing so: I took physics as a senior in high school and did not fail.

That's it. That's as far as it goes. I know how a fulcrum works and I know how to make the cue ball roll backward when I shoot pool. I know that "quantum mechanics" means "extremely small mechanics." I understand the concepts of *lift* and *drag* just enough to be continually amazed every time an airplane doesn't crash during takeoff. But that's the extent of my expertise. I don't own a microscope or a Bunsen burner. So when I write about science, I'm not really writing about "science." I'm not pretending to refute anything we currently believe about the natural world, particularly since my natural inclination is to reflexively accept all of it. I am, however, willing to reconsider the *idea* of science, and the way scientific ideas evolve. Which—in many contradictory ways—is at the center of every question this book contains.

There is, certainly, an unbreachable chasm between the subjective and objective world. A reasonable person expects subjective facts to be overturned, because subjective facts are not facts; they're just well-considered opinions, held by multiple people at the same time. Whenever the fragility of those beliefs is applied to a specific example, people bristle—if someone says, "It's possible that Abraham Lincoln won't always be considered a great president," every presidential scholar scoffs. But if you remove the specificity and ask, "Is it possible that someone currently viewed as a historically great president will have that view reversed by future generations?" any smart person will agree that such a scenario is not only plausible but inevitable. In other words, everyone concedes we have the potential to be subjectively wrong about anything, as long as we don't explicitly name whatever that something is. Our sense of subjective reality is simultaneously based on an acceptance of abstract fallibility ("Who is to say what constitutes good art?") and a casual certitude that we're right about exclusive assertions that *feel* like facts ("*The Wire* represents the apex of television").

But the objective world is different. Here, we traffic in literal facts—but the permanence of those facts matters less than the means by which they are generated. What follows is an imperfect example, but it's one of the few scientific realms that I (and many people like me) happen to have an inordinate amount of knowledge about: the Age of Dinosaurs.

In 1981, when I was reading every dinosaur book I could locate, the standard belief was that dinosaurs were cold-blooded lizards, with the marginalized caveat that "some scientists" were starting to believe they may have been more like warm-blooded birds. There were lots of reasons for this alternative theory, most notably the amount of time in the sun required to heat the blood of a sixty-ton sauropod and the limitations of a reptilian two-chambered heart. But I rejected these alternatives. When I was nine, people who thought dinosaurs were warm-blooded actively made me angry. By the time I hit the age of nineteen, however, this line of thinking had become accepted by everyone, myself included. Dinosaurs were warm-blooded, and I didn't care that I'd once thought otherwise. Such intellectual reinventions are just part of being interested in a group of animals that were already extinct ten million years before the formation of the Himalayan mountains. You naturally grow to accept that you can't really know certain things everyone considers absolute, since these are very hard things to know for sure. For almost one hundred years, one of the earmarks of a truly dino-obsessed kid was his or her realization that there actually wasn't such a thing as a *brontosaurus*—that beast was a fiction, based on a museum's nineteenth-century mistake. The creature uninformed dilettantes referred to as a "brontosaurus" was technically an "apatosaurus" . . . until the year 2015. In 2015, a paleontologist in Colorado declared that there really *was* a species of dinosaur that should rightfully be classified as a brontosaurus, and that applying that name to the long-necked animal we imagine is totally acceptable, and that all the dolts[1] who had used the wrong term out of ignorance for all those years had been correct the whole time. What was (once) always true was (suddenly) never true and then (suddenly) accidentally true.

Yet these kinds of continual reversals don't impact the way we think about paleontology. Such a reversal doesn't impact the way we think about anything, outside of the specialized new data that replaced the specialized old data. If any scientific concept changes five times in five decades, the perception is that we're simply refining what we thought we knew before, and every iteration is just a "more correct" depiction of what was previously considered "totally correct." In essence, we anchor our sense of objective reality in science itself—its laws and methods and sagacity. If certain

----

1 Also known as "kids who were mostly interested in other kids, or at least dogs and cats."

ancillary details turn out to be specifically wrong, it just means the science got better.

But what if we're *really* wrong, about something *really* big?

I'm not talking about things like the relative blood temperature of a stegosaurus or whether Pluto can be accurately classified as a planet, or even the nature of motion and inertia. What I'm talking about is the possibility that we think we're playing checkers when we're really playing chess. Or maybe even that metaphor is too conservative for what I'm trying to imagine—maybe we think we're playing checkers, but we're actually playing goddamn Scrabble. Every day, our understanding of the universe incrementally increases. New questions are getting answered. But are these the right questions? Is it possible that we are mechanically improving our comprehension of principles that are all components of a much larger illusion, in the same way certain eighteenth-century Swedes believed they had *finally* figured out how elves and trolls caused illness? Will our current understanding of how space and time function eventually seem as absurd as Aristotle's assertion that a brick doesn't float because the ground is the "natural" place a brick wants to be?

No. (Or so I am told.)

"The only examples you can give of complete shifts in widely accepted beliefs—beliefs being completely thrown out the window—are from before 1600," says superstar astrophysicist Neil deGrasse Tyson. We are sitting in his office in the upper deck of the American Museum of Natural History. He seems mildly annoyed by my questions. "You mentioned Aristotle, for example. You could also mention Copernicus and the Copernican Revolution. That's all before 1600. What was different from 1600 onward was how science got conducted. Science gets conducted by experiment. There is no truth that does not exist without experimental verification of that truth. And not only one person's experiment, but an ensemble of experiments testing the same idea. And only when an ensemble of experiments statistically agree do we then talk about an emerging truth within science. And that emerging truth does not change, because it was verified. Previous to 1600—before Galileo figured out that experiments matter—Aristotle had no clue about experiments, so I guess we can't blame him. Though he was so influential and so authoritative, one might say some damage was done, because of how much confidence people placed in his writing and how smart he was and how deeply he thought about the world . . . I will add that in 1603 the microscope was invented, and in 1609 the telescope was invented. So these things gave us tools to replace our own senses, because our own senses are quite feeble when it comes to recording objective reality. So it's not like this is a *policy*. This is, 'Holy shit, this really works. I can establish an objective truth that's not a function of my state of mind, and you can do a different experiment and come up with the same result.' Thus was born the modern era of science."

This is all accurate, and I would never directly contradict anything Neil deGrasse Tyson says, because—compared to Neil deGrasse Tyson—my skull is a bag of hammers. I'm the functional equivalent of an idiot. But maybe it takes an idiot to pose this non-idiotic question: How do we know we're not currently living in our own version of the year 1599?

According to Tyson, we have not reinvented our understanding of scientific reality since the seventeenth century. Our beliefs have been relatively secure for roughly four hundred years. That's a long time—except in the context of science. In science, four hundred years is a grain in the hourglass. Aristotle's ideas about gravity were accepted for more than twice that long. Granted, we're now in an era where repeatable math can confirm theoretical ideas, and that numeric confirmation creates a sense that—*this time*—what we believe to be true is not going to change. We will learn much more in the coming years, but mostly as an extension of what we already know now. Because—*this time*—what we know is actually right.

Of course, we are not the first society to reach this conclusion.

[2] If I spoke to one hundred scientists about the topic of scientific wrongness, I suspect I'd get one hundred slightly different answers, all of which would represent different notches on a continuum of confidence. And if this were a book *about science*, that's what I'd need to do. But this is not a book about science; this is a book about continuums. Instead, I interviewed two exceptionally famous scientists who exist (or at least *appear* to exist) on opposite ends of a specific psychological spectrum. One of these was Tyson, the most conventionally famous astrophysicist alive.[2] He hosted the Fox reboot of the science series *Cosmos* and created his own talk show on the National Geographic Channel. The other was string theorist Brian Greene at Columbia University (Greene is the person mentioned in this book's introduction, speculating on the possibility that "there is a very, very good

---

2 Unless you count Stephen Hawking, who is technically a cosmologist.

chance that our understanding of gravity will not be the same in five hundred years").

Talking to only these two men, I must concede, is a little like writing about debatable ideas in pop music and interviewing only Taylor Swift and Beyoncé Knowles. Tyson and Greene are unlike the overwhelming majority of working scientists. They specialize in translating ultra-difficult concepts into a language that can be understood by mainstream consumers; both have written best-selling books for general audiences, and I assume they both experience a level of envy and skepticism among their professional peers. That's what happens to any professional the moment he or she appears on TV. Still, their academic credentials cannot be questioned. Moreover, they represent the competing poles of this argument almost perfectly. Which might have been a product of how they chose to hear the questions.

When I sat down in Greene's office and explained the premise of my book—in essence, when I explained that I was interested in considering the likelihood that our most entrenched assumptions about the universe might be wrong—he viewed the premise as playful. His unspoken reaction came across as "This is a fun, non-crazy hypothetical." Tyson's posture was different. His unspoken attitude was closer to "This is a problematic, silly supposition." But here again, other factors might have played a role: As a public intellectual, Tyson spends a great deal of his time representing the scientific community in the debate over climate change. In certain circles, he has become the face of science. It's entirely possible Tyson assumed my questions were veiled attempts at debunking scientific thought, prompting him to take an inflexibly hard-line stance. (It's also possible this is just the stance he always takes with everyone.) Conversely, Greene's openness might be a reflection of his own academic experience: His career is punctuated by research trafficking on the far edges of human knowledge, which means he's accustomed to people questioning the validity of ideas that propose a radical reconsideration of everything we think we know.

One of Greene's high-profile signatures is his support for the concept of "the multiverse." Now, what follows will be an oversimplification—but here's what that connotes: Generally, we work from the assumption that there is one universe, and that our galaxy is a component of this one singular universe that emerged from the Big Bang. But the multiverse notion suggests there are infinite (or at least numerous) universes beyond our own, existing as alternative realities. Imagine an endless roll of bubble wrap; our universe (and everything in it) would be one tiny bubble, and all the other bubbles would be other universes that are equally vast. In his book *The Hidden Reality*, Greene maps out nine types of parallel universes within this hypothetical system. It's a complicated way to think about space, not to mention an inherently impossible thing to prove; we can't get (or see) outside our own universe any more than a man can get (or see) outside his own body. And while the basic concept of a limited multiverse might not seem particularly insane, the logical extensions of what a limitless multiverse would entail are almost impossible to fathom.

Here's what I mean: Let's say there are infinite universes that exist over the expanse of infinite time (and the key word here is "infinite"). Within infinity, everything that *could* happen *will* happen.[3] Everything. Which would mean that—somewhere, in an alternative universe—there is a planet exactly like Earth, which has existed for the exact same amount of time, and where every single event has happened exactly as it has on the Earth that we know as our own . . . except that on Christmas Eve of 1962, John F. Kennedy dropped a pen. And there is still another alternative universe with a planet exactly like Earth, surrounded by an exact replica of our moon, with all the same cities and all the same people, except that—in this reality—you read this sentence yesterday instead of today. And there is still another alternative universe where everything is the same, except you are slightly taller. And there is still another alternative universe beyond that one where everything is the same, except you don't exist. And there is still another alternative reality beyond that where a version of Earth exists, but it's ruled by robotic wolves with a hunger for liquid cobalt. And so on and so on and so on. In an infinite multiverse, everything we have the potential to imagine—as well as everything we *can't* imagine—would exist autonomously. It would require a total recalibration of every spiritual and secular belief that ever was. Which is why it's not surprising that many people don't dig a transformative hypothesis that even its proponents concede is impossible to verify.

"There really are some highly decorated physicists[4] who

---

3 As a species, the concept of "infinity" might be too much for us. We can define it and we can accept it—but I don't know if it's possible for humans to truly comprehend a universe (or a series of universes) where everything that *could* happen *will* happen. I suspect the human conception of infinity is akin to a dog's conception of a clock.

4 Greene is not exaggerating: He said he's had the same argument at least ten times with David Gross, the winner of the Nobel Prize for physics in 2004. "Because we can't falsify the idea," Gross writes of the multiverse, "it isn't

have gotten angry with me, and with people like me, who have spoken about the multiverse theory," Greene says. "They will tell me, 'You've done some real damage. This is nuts. Stop it.' And I'm a completely rational person. I don't speak in hyperbole to get attention. My true feeling is that these multiverse ideas could be right. Now, why do I feel that way? I look at the mathematics. The mathematics lead in this direction. I also consider the history of ideas. If you described quantum physics to Newton, he would have thought you were insane. Maybe if you give Newton a quantum textbook and five minutes, he sees it completely. But as an idea, it would seem insane. So I guess my thinking is this: I think it's extraordinarily unlikely that the multiverse theory is correct. I think it's extraordinarily likely that my colleagues who say the multiverse concept is crazy are right. But I'm not willing to say the multiverse idea is *wrong*, because there is no basis for that statement. I understand the discomfort with the idea, but I nevertheless allow it as a real possibility. Because it *is* a real possibility."

Greene delivered a TED talk about the multiverse in 2012, a twenty-two-minute lecture translated into more than thirty languages and watched by 2.5 million people. It is, for all practical purposes, the best place to start if you want to learn what the multiverse would be like. Greene has his critics, but the concept is taken seriously by most people who understand it (including Tyson, who has said, "We have excellent theoretical and philosophical reasons to think we live in a multiverse"). He is the

----

science." In other words, because there's no way for the multiverse theory to be proven untrue, it can't be examined through the scientific method.

recognized expert on this subject. Yet he's still incredulous about his own ideas, as illustrated by the following exchange:

Q: *What is your level of confidence that—in three hundred years—someone will reexamine your TED talk and do a close reading of the information, and conclude you were almost entirely correct?*

A: Tiny. Less than one percent. And you know, if I was really being careful, I wouldn't have even given that percentage a specific number, because a number requires data. But take that as my loose response. And the reason my loose response is one percent just comes from looking at the history of ideas and recognizing that every age thinks they were making real headway toward the ultimate answer, and every next generation comes along and says, "You were really insightful, but now that we know X, Y, and Z, here is what we actually think." So, humility drives me to anticipate that we will look like people from the age of Aristotle who believed stones fell to earth because stones wanted to be on the ground.

Still, as Greene continues to explain the nature of his skepticism, a concentration of optimism slowly seeps back in.

In the recesses of my mind, where I would not want to be out in public—even though I realize you're recording this, and this is a public conversation—I do hold out hope that in one hundred or five hundred years, people will look back on our current work and say, "Wow." But I love to be conservative in my estimates. Still, I sometimes think I'm being too conservative, and that makes me excited. Because look at quantum mechanics. In quantum mechanics, you can do a calculation and predict esoteric properties of electrons. And you can do the calculation—and people have done these calculations, heroically, over the span of decades—and compare [those calculations] to actual experiments, and the numbers agree. They agree up to the tenth digit beyond the decimal point. That is unprecedented—that we can have a theory that agrees with observation to that degree. That makes you feel like "This is different." It makes you feel like you're closing in on truth.

So here is the hinge point where skepticism starts to reverse itself. Are we the first society to conclude that *this time* we're finally right about how the universe works? No—and every previous society who thought they were correct ended up hopelessly mistaken. That, however, doesn't mean that the goal is innately hopeless. Yes, we are not the first society to conclude that our version of reality is objectively true. But we could be the first society to express that belief and is never contradicted, because we might be the first society to really get there. We might be the *last* society, because—now—we translate absolutely everything into math. And math is an obdurate bitch.

[3] The "history of ideas," as Greene notes, is a pattern of error, with each new generation reframing and correcting the mistakes of the one that came before. But "not in physics, and not since 1600," insists Tyson. In the ancient world, science was fundamentally connected to philosophy. Since the age of Newton, it's become fundamentally connected to math. And in any situation where the math zeroes out, the possibility of overturning the idea becomes borderline impossible. We don't know—and we *can't* know—if the laws of physics are the same everywhere in the universe, because we can't access most of the universe. But there are compelling reasons to believe this is indeed the case, and those reasons can't be marginalized as egocentric constructions that will wax and wane with the attitudes of man. Tyson uses an example from 1846, during a period when the laws of Newton had seemed to reach their breaking point. For reasons no one could comprehend, Newtonian principles were failing to describe the orbit of Uranus. The natural conclusion was that the laws of physics must work only within the inner solar system (and since Uranus represented the known edge of that system, it must be operating under a different set of rules).

"But then," Tyson explains, "someone said: 'Maybe Newton's laws still work. Maybe there's an unseen force of gravity operating on this planet that we have not accounted for in our equations.' So let's assume Newton's law is correct and ask, 'If there is a hidden force of gravity, where would that force be coming from? Maybe it's coming from a planet we have yet to discover.' This is a very difficult math problem, because it's one thing to say, 'Here's a planetary mass and here's the value of its gravity.' Now we're saying we have the value of gravity, so let's infer the existence of a mass. In math, this is called an inversion problem, which is way harder than starting with the object and calculating its gravitational field. But great mathematicians engaged in this, and they said, 'We predict, based on Newton's laws that work on the inner solar system, that if Newton's laws are just as accurate on Uranus as they are anywhere else, there ought to be a planet right *here*—go look for it.' And the very night they put a telescope in that part of the sky, they discovered the planet Neptune."

The reason this anecdote is so significant is the sequence. It's easy to discover a new planet and then work up the math proving that it's there; it's quite another to mathematically insist a massive undiscovered planet should be precisely where it ends up being. This is a different level of correctness. It's not interpretative, because numbers have no agenda, no sense of history, and no sense of humor. The Pythagorean theorem doesn't need the existence of Mr. Pythagoras in order to work exactly as it does.

I have a friend who's a data scientist, currently working on the economics of mobile gaming environments. He knows a great deal about probability theory,[5] so I asked him if our contemporary

----

5 When I first met this guy (his name is Mike Mathog), the only thing I knew about him was how much he hated an absurdist joke I'd made in one of my early books, where I claimed the probability of *everything* was always 50-50 ("Either something will happen, or something will not"). Mike has since invested a lot of conversational effort into proving I am empirically wrong about this, which means he's invested a lot of conversational effort into proving I was incorrect about something I never actually believed in the first place. In fact, I feel like he's brought this up in half the conversations we've had ever since the very first night we met. So every time I see him, the odds of this specific interaction happening again are 50-50.

understanding of probability is still evolving and if the way people understood probability three hundred years ago has any relationship to how we will gauge probability three hundred years from today. His response: "What we think about probability in 2016 is what we thought in 1716, for sure . . . probably in 1616, for the most part . . . and probably what [Renaissance mathematician and degenerate gambler Gerolamo] Cardano thought in 1564. I know this sounds arrogant, but what we've believed about probability since 1785 is still what we'll believe about probability in 2516."

If we base any line of reasoning around consistent numeric values, there is no way to be wrong, unless we are (somehow) wrong about the very nature of the numbers themselves. And that possibility is a non-math conversation. I mean, can 6 *literally* turn out to be 9? Jimi Hendrix imagined such a scenario, but only because he was an electric philosopher (as opposed to a pocket calculator).

"In physics, when we say we know something, it's very simple," Tyson reiterates. "Can we predict the outcome? If we can predict the outcome, we're good to go, and we're on to the next problem. There are philosophers who care about the understanding of *why* that was the outcome. Isaac Newton [essentially] said, 'I have an equation that says why the moon is in orbit. I have no fucking idea how the Earth talks to the moon. It's empty space—there's no hand reaching out.' He was uncomfortable about this idea of action at a distance. And he was criticized for having such ideas, because it was preposterous that one physical object could talk to another physical object. Now, you can certainly have that conversation [about why it happens]. But an equation properly predicts what it does. That other conversation is for people having a beer. It's a beer conversation. So go ahead—have that conversation. 'What is the nature of the interaction between the moon and the Earth?' Well, my equations get it right every time. So you can say that gremlins do it—it doesn't matter to my equation . . . Philosophers like arguing about [semantics]. In physics, we're way more practical than philosophers. Way more practical. If something works, we're on to the next problem. We're not arguing *why*. Philosophers argue *why*. It doesn't mean we don't like to argue. We're just not derailed by *why*, provided the equation gives you an accurate account of reality."

In terms of speculating on the likelihood of our collective wrongness, Tyson's distinction is huge. If you remove the deepest question—the question of why—the risk of major error falls through the floor. And this is because the problem of *why* is a problem that's impossible to detach from the foibles of human nature. Take, for example, the childhood question of why the sky is blue. This was another problem tackled by Aristotle. In his systematic essay "On Colors," Aristotle came up with an explanation for why the sky is blue: He argued that all air is *very slightly* blue, but that this blueness isn't perceptible to the human eye unless there are many, many layers of air placed on top of each other (similar, according to his logic, to the way a teaspoon of water looks clear but a deep well of water looks black). Based on nothing beyond his own powers of deduction, it was a genius conclusion. It explains why the sky is blue. But the assumption was totally wrong. The sky is blue because of the way sunlight is refracted. And unlike Aristotle, the person who realized this truth didn't care why it was true, which allowed him to be right forever. There will never be a new explanation for why the sky is blue.

Unless, of course, we end up with a new explanation for *everything*.

[**4**] A few pages back, I positioned two scientists—Tyson and Greene—on opposite ends of a continuum of confidence, constructed inside my own mind. But even in the context of this fabricated binary, they agree on things far more than they differ. Since the dawn of civilization, people have argued about (and continually increased) the age of the known universe; when I asked both men if there was any chance the current age of our universe will be recalculated again, they both had the same answer. "It will not happen," says Tyson. "That number [13.79 billion years, plus or minus 0.2] is actually quite stable," reiterates Greene. Even on points of conflict, they generally force themselves into alignment: When I told Tyson that Greene was open to the possibility that our understanding of gravity might drastically change, Tyson implied that I may have phrased the question incorrectly.

"He's pointing forward to a time when our understanding of gravity includes our understanding of dark matter," said Tyson. "That there will be some other understanding of gravity, but it will still enclose Newton's laws of gravity and Einstein's general relativity. So he may have presumed your question meant, 'Is there anything *left* to be discovered about gravity?' And that question is not clear to someone who researches gravity."

This kind of willful, unilateral agreement is not unique to famous scientists—most of the unfamous scientists would agree, too. You're not really a scientist if you don't. The core components of science—say, the structure of DNA or the speed of light or the weight of carbon—have to be uniform. This is a card game that can be played with only one specific deck, and that should increase our confidence in what we believe to be true. If everyone is using the same information to do different things and still coming to the same reliable conclusions, there isn't much room for profound wrongness.

Yet there is something about the depth of this consensus that makes me slightly *less* confident.

Can I point to a specific example? I can't point to any specific example. If someone demanded I outline an unambiguous scientific truth that seems dangerously misguided, I could not do it (and if someone else did so, my contradictory inclination would be to immediately disagree). But herein lies the problem. If we're playing a card game that works with only one deck, we can interrogate only the deck itself. If we assert, "This Queen of Diamonds is actually a Joker," the rest of the cards will prove the assertion is wrong. What we can't do is allege that we're all playing the game wrong, because this is the only game anyone plays. We can't assert that this card game is actually a board game, because nobody knows what that would mean if we can't visualize the board. This is the ultimate model for naïve realism: It's irrational to question any explicit detail within a field of study that few rational people classify as complete.

"There are certainly some ideas that many of us are starting to anticipate will be jettisoned, even if we can't quite jettison them just yet," Greene says. "The most basic being that space and time are ingredients that are somehow fundamental, and that space and time will be the starting point for any understanding of physics. Even going back to Aristotle, there is this basic assumption that physics take place in an arena—basically, inside a container. And that container involves some expanse that we call *space*, and events in the space take place over a duration we call *time*. Now, it's certainly the case that our view of space and time has shifted, mostly because of Einstein. We now see space and time as much more malleable. But we still see them as 'being there,' for lack of a better term. But some of us anticipate that—in the future—our theories will not start with space and time. They will start with something more fundamental. What that fundamental thing is—we still don't know. Sometimes we give it names like 'the atoms of space and time' or 'the constituents of space and time.' We don't really have a name for whatever this is, because it's not necessarily a particle, per se. It's an even more basic entity. It's something that—when arranged in a specific way—*builds* space and time. But if those ingredients were somehow arranged differently, the concepts of space and time wouldn't even apply."

Whether or not you take Greene's position as radical is open to interpretation (some might classify it as inordinately safe). I'm in no position to adequately consider what it would mean if physics were no longer based on space and time, or what that would change about day-to-day life. But his central point is my obsession: the possibility that we are unable to isolate or imagine something *fundamental* about the construction of reality, and that the eventual realization of whatever that fundamental thing is will necessitate a rewrite of everything else. Here again, I'm not the first person to fantasize about this possibility. It's the controversial premise of Thomas Kuhn's 1962 masterwork *The Structure of Scientific Revolutions*. Kuhn's take was that science does not advance through minor steps, but through major ones—basically, that everyone believes all the same things for long stretches of time, only to have the entire collective worldview altered by a paradigm shift[6] transforming the entire system. Prior to these massive shifts, researchers conduct what Kuhn called "normal science," where scientists try to solve all the puzzles inside the existing paradigm, inadvertently propping up its dominance. In essence, Kuhn saw science as less coldly objective than scientists prefer to believe.

It's easy to recognize why *The Structure of Scientific Revolutions* annoys a lot of people who earn a living trying to figure out why and how the world works. There's something a little insulting about the term "normal science," in the same way it's insulting to describe a woman's outfit as "basic." There's also a high degree of intellectual hopelessness ingrained within this philosophy—it makes it seem like whatever science is happening at any given time is just a placeholder, and that the main purpose of any minor scientific advance is to wait for its inevitable obsolescence. Tyson strongly criticized the book, noting that its main arguments are (again) stuck in the seventeenth century.

"[*The Structure of Scientific Revolutions*] was hugely influential," Tyson tells me, "especially on the liberal arts, giving them ammunition to suggest that science was no better way of knowing the truth than any other way of investigating. It made a huge case of scientists gathering around one truth, and then there's a tipping point and everyone moves away from that truth to gather around another truth. Hence the title of the book. And this left people

----
6 If you're the type who hates seeing buzzwords like "paradigm shift" in every piece of cultural analysis you encounter, blame Kuhn. He didn't invent the term, but he introduced it to most normal people. Some have argued that *The Structure of Scientific Revolutions* is the most-read science book of all time, among non-scientists.

with the sense that science is just whatever is in fashion. Kuhn used, as his best example of this, Copernicus. That's half his book . . . almost half of that book describes the Copernican Revolution as an example of the way science works. But that's not how science works. It's just not. It's how things happened until 1600."

Kuhn died in 1996, so he can't respond to this accusation. But I assume his response would be something in the neighborhood of "Well, of course *you* think that. You have to. You're a scientist." A philosopher can simultaneously forward an argument's impregnable logic and its potential negation within the same sentence; a scientist can't do that. There is no practical purpose to fungible physics. If Tyson were to validate the possibility that his entire day-to-day vocation is just "normal science" that will eventually be overwritten by a new paradigm, it would justify the lethargic thinking of anyone who wants to ignore the work that he does (work that he believes is too important to ignore). It is, in many ways, a completely unbalanced dispute. Tyson (or Greene, or any credible scientist) can present ten thousand micro arguments that demonstrate why our current structure of scientific inquiry is unique and unassailable. A Kuhnian disciple need only make one macro argument in response: *Well, that's how it always seems, until it doesn't.*

My limited brain tells me that ten thousand micro arguments are better than one macro abstraction. My limited sense of reality tells me that Kuhn's abstraction is reasonable and unavoidable, and that the attacks against it define naïve realism. And it's that latter sensation that prompts me to pose the following: If we're destined (as Kuhn would argue) for an inevitable paradigm shift, what would that shift feel like?

[5] Here's the thing with paradigm shifts: They tend to be less dramatic than cultural memory suggests. There's a tendency to imagine that all those who upend the nature of existence are marginalized as heretics and crucified by crazed mobs, because drama confirms the importance of what those people thought. But it rarely happens like that, and the last monster shift in science—the Copernican Revolution—was a textbook example.

Nicolaus Copernicus surmised that the Earth rotated around the sun in about 1514, and no one killed him for thinking that. He lived another twenty-nine years and died at the age of seventy. Throughout those final twenty-nine years, his revolutionary description of outer space mostly seemed like an unprovable thought experiment that had the ancillary benefit of making the calendar more accurate, which made it easier to schedule Easter. When Galileo later declared that Copernicus was right (and that the Bible was therefore wrong) in the seventeenth century, he was eventually arrested by the Inquisition and forced to recant—but not before the Catholic Church told him (and I'm paraphrasing here): "Hey, man. We all know you're probably correct about this. We concede that you're a wizard, and what you're saying makes sense. But you gotta let us explain this stuff to the rest of the world very, very slowly. We can't suddenly tell every pasta-gorged plebeian in rural Italy that we live in a heliocentric universe. It will blow their minds and fuck up our game. Just be cool for a while." Galileo famously refused to chill and published his *Dialogue Concerning the Two Chief World Systems* as soon as he possibly could, mocking all those who believed (or claimed to believe) that the

Earth was the center of the universe. The pope, predictably, was not stoked to hear this. But the Vatican still didn't execute Galileo; he merely spent the rest of his life under house arrest (where he was still allowed to write books about physics) and lived to be seventy-seven.

I don't mention this to negate what these guys learned, the adversity they faced, or what they accomplished. But it does serve to illustrate the pace at which ideological transformations actually occur: This revolution took over one hundred years, invisible to the vast majority of the planet. Granted, a revolution within our accelerated culture would happen far faster. The amount of human information exchanged is exponentially different, as is the overall level of literacy. But that still doesn't mean a transformative period would be transparent to the people actually experiencing it; this is why I ask how a modern paradigm shift would *feel*, as opposed to what it would look like or how it would operate. Like a fifteenth-century monk, my perspective is locked by fixed boundaries. I cannot depict a transformation I don't have the ability to visualize. But I can envision the *texture* of how such an experience might feel. I can imagine the cognition of my current worldview slowly dissolving, in the same way certain dreams dissolve within the same instant I wake up and realize that I was not experiencing my actual life.

Every so often, minor news stories will surface suggesting something major about science is already shifting. "NASA successfully tests engine that uses no fuel [and] violates the laws of physics," read an August 1, 2014, headline in the citizen-journalist-run *Examiner*. Nine months later, the Silicon Valley–based *Tech Times* proclaimed, "NASA may have accidentally discovered faster-than-light travel." Both articles were about the EmDrive, an experimental rocket thruster that supposedly violates Newton's Third Law (the conservation of momentum). By the time any reader reached the conclusion of these articles, it was clear that the alleged breakthroughs were more interesting than practical. But if a series of similar stories kept appearing in greater depth, and if they ran in places like *The Guardian* and *Scientific American* and *Wired*, there'd be a general sense that a rethinking[7] of how we viewed space and time was necessary. This is not the type of paradigm shift I try to imagine, however. To me, this feels closer to a typical conversation about technology (which is, obviously, always advancing). Instead, I tend to think about two distinct varieties of potential shifts: the world beyond us, and the world around us.

What I classify as "the world beyond us" are notions like the aforementioned multiverse—the possibility of a cosmos that is way more complicated than the cosmos we conceive. Does such a cosmos seem plausible? Sure. It almost seems likely. I cautiously suspect there are universes beyond our universe, the laws of which might contradict the most basic things we believe. But what is the *feeling* that would accompany the validation of this hypothesis?

Nothing.

There would be no feeling at all. It would just be an interesting thing to know. I mean, even if NASA did "accidentally" invent faster-than-light travel, it wouldn't even be a useful tool for

---

7 Or maybe just a different context for the word "law." When people mention Newton's laws, they use the term "laws" because the rules are unbreakable. But perhaps they are unbreakable only in nature. Maybe the barriers they represent are real, but *we can still break them*, as technology advances beyond the parameters of the natural world.

exploring these particular possibilities. Depending on what estimate you use, Earth is somewhere[8] between 24,000 and 94,000
light-years away from the edge of the Milky Way galaxy. Even if
EmDrive technology allowed us to travel at the improbable top
speed of the USS *Enterprise* from *Star Trek: The Next Generation*
(1.04 light-years per hour), and even if we used the low end of
the distance estimate, it would still take 2.6 years just to reach
the Milky Way's edge. The distance to the next major galaxy is
another 2.5 million light-years, so that would be a 26-year trip.
Most critically, the known universe is over 90 billion light-years
in diameter (and that's just the observable part, which—even in
a non-multiverse theory—might be one-thousandth of its actual
size). Even if we irrefutably knew[9] there was a cosmos beyond our
cosmos, it could never be reached by anything except a wormhole,
the likes of which have been found only in fiction. The multiverse
could not be seen or described, and certainly not visited. Which
means incontrovertible proof of an infinite multiverse would be
like incontrovertible proof of purgatory—we'd just have to dogmatically accept it, with no functional application to our daily
lives. For non-scientists, the same could be said for a similar super-
discovery in quantum mechanics: If we realized something profound and insane about atomic structure, happening on a level so
microscopic that it could never be touched or observed or manipulated, the only thing it would really change is the language of
textbooks. Here again, the (very real) paradigm shift would *feel*

----

8 As far as I can tell, the official "edge" of the galaxy cannot be defined.

9 No clue as to how this would become irrefutably known. I guess it would require
an anonymous, untraceable transmission from aliens?

like nothing at all. It would mirror the reaction of a seventeenth-century shepherd who had just been told we live in a heliocentric universe: "Oh."

But what if we told that seventeenth-century shepherd something even crazier?

What if we told him that he did not exist? And that his sheep didn't exist, and neither did the pasture he was standing in, nor the moon, nor the sun? Or even the person who was telling him this?

This is a shift in the world around us.

This is a shift in "the (simulated) world around us."

[**6**] Like most people who enjoy dark rooms and Sleep's *Jerusalem*, I dig the simulation argument. It is, as far as I can tell, the most reasonable scientific proposition no one completely believes. I have yet to encounter anyone who totally buys it; even the man most responsible for its proliferation places the likelihood of its validity at roughly 20 percent. But even a one-in-five chance presents the potential for a paradigm shift greater than every other historical shift combined. It would place the Copernican Revolution on a par with the invention of Velcro.

The man to whom I refer is existential Swedish philosopher Nick Bostrom, currently directing the Future of Humanity Institute at the University of Oxford. He's relatively young (born in '73), balding, and slightly nervous that the human race will be annihilated by robots. Yet it is his simulation hypothesis (building off the earlier work of Austrian roboticist Hans Moravec) that really moves the stoner needle. The premise of his hypothesis started showing up in places like *The New York Times* around 2007, and it boils down to this: What we believe to be reality is actually a computer simulation, constructed in a future where artificial intelligence is so advanced that those living inside the simulation cannot tell the difference. Essentially, we would all be characters in a supernaturally sophisticated version of The Sims or Civilization, where the constructed characters—us—are self-aware and able to generate original thoughts and feelings. But none of this would be *real*, in the way that term is traditionally used. And this would be true for all of history and all of space.[10]

What Bostrom is asserting is that there are three possibilities about the future, one of which must be true. The first possibility is that the human race becomes extinct before reaching the stage where such a high-level simulation could be built. The second possibility is that humans *do* reach that stage, but for whatever reason—legality, ethics, or simple disinterest—no one ever tries to simulate the complete experience of civilization. The third possibility is that we are living in a simulation right now. Why? Because if it's possible to create this level of computer simulation (and if it's legally and socially acceptable to do so), there won't just be *one* simulation. There will be an almost limitless number of competing simulations, all of which would be disconnected from each other. A computer program could be created that does nothing

----

10 Though some are tempted to connect this theory to the scenario described in *The Matrix*, there is no relationship. *The Matrix* suggests real human bodies could serve as batteries for the projection of a simulated world. This theory suggests "real humans" are not involved at all, at least within the projection itself.

except generate new simulations, all day long, for a thousand consecutive years. And once those various simulated societies reach technological maturity, they would (assumedly) start creating simulations of their own—simulations inside of simulations. Eventually, we would be left with the one original "real" reality, along with billions and billions of simulated realities. Simple mathematical odds tell us that it's far more likely our current reality would fall somewhere in the latter category. The chance that we are living through the immature stages of the original version is certainly possible, but ultra-remote.

If you're the type of person who first read about the simulation argument in 2007 and stopped thinking about it by 2008, your reaction to the previous paragraph is probably, "This incomprehensible nonsense again?" If you've never heard of the simulation argument before today, you're probably trying to imagine how any of this could possibly be true. There's always an entrenched psychological hurdle with this hypothesis—it's just impossible for any person to circumvent the sense that what appears to be happening *is really happening*, and that the combination of strangeness and comfort within this experience makes the sensation of "being alive" too uncanny to be anything but genuine. But this sensation can't be trusted (in fact, it might be baked into the simulation). And what's most compelling about this concept is how rational it starts to seem, the longer you think about it. Bostrom is a philosopher, but this hypothesis is not really an extension of philosophy. This is not a situation where we start from the premise that we don't exist and demand someone prove that we do. It follows a basic progression:

1. We have computers, and these computers keep getting better.
2. We can already create reality simulations on these computers, and every new generation of these simulations dramatically improves.
3. There is no reason to believe that these two things will stop being true.

In a limited capacity, artificial intelligence already exists. Even if mankind is never able to create a digital character that's fully conscious, it seems possible that mankind could create a digital character that *assumes* it is conscious, within the context of its program. Which actually sounds a lot like the experience we're all having here, right now, on "Earth." That actually sounds a lot like life.

Certainly, it takes a mental leap to imagine how this circumstance would have transpired. But that leap is less than you might think. Here's one possible scenario, described by Brian Greene: At the time, Greene was discussing a collection of (roughly) twenty numbers that seem to dictate how the universe works. These are constants like "the mass of an electron" and "the strength of gravity," all of which have been precisely measured and never change. These twenty numbers appear inconceivably fine-tuned—in fact, if these numbers didn't have the exact value that they do, nothing in the universe would exist. They are so perfect that it almost appears as if someone *set* these numbers. But who could have done that? Some people would say God. But the simulation hypothesis presents a secular answer: that these numbers were set by the simulator.

"That's a rational possibility: that someday, in the future, we'll be able to simulate universes with such verisimilitude that the beings within those simulations believe they are alive in a conventional sense. They will not know that they are inside a simulation," says Greene. "And in that case, there *is* a simulator—maybe some kid in his garage in the year 4956—who is determining and defining the values of the constants in this new universe that he built on a Sunday morning on a supercomputer. And within that universe, there are beings who will wonder, 'Who set the values of these numbers that allow stars to exist?' And the answer is the kid. There *was* an intelligent being outside that universe who was responsible for setting the values for these essential numbers. So here is a version of the theological story that doesn't involve a supernatural anything. It only involves the notion that we will be able to simulate realistic universes on futuristic computers."

Part of what makes the simulation argument so attractive is the way its insane logic solves so many deep, impossible problems. Anything we currently classify as unexplainable—ghosts, miracles, astrology, demonic possession—suddenly has a technological explanation: They are bugs in the program (or, in the case of near-death experiences, cheat codes). Theologians spend a lot of time trying to figure out how a righteous God could allow the Holocaust to happen, but that question disappears when God is replaced by Greene's teenager in the year 4956 (weird kids love death). Moreover, the simulation hypothesis doesn't contradict God's existence in any way (it just inserts a middle manager).

The downside to the simulation hypothesis is that it appears impossible to confirm (although maybe not totally[11] impossible).

----

11 "There have been suggestions that there might be actual evidence [of this] rather than supposition," Tyson told me, much to my surprise. "The evidence is this: There is something called cosmic rays that are high-energy particles moving

Such a realization wouldn't be like Jim Carrey's character's recognition of his plight in *The Truman Show*, because there would be no physical boundary to hit; it would be more like playing Donkey Kong and suddenly seeing Mario turn toward the front of the monitor in order to say, "I know what's going on here." Maybe speculating on the mere possibility of this simulacrum is the closest we could ever come to proving that it's real. But this is a book, so those limitations don't apply. For my purposes, the *how* is irrelevant. I'm just going to pretend we all collectively realized that we are simulated digital creatures, living inside a simulated digital game. I'm going to pretend our reality is a sophisticated computer simulation, and that we all know this.

If this were true, how should we live? Or maybe: How should we "live"?

[7] Imagine two men in a bar, having (in Neil deGrasse Tyson's parlance) a "beer conversation." One man believes in God and the other does not, and they are debating the nature of morality. The man who believes in God argues that

----

through the universe, and they're accelerated to very high energies in the centers of galaxies by astrophysical phenomena we think we understand—though there are a lot of holes in this. It was noticed that there was an upper limit to the energy produced by these cosmic rays. Now, in practically anything else we've ever measured, there's sort of a bell curve of how such things appear. Most are in some group, then there's a tail, and it continues off to zero. With cosmic rays, the tail's off and there's no broad cutoff. It was suggested that if we were a simulation, you'd have to put in a limit to something that goes on within it. And this cutoff could be the program's pre-calculated limit for the energy level of these cosmic rays. We could be up against that boundary. It's an intriguing thought that we're all just one big simulation. That being said . . . it would be hard to swallow."

without the existence of a higher power, there would be no reason for living a moral life, since this would mean ethics are just slanted rules arbitrarily created by flawed people for whatever reason they desire. The man who does not believe in God disagrees and insists that morality matters *only* if its tenets are a human construct, since that would mean our ethical framework is based not on a fear of supernatural punishment but on a desire to give life moral purpose. They go back and forth on this for hours, continually restating their core position in different ways. But then a third man joins their table and explains the new truth: It turns out our moral compass comes from neither God nor ourselves. It comes from Brenda. Brenda is a middle-aged computer engineer living in the year 2750, and she designed the simulation that currently contains all three of their prefab lives. So the difference between right and wrong *does* come from a higher power, but that higher power is just a mortal human. And the ethical mores ingrained in our society are *not* arbitrary, but they're also not communal or fair (they're just Brenda's personal conception of what a society should believe and how people should behave).

The original two men finish their beers and exit the tavern. Both are now aware they've been totally wrong about everything. So what do they do now? For a moment, each man is overcome with suicidal tendencies. "If we are not even real," they concurrently think, "what is the meaning of any of this?" But these thoughts quickly fade. For one thing, learning you're not real doesn't *feel* any different from the way you felt before. Pain still hurts, even though no actual injury is being inflicted; happiness still feels good, even if the things making you happy are as fake as you are. The "will to live" still subsists, because that will was programmed into your character (and so was a fear of death). Most critically, the question of "What is the meaning of any of this?" was just as present yesterday as it is today—the conditions are different, but the confusion is the same.

Even if you're not alive, life goes on. What changes is the purpose.

Think of a video game that immerses the player in an alternative reality—I'll use Grand Theft Auto as an example, simply because of its popularity. When a casual gamer plays any new version of GTA, they typically work through three initial steps. The first is to figure out the various controls and to develop a general sense of how to move around the virtual sandbox. The second is a cursory examination of the game's espoused plot, done mostly to gauge its level of complexity and to get a fuzzy sense of how long it will take to complete. And then—and particularly if the game looks like it will be time-consuming and hard—the player enters a third phase: a brief, chaotic attempt at "breaking the game." Can I drive my car into the ocean? Can I shoot people who are trying to help me? Can I punch animals? What, exactly, are the limits here?

When I first played the crime-solving video game L.A. Noire, I realized that the main character (voiced by *Mad Men*'s Ken Cosgrove) would sometimes fall through the floor of certain buildings and disappear into the middle of the earth. I had no idea why this happened, so I spent a lot of time searching for floors to inexplicably fall through. And if I knew that my actual life was similarly unreal, I'd do the same thing: I'd look for ways to break the simulation. Obviously, I could not be as militant as I was while playing L.A. Noire, because I wouldn't have unlimited lives. I wouldn't want my character to die. When I use my Xbox, I'm an extension of the simulator (which means I could let my little Cosgrove fall through the floor a hundred times, knowing he'd always return). Were I actually living inside the simulation hypothesis, I'd be a one-time avatar. So the boundaries I would try to break would not be physical. In fact, I'd say the first principle to adopt in this scenario would be the same as the one we use in regular life—don't get terminated. Stay alive. But beyond that? I'd spend the rest of my "life" trying to figure out what I *can't* do. What are the thoughts I can't have? What beliefs are impossible for me to understand or express? Are there aspects of this simulation that its creator never considered? Because if this simulation is all there is (and there's no way to transcend beyond it), I would have to look for the only possible bright side: A simulated world is a *limited* world. It's a theoretically *solvable* world, which is not something that can be said of our own.

The only problem is that anyone capable of building such a world would likely consider this possibility, too.

"You could try to 'break' the simulation, but if the simulators did not want the simulation to be broken, I would expect your attempts to fail," Bostrom e-mails me from England. I suspect this is not the first time he's swatted this argument into the turf. "I figure they would be vastly superior to us in intelligence and technological capability (or they could not have created this kind of simulation in the first place). And so they could presumably prevent their simulated creatures from crashing the simulation or discovering its limitations."

Well, fine. I give up. Pour me a drink. Simulate me, don't simulate me—it's all equally hopeless. We're just here, and there's nowhere else to be.

[**8**] *Particle Fever* is a 2013 documentary about the Large Hadron Collider in Switzerland. It depicts the final seven years of the five-decade search for the Higgs boson, the so-called God particle at the core of everything we believe about deep physics and the origin of existence. The film is elucidated through the words of many perceptibly brilliant people, a few of whom spend much of the movie expressing dark apprehension over what will happen if the massive $9 billion LHC does not locate the Higgs particle. The person most openly nervous is the theorist identified as the academic star of his generation: Nima Arkani-Hamed. Born to a pair of Iranian doctors in 1972 and raised in Canada, the long-haired Arkani-Hamed directly states that if the Higgs particle can't be found, he will have wasted at least fifteen years of his life. Later, when discussing the bizarre numeric perfection of the "cosmological constant,"[12] he says something that guys in his position don't usually say.

"This is the sort of thing that really keeps you up at night," Arkani-Hamed says. "It really makes you wonder if we've got something about the whole picture—the big picture—totally, totally, totally wrong."

Or maybe not. Spoiler alert: They find the particle. The experiment works. The previous fifteen years of Arkani-Hamed's life

---

12 The *cosmological constant* is the value of the energy density of the vacuum of space. Now, I don't understand what that means. But it's one of those "twenty numbers" Brian Greene mentioned a few pages back—a number that has a value so specific and so inimitable that the universe as we know it could not exist if it were even .0001 percent different.

were not in vain. But the discovery of the Higgs doesn't prove we are necessarily *right* about the origin of life; it just means that we're still not wrong. Moreover, the unexpected mass of the Higgs particle—125 GeV—doesn't corroborate the likelihood of a multiverse or the likelihood of its competing theory (a more elegant, less chaotic vision of the universe called "supersymmetry"). Still, this ninety-five-yard drive ends with a touchdown: The scientific community believed that something they could not see was there, and it ultimately was. It's an indicator that we are not wrong, and that the current path might be the final path.

And yet, even within this success, I can't help but wonder . . . if the finest physicist in North America was willing to publicly express anxiety over his entire life's work, how stable can any of this be? When Arkani-Hamed finds himself awake in his bed, wondering about his potential wrongness, is he being insecure or pragmatic? And what if the Higgs particle had *not* been found? Would any of the geniuses involved in its search quit their jobs? Would they have rebooted the entire concept? No way. They would have merely viewed the experiment itself as a failure, or the LHC as too small, or the particle as too crafty. They would have to double down on their commitment to certitude and we would have to agree with them. Philosophically, as a species, we are committed to this. In the same way that religion defined cultural existence in the pre-Copernican age, the edge of science defines the existence we occupy today.

Do I believe we are right? I believe we are right. But even if I didn't, what would I do?

The World That Is Not There

The term "conspiracy theory" has an irrevocable public relations problem. Technically, it's just an expository description for a certain class of unproven scenario. But the problem is that it can't be self-applied without immediately obliterating whatever it's allegedly describing. You can say, "I suspect a conspiracy," and you can say, "I have a theory." But you can't say, "I have a conspiracy theory." Because if you do, it will be assumed that even you don't entirely believe the conspiracy you're theorizing about. There's also a growing belief that conspiracy theories aren't merely goofy; some would argue they're politically detrimental. Early in his book *Voodoo Histories: The Role of the Conspiracy Theory in Shaping Modern History*,[1] British journalist David Aaronovitch asserts, "The belief

---

1 This is a super-fun book, but I don't understand how the publisher was supposed to market it: It rejects every possible conspiracy theory, yet would only be of interest to people who are actively obsessed with conspiracy theories (and who would read this book with the sole purpose of examining the details of theories

in conspiracy theories is, I hope to show, harmful in itself. It distorts our view of history and therefore of the present, and—if widespread enough—leads to disastrous decisions." A smart person is supposed to recognize that the term "conspiracy theory" has only one conversational utility: It's a way to marginalize undesirable possibilities as inherently illogical, along with the people who propose them.

But I want to consider a conspiracy theory (so I will). And by virtue of my previous argument, this means I want to consider a theory that I don't actually believe (and I don't). It is, however, my favorite theory about anything. It's the largest possible conspiracy, and perhaps the least plausible. It's also the hardest to disprove, and—if it *were* true—the least socially damaging. It's referred to as the Phantom Time Hypothesis, and the premise is as straightforward as it is insane: It suggests that the past (or at least the past as we know it) never happened at all.

There are two strains of the Phantom Time Hypothesis, both of which have been broadly discredited. The first version is the "minor theory," proposed by the German historian Heribert Illig and extended by engineer Hans-Ulrich Niemitz. The German version of Phantom Time proposes that the years AD 614 to 911 were falsified, ostensibly by the Catholic Church, so that rulers from the period could begin their reign in the year 1000 (which would thereby allow their lineage to rule for the next millennium, based on the superstition that whoever was in power in the year 1000 would remain in that position for the next ten centuries).

----

the author is illustrating to be false). It would be kind of like if I wrote and researched a 390-page book about Fleetwood Mac's *Rumours* LP, but my whole point was that Fleetwood Mac is not worth listening to.

The second version is the "major theory," hailing from Russia, developed by Marxist revolutionary Nikolai Morozov and outlined in detail by mathematician Anatoly Fomenko. In this so-called New Chronology, everything that supposedly happened prior to the eleventh century is a historical forgery; the historical record we currently accept was constructed in the fifteenth century by French religious scholars. The argument is not that history *begins* in the eleventh century, but that we simply don't know what happened before that, so powerful French historians[2] attempted to re-create and insert various events from the Middle Ages upon the expanse of our unknown pre-history. This would mean that many historical figures are simply different mythological versions of the same root story (for example, Attila the Hun, Genghis Khan, and Tamerlane would all be roughly based on the same person). The life of Jesus Christ, surmises Fomenko, is a hagiographic interpretation of the reign of a likable twelfth-century Byzantine emperor who tried to destroy the aristocracy and empower the underclass. In short, everything we think we know about the ancient world is a fictional story, based on things that happened less than a thousand years ago.

Now, if you want to view these competing theories as totally crazy, you will not have to work particularly hard (it says a lot that the notion's "minor" version would still mean I'm unknowingly writing this book in the year 1718). There is an avalanche of data that disputes these suppositions, some of which is astrological (e.g., the record of when certain comets and eclipses were seen that

----

2 In his seven-volume collection *History: Fiction or Science?* Fomenko specifically cites Joseph Justus Scaliger, although it appears the Jesuits would also be involved here.

concur with our standard timeline) and some of which is archaeological (the major hypothesis would mean that hundreds of historical artifacts supporting our conventional view of history are brilliant forgeries, secretly produced by fifteenth-century monks). There's also the question of motive: Fomenko's revisionist timeline places the center of all "real history" inside Russia, which is probably why the only people who take it seriously are Russian (most notably grandmaster chess champion Garry Kasparov, who wrote a long essay in support of the theory titled "Mathematics of the Past"). Yet the brilliance of these theories—and particularly the larger, Russo-centric hypothesis—is the unassailability of its scope. If you believe that all of history is a fabrication, every piece of evidence disputing that claim is *also* a fabrication. For example, Halley's Comet was spotted in AD 837 (in multiple countries), which is exactly when it should have been seen, which indicates that the year 837 must have happened the way we generally assume . . . unless, of course, you believe that the Dark Ages are classified as "dark" because they didn't happen at all, and all the ancillary details they encompass were manufactured by sinister people who made sure the math worked out. There is no way to irrefutably disprove either strain of the Phantom Time Hypothesis, as both are fundamentally grounded in the belief that all the information we possess about the distant past is unreal. Anything contradicting the possibility of established human history being false is proof that the plot succeeded. It's an inane argument that cannot be defeated.

So why consider it at all?

I consider it because of the central principle. Phantom Time inadvertently prompts a greater question that is not inane at all. Granted, it's the kind of question someone like David Aaronovitch hates to hear, and it opens the door to a lot of troubling, misguided conjecture. But it still must be asked: *Discounting those events that occurred within your own lifetime, what do you know about human history that was not communicated to you by someone else?*

This is a question with only one possible answer.

[2] Arguing with a Phantom Time advocate is a little like arguing with someone who insists that your life is not really happening, and that you're actually asleep right now, and that everything you assume to be reality is just a dream that will disappear when you awake. How does one dispute such an accusation? It can't be done (unless you consider "scoffing" to be a valid forensic technique). You can disagree with the claim that any specific world condition is illusionary, but you can't refute that the world itself is an illusion; there's no other world to compare it against. The closest equivalent we have *is* the dream world—which, somewhat curiously, has never been viewed as less important than it is right now.

For most of human history, the act of dreaming was considered deeply important, almost like a spiritual interaction with a higher power. Three thousand years ago (assuming Fomenko was wrong), Tibetan monks would teach themselves to lucid dream in order to pursue enlightenment through a process called Dream Yoga. Around 1619, philosopher René Descartes forwarded his take on the so-called Dream Argument, the quintessential distillation[3]

---

3 The "Dream Argument" is a two-pronged proposition: The first prong is that dreams sometimes seem so real to us that there's no way to know when we're dreaming and when we are not. The second prong is that—in the same way we

of the "Maybe this isn't really happening" dorm room conversation. The zenith of dream seriousness occurred at the turn of the
twentieth century, defined by the work of Sigmund Freud (who
thought dreams were everything) and his adversarial protégé Carl
Jung (who thought dreams were *more* than everything—they were
glimpses into a collective unconscious, shared by everyone who's
ever lived). But soon after World War I, this mode of thinking
slowly started to crumble. The ability to map the brain's electrical
activity started in 1924—and from that point forward, dreams
increasingly mattered less. The last wide-scale attempt at catalog-
ing a database of human dreams dissipated in the sixties. In 1976,
two Harvard psychiatrists[4] proposed the possibility that dreams
were just the by-product of the brain stem firing chaotically during
sleep. Since then, the conventional scientific sentiment has become
that—while we don't *totally* understand why dreaming happens—
the dreams themselves are meaningless.[5] They're images and

----

usually don't recognize we're dreaming until we begin to wake up—it's possible
that what currently appears to be regular day-to-day reality will disintegrate the
moment we reach lucidity. In other words, you may think you're reading a
footnote right now, but maybe you're just having a nonlucid dream where a
footnote is being read. And as soon as you realize this, the page will start to
dissolve.

4 These psychiatrists are referred to as Hobson-McCarley (John Allan Hobson
and Robert McCarley), the Lennon-McCartney of not caring about dreams.

5 This belief is so pervasive that even those who believe otherwise feel obli-
gated to concede its prevalence. "In Western society, most people don't pay too
much attention to their dreams," said Deirdre Barrett, an assistant professor
of psychology at Harvard Medical School. Barrett has studied dreaming for
forty years.

sounds we unconsciously collect, almost at random.[6] The psyche-delic weirdness of dreaming can be explained by the brain's topography: The part of your mind that controls emotions (the limbic system) is highly active during dreams, while the part that controls logic (the prefrontal cortex) stays dormant. This is why a dream can feel intense and terrifying, even if what you're seeing within that dream wouldn't sound scary if described to someone else. This, it seems, has become the standard way to compartmentalize a collective, fantastical phenomenon: Dreaming is just something semi-interesting that happens when our mind is at rest—and when it happens in someone else's mind (and that person insists on describing it to us at breakfast), it isn't interesting at all.

Which seems like a potentially massive misjudgment.

Every night, we're all having multiple metaphysical experiences, wholly constructed by our subconscious. Almost one-third of our lives happens inside surreal mental projections we create without trying. A handful of highly specific dreams, such as slowly losing one's teeth, are experienced unilaterally by unrelated people in unconnected cultures. But these events are so personal and inscrutable that we've stopped trying to figure out what they mean.

"We have come to the conclusion that dreams are something that can be explained away scientifically," Richard Linklater tells me over the phone. He's calling from his studio in Texas, and I

---

6 This is mirrored by the growth of cognitive behavioral therapy, a model of psychoanalysis that suggests many thoughts are merely "automatic thoughts" that should not be taken as literal depictions of what we truly believe or desire. For example, just because you spontaneously imagine killing someone should not be taken as an indication that you secretly want to do this.

sense he's sweeping the floor of a very large room as we chat—his sentences are periodically punctuated by the dulcet *swoosh* of a broom. "Dreams used to have a much larger role in the popular culture—people would discuss dreams in normal conversation and it was common for people to keep dream diaries. So why did that drop off, but things like astrology somehow stayed popular? I mean, one is an actual thing that happens to everyone, and the other is a system put in place that obviously can't be real. This idea that we're connected to other realities is somehow no longer worth considering at all, even though the multiverse theory and string theory is increasingly prominent, and more and more scientists are reluctantly conceding that certain things about the universe lead to that very possibility. So two things are happening simulta- neously: We're moving into this period where our view of the uni- verse is kind of a 'What the fuck? How could that be?' scenario, where there's this possibility of endless alternative realities across space, totally based on conjecture—yet our dreams are supposed to mean *nothing*? The fact that we're in a parallel world every night is just supposed to be *meaningless*? I mean, the same scientists that are trying to explain away our dreams are also telling us things about the universe that are so mind-boggling that we almost can't describe them."

Linklater is an Austin-based director who's best known to casual audiences for *Boyhood*, a fictional narrative he shot over the course of twelve years that was nominated for an Academy Award. His most successful film was *School of Rock*, his most intimate films comprise a cultic romantic trilogy, and his most canonically sig- nificant film is *Dazed and Confused*. But I wanted to interview Link- later about two of his less commercial projects: his nonlinear 1991 debut *Slacker* and the 2001 animated film *Waking Life*. The former opens with a nameless character (played by Linklater) speculating on the nature of dreaming, specifically the thought that dreams are glimpses into alternative realities running parallel to our own. The latter film is perhaps the most immersive dream experience ever transferred to celluloid—the rotoscoped re-creation of a sprawling lucid dream Linklater had when he was eighteen. Now in his mid-fifties, Linklater concedes that his willingness to view dreams as literal pathways to alternative worlds has "fallen off." But he still thinks we're underrating the psychological importance of nocturnal narratives. The lucid dream that inspired *Waking Life* was encapsulated in the span of twelve real-time minutes of sleep, but—inside Linklater's mind—the dream lasted for days, to the point where he truly believed he had died. Is it possible that this serves a function? Do we need to create unconscious interior experiences in order to manage our conscious, exterior existence?

"Here's something I still think about: the near-death experience," Linklater continues. "There are several bestselling books about this topic, usually from a very Christian perspective. But I talk about this concept very specifically in *Waking Life*. You have this chemical in your brain, dimethyltryptamine,[7] this never-ending chemical that is always there until you die. And there is this thinking that at the moment you die, maybe all the

----

7   Dimethyltryptamine (usually referred to as DMT) can also be smoked recreationally. Manufactured DMT crystals are sprinkled atop marijuana buds and inhaled in one hit, generating a heavy, optical trip that lasts around ten minutes. Because the experience is so brief and fleeting, DMT is sometimes called "the businessman's hallucinogen." It doesn't demand a lot of free time. But in the same way that dream time is elastic, ten minutes on DMT can feel much, much longer.

dimethyltryptamine that remains in your brain tissue gets used at once. And what's interesting is that all the bestselling books about near-death experiences are always about people getting close to God and seeing relatives and having this calm, wonderful experience. What they never tell you about are the people who have near-death experiences that are not good, and in fact incredibly unsettling. Which really just tells me that we bring so much of ourselves to these so-called afterlife moments, and that maybe this is something we need to prepare ourselves for."

What Linklater is describing is an unrealized relationship between sleeping and dying, specifically the sensation of having one's life "flash before your eyes" in a near-death episode. That event is the ultimate dream experience, possibly driven by a flood of dimethyltryptamine. Is it possible that our normal nightly dreams are vaguely connected to this dramatic eventuality? If so, a spiritual person might argue this means dreams are preparing us for something quite important; using the same information, a secular person might argue this means dreams are micro-versions of a massive chemical event that happens only at the very end of life. But either way, such a scenario should drastically alter the significance we place on the *content* of dreams. Right now, we don't think the content of dreams matters at all. If we end up being wrong about the psychological consequence of dreaming, it will be the result of our willingness to ghettoize an acute cognitive experience simply because it seems too difficult to realistically study. The problem with studying the subject matter of dreams is straightforward: We can map the brain's electrical activity, but we can't *see* other people's dreams. The only way we can analyze the content of a dream is to ask the dreamer what she remembers.

That makes the entire endeavor too interpretive to qualify as regular science. Every detail can prove or disprove the same thesis.

While talking with Linklater, I mentioned an anxiety dream my wife had had two nights previous: She dreamed I had been beaten by drug dealers as a result of her failure to pick up our son from day care. There were a few details from her actual life that clearly fed into this dream—she'd come home late from work the day before, I'd just experienced an unusually gruesome dental appointment, and we both watched an episode of *Bloodline* (a TV show about drug dealers) before going to bed. But these connections could go either way. It could mean the dream matters more than we think, because the narrative details closely mirror things that were happening in her day-to-day life; it could also mean that the dream is meaningless, since the details were just the detritus of the many assorted thoughts she considered and discarded. Both possibilities raise a host of related questions that we simply can't access without getting inside her brain (and since we can't do that, we've essentially stopped asking). Case in point: We know this dream was manufactured by my wife's mind, so every detail of the dream had to have come from that same mind. My wife could not (for example) dream about a specific character from an obscure modernist novel if she had no knowledge that the book itself had ever been written. But could she dream about something *she does not know* that she knows? Robert Louis Stevenson famously (or at least supposedly) wrote *The Strange Case of Dr. Jekyll and Mr. Hyde* after a dream he experienced in the autumn of 1885. He'd been interested in the subject of personality for years, but it was the dream that allowed him to suddenly craft an intricate fictional plot in a matter of days. The story came from his brain, no differently from any other story he ever wrote. But could he have written this novel without that dream? Are we—as a society—discounting our only natural means of interacting with all the subterranean thoughts we don't realize we have?

Before ending our conversation, Linklater told me about a dream he'd had a week prior: He dreamed he was backstage at an Alice Cooper concert and saw the musician's son in a wheelchair (Alice Cooper does have two sons, but neither is paralyzed and Linklater has no relationship with either). In the dream, Linklater walks over to the son and asks him how old he is, assuming the child must be in his mid-thirties. From his wheelchair, the son says, "I'm eighteen." The response made no sense and seemed to have no meaning. But two days later, it dawned on Linklater that "I'm Eighteen" was the title of Alice Cooper's breakthrough single, a song he's heard hundreds of times throughout his life.

"So I thought that was kind of witty," Linklater said. "Here was an inside joke in my own dream that I didn't even get for two days. Not to get too far out there on this, but either it all matters or none of it matters. That's just sort of a view about life, and about how thoughts work."

[3] For a moment, let's get nutzo. Let's imagine the Phantom Time Hypothesis was proven to be true (this could never happen, but—at the risk of sounding like some kind of conspiracy Yoda—lots of things could never happen, until they do). To keep things conservative, let's stick with the "minor theory," since it's less radical (in that it only negates three centuries) and is at least marginally explicable (we already accept that the Catholic

Church *slightly* manipulated the Gregorian calendar when it was invented, so it's not like the desire to change time doesn't exist). Let's assume the evidence for this event is compelling, and the theory gets support from all the necessary places—the scientific community, historians, the media, the Vatican. We accept that it happened. However, nobody wants to mechanically roll the calendar back, so life continues as it currently is. The only difference is that most informed people now accept that the Dark Ages were a myth and that the historical stories from that period either happened at a different time or never happened at all.

Why would this matter?

Yes, very old things would now be slightly less old, and distant human events (like the crucifixion of Christ) would be slightly less distant. And—sure—history books would require corrections, and *Monty Python and the Holy Grail* would be a little less funny, and the Steely Dan song "Kid Charlemagne" would have a weirder subtext. But the only real problem would be the subsequent domino effect: If we were wrong about something this fundamental, we could theoretically be wrong about anything. Proof of Phantom Time would validate every possible skeptic, including those skeptical about Phantom Time; almost certainly, a new conspiracy theory would instantly emerge, this time positing that the Dark Ages *did* happen and that the revisionists were trying to remove those 297 years for nefarious, self-interested motives. A sliver of the populace would never believe those years didn't exist, in the same way a similarly sized sliver currently can't accept that they did. But the day-to-day life of those in either camp would not change at all.

Conflicting conceptions of "reality" have no impact on *reality*.

And this does not apply exclusively to conspiracy theorists. It applies to everyone, all the time.

[**4**] On the evening of February 26, 2015, I (along with millions of other people) experienced a cultural event that— at least for a few hours—seemed authentically unexplainable. By March of that year, most of the world had moved on from this. But I still think about that night. Not because of what happened, but because of how it felt while it was transpiring.

A woman on the Internet posted a photograph of a dress. The dress was potentially going to be worn by someone's mother at a Scottish wedding, but that detail is irrelevant. What mattered was the color of the dress. The image of the garment was tagged with the following caption:

> *guys please help me—is this dress white and gold, or blue and black? Me and my friends can't agree and we are freaking the fuck out*

When my wife saw this image, she said, "I don't get what the joke is here. This is just a picture of a white and gold dress." When I glanced at the image and told her it was plainly black and blue, she assumed I was playfully lying (which, to be fair, is not exactly outside my character). But I wasn't. We were looking at the same thing and seeing something completely different. I texted a friend in California, who almost seemed pissed about this—he assumed everyone on Twitter claiming it was anything except blue (specifically periwinkle) and black was consciously trolling society. "I don't know about that," I responded. "Something is happening here." And something *was* happening. Random pairs of people had differing opinions about something they both perceived to be independently obvious. At first, unscientific surveys suggested that most people thought the dress was gold and white, but the gap rapidly shrank to almost 50-50 (which might have been partially due to the discovery that the actual dress actually *was* blue and black).

The next day, countless pundits tried to explain why this had transpired. None of their explanations were particularly convincing. Most were rooted in the idea that this happened because we were all looking at a photo of a dress, as opposed to the dress itself. But that only shifts the debate, without really changing it—why, exactly, would two people see the same photograph in two completely different ways? There was a momentary sense that this stupid dress had accidentally collided with some previously unknown optic frequency that lay exactly between the two ways in which color can be perceived, and that—maybe, possibly, somehow—the human race did not see "blue" and "gold" (and perhaps every color) in the same, unified way. Which would mean that *color* is not a real thing, and that our perception of the color wheel is subjective, and that what we currently classify as "blue" might not be classified as "blue" in a thousand years.

But this, it seems, is not exactly a new debate.

The argument that color is not a static property has been gingerly waged for decades, and it always seems to hinge on the ancient work of a possibly blind, probably imaginary, thoroughly unreliable poet. In both *The Iliad* and *The Odyssey*, Homer describes the Aegean Sea. Again and again, he describes this sea as "wine-dark." He unswervingly asserts that the ocean is the same color as red wine. To some, this suggests that the way we saw and understood color three thousand years ago was radically different from the way we see and understand it now. To others, this is just an example of a poet being poetic (or maybe an example of a blind poet getting bad advice). It's either meaningful or meaningless, which is probably why no one will ever stop talking about it.

"I think people really overstate the significance of that passage from Homer. He's mostly just being evocative," says Zed Adams, an assistant professor of philosophy at the New School for Social Research. "But I think it does hint at one important difference between the Greek use of certain 'color words' and our own. The shiny/matte distinction seems like it might have been more central for them than it is for us, so Homer might have been thinking of water and wine as similarly colored, in the sense that they are both shiny. But, beyond that, I think the ocean *is* sometimes wine-colored, so I don't think the passage is that big of a deal."

Adams is the author of *On the Genealogy of Color*. He believes the topic of color is the most concrete way to consider the question of how much—or how little—our experience with reality is shared with the experience of other people. It's an unwieldy subject that straddles both philosophy and science. On one hand, it's a physics argument about the essential role light plays in our perception of color; at the same time, it's a semantic argument over how color is linguistically described differently by different people. There's also a historical component: Up until the discovery of color blindness in the seventeenth century, it was assumed that everyone saw everything the same way (and it took another two hundred years before we realized how much person-to-person variation there is).

What really changed four hundred years ago was due (once again) to the work of Newton and Descartes, this time in the field of optics. Instead of things appearing "red" simply because of their intrinsic "redness" (which is what Aristotle[8] believed), Newton and Descartes realized it has to do with an object's relationship to light. This, explains Adams, led to a new kind of separation between the mind and the world. It meant that there are all kinds of things we can't understand about the world through our own observation, and it made it intellectually conceivable that two people could see the same thing differently.

What's particularly interesting here is that Adams believes Descartes misunderstood his own discovery about light and experience. The basis for his argument is extremely wonky (and better explained by his own book). But the upshot is this: Adams suspects the way we'll talk about color in a distant future will be different from the way we talk about it now. And this will be because future conversations will be less interpretative and more precise. It's an optimistic view of our current inexact state of perception—someday, we might get this right. We might actually agree that "blue" is *blue*, and arguments about the hue of online dresses will last all of three seconds.

"Descartes thought that the mind, and specifically 'what mental experience is like,' somehow stood outside of the physical world, such that [this mental experience] could vary while everything physical about us would stay the same," Adams says. "I think that idea will gradually become less and less intuitive, and will just

- - - - - - - - - - - - - - - - - - -

8 I sometimes think I should have titled this book *Aristotle: The Genius Who Was Wrong About Fucking Everything.*

start to seem silly. I'd like to imagine that in a hundred years, if I said to you, 'But how could I ever *really* know whether your color experience is the same as mine?' your response would just be, 'Well, if our eyes and brains are the same, then our color experiences are the same.' End of story."

[5] Metaphoric sheep get no love. There's no worse thing to be compared to, at least among conspiracy theorists. "You're just a sheep," they will say. "You believe what they want you to believe." But this implies that *they*—the metaphoric shepherds—have something they want you to accept. It implies that these world-altering shepherds are consciously leading their sheeple to a conclusion that plays to their benefit. No one considers the possibility of a shepherd just aimlessly walking around the meadow, pointing his staff in whatever direction he happens to be facing.

On the same day I spoke with Linklater about dreams, there was a story in *The New York Times* about a violent incident that had occurred a few days prior in Manhattan. A man had attacked a female police officer with a hammer and was shot by the policewoman's partner. This shooting occurred at ten a.m., on the street, in the vicinity of Penn Station. Now, one assumes seeing a maniac swinging a hammer at a cop's skull before being shot in broad daylight would be the kind of moment that sticks in a person's mind. Yet the *Times* story explained how at least two of the eyewitness accounts of this event ended up being wrong. Linklater was fascinated by this: "False memories, received memories, how we fill in the blanks of conjecture, the way the brain fills in those spaces with something that is technically incorrect—all of these errors allow us to make sense of the world, and are somehow accepted enough to be admissible in a court of law. They are accepted enough to put someone in prison." And this, remember, was a violent incident that had happened only hours before. The witnesses were describing something that had happened that same day, and they had no incentive to lie. But video surveillance proved their depictions of reality were inaccurate.

This is a level of scrutiny that can't be applied to the distant past, for purely practical reasons. Most of history has not been videotaped. But what's interesting is our communal willingness to assume most old stories *may as well be true*, based on the logic that (a) the story is already ancient, and (b) there isn't any way to confirm an alternative version, despite the fact that we can't categorically confirm the original version, either.

A week before Manhattan cops were being attacked by hammer-wielding schizophrenics, Seymour Hersh published a ten-thousand-word story in the *London Review of Books* headlined "The Killing of Osama bin Laden." Hersh's wide-ranging story boiled down to this: The accepted narrative of the 2011 assassination of bin Laden was a fabrication, deliberately perpetrated by the Obama administration. It was not a clandestine black ops attack by Navy SEALs, working off the CIA's meticulous intelligence gathering; it was the result of a former Pakistani intelligence officer exchanging the whereabouts of bin Laden for money, thereby allowing the SEALs to just walk into his compound and perform an execution. It was not a brazen military gamble; the government of Pakistan knew it was going to happen in advance and quietly allowed the cover-up. During the first thirty-six hours of the story's publication, it felt like something unthinkable was suddenly transparent: Either we were being controlled by a shadow government where nothing was as it seemed, or the finest investigative reporter of the past half century had lost his goddamn mind. By the end of the week, most readers leaned in the direction of the latter. Some of this was due to a follow-up interview Hersh gave to *Slate* that made him seem unreliable, slightly crazy, and very old. But most of the skepticism came from a multitude of sources questioning the validity of specific particulars in Hersh's account, even though the refutation of those various details did not really contradict the larger conspiratorial thesis. Hersh's alternative narrative was scrutinized far more aggressively than the conventional narrative, even though the mainstream version of bin Laden's assassination was substantially more dramatic (if film director Kathryn Bigelow had used Hersh's story as the guide for *Zero Dark Thirty*, it might have qualified as mumblecore).

By the first week of June, "The Killing of Osama bin Laden" had been intellectually discarded by most people in the United States. Every subsequent conversation I had about the Hersh story (and I had many) drifted further and further from seriousness. More than a year later, journalist Jonathan Mahler wrote a story for *The New York Times Magazine* reexamining the dispute from a media perspective. "For many," wrote Mahler, "[the official bin Laden story] exists in a kind of liminal state, floating somewhere between fact and mythology." Considering what can be conclusively verified about the assassination, that's precisely where the story should float. But I don't believe that it does. Judging from the (mostly incredulous) reaction to Mahler's story, I don't think a sizable chunk of US citizenry distrusts the conventional depiction of how bin Laden was killed. This acceptance is noteworthy for at least two reasons. The first is that—had this kind of alternative story emerged from a country like Russia, and if the man orchestrating the alleged conspiracy was Vladimir Putin—nobody in America would question it at all. It would immediately be accepted as plausible, and perhaps even probable. The second is a discomfiting example of how "multiple truths" don't really mesh with the machinations of human nature: Because we were incessantly told one version of a story before hearing the second version, it's become impossible to overturn the original template. It was unconsciously assumed that Hersh's alternative story had to both prove itself *and* disprove the primary story, which automatically galvanizes the primary version as factual. It took only four years for that thinking to congeal. Extrapolate that phenomenon to forty years, or to four hundred years, or to four thousand years: How much of history is classified as true simply because it can't be sufficiently proven false? In other words, there's no way we can irrefutably certify that an event from 1776 didn't happen in the manner we've always believed, so there's no justification for presenting a counter-possibility. Any counter-possibility would have to use the same methodology, so it would be (at best) equally flawed. This becomes more and more ingrained as we move further and further from the moment of the event. So while it's absurd to think that all of history never really happened, it's almost as absurd to think that everything we know about history is real. All of which demands a predictable question: What significant historical event is most likely wrong? And not because of things we know that contradict it, but because of the way wrongness works.

We understand the past through the words of those who experienced it. But those individuals aren't necessarily reliable, and we are reminded of this constantly. The average person can watch someone attack a cop with a hammer and misdescribe what he saw twenty minutes after it happened. But mistakes are only a fraction of the problem. There's also the human compulsion to lie—and not just for bad reasons, but for good reasons, and sometimes for *no* reasons, beyond a desire to seem interesting. When D. T. Max published his posthumous biography of David Foster Wallace, it was depressing to discover that many of the most memorable, electrifying anecdotes from Wallace's nonfiction were total fabrications. Of course, that accusation would be true for countless essays published before the fact-checking escalation of the Internet. The defining works of Joseph Mitchell, Joan Didion, and Hunter Thompson all contain moments of photographic detail that would never withstand the modern verification process[9]—we've just collectively decided to accept the so-called larger truth and ignore the parts that skew implausible. In other words, people who don't know better are often wrong by accident, and people who do know better

----

9   Some might question the espoused veracity of "the modern verification process," on the basis of the publication of Stephen Glass's imaginary exposés in *The New Republic*, Jayson Blair's tenure at *The New York Times*, and the unreal University of Virginia rape account in *Rolling Stone*. But two things must be considered here. The first is that the process of fact-checking does have one unavoidable problem—there's almost no way to verify a story that the writer has fabricated *entirely*, because you can't disprove a negative. It's unreasonable for a magazine fact-checker to start from the premise that the reporter concocted a story out of thin air, since only a psychopath would do so. It would be like a doctor initiating every medical examination by asking the patient if she's lying about feeling sick. The second point is that all these stories *were*, eventually, proven to be false. It just took a little longer than we'd prefer.

are sometimes wrong on purpose—and whenever a modern news story explodes, everyone recognizes that possibility. But we question this far less when the information comes from the past. It's so hard to get viable info about pre-twentieth-century life that any nugget is reflexively taken at face value. In Ken Burns's documentary series *The Civil War*, the most fascinating glimpses of the conflict come from personal letters written by soldiers and mailed to their families. When these letters are read aloud, they almost make me cry. I robotically consume those epistles as personal distillations of historical fact. There is not one moment of *The Civil War* that feels false. But why is that? Why do I assume the things Confederate soldiers wrote to their wives might not be wildly exaggerated, or inaccurate, or straight-up untruths? Granted, we have loads of letters from lots of unrelated Civil War veterans, so certain claims and depictions can be fact-checked against each other. If multiple letters mention that there were wheat weevils in the bread, we can concede that the bread was infested with wheat weevils. But the American Civil War isn't exactly a distant historical event (amazingly, a few Civil War veterans were still alive in the 1950s). The further we go back, the harder it becomes to know how seriously any eyewitness account can be taken, particularly in cases where the number of accounts is relatively small.

There's a game I like to play with people when we're at the bar, especially if they're educated and drunk. The game has no name, but the rules are simple: The player tries to answer as many of the following questions as possible, without getting one wrong, without using the same answer twice, and without looking at a phone. The first question is, "Name any historical figure who was alive in the twenty-first century." (No one has ever gotten this one wrong.) The second question is, "Name any historical figure who was alive in the twentieth century." (No one has ever gotten this one wrong, either.) The third question is, "Name any historical figure who was alive in the nineteenth century." The fourth question is, "Name any historical figure who was alive in the eighteenth century." You continue moving backward through time, in centurial increments, until the player fails. It's mildly shocking how often highly intelligent people can't get past the sixteenth century; if they make it down to the twelfth century, it usually means they either know a lot about explorers or a shitload about popes. What this game illustrates is how vague our understanding of history truly is. We know all the names, and we have a rough idea of what those names accomplished—but how much can that be trusted if we can't even correctly identify when they were alive? How could our abstract synopsis of what they did be internalized if the most rudimentary, verifiable detail of their lives seems tricky?

It's hard to think of a person whose portrait was painted more than Napoleon. We should definitely know what he looked like. Yet the various firsthand accounts of Napoleon can't even agree on his height, much less his actual appearance. "None of the portraits that I had seen bore the least resemblance to him," insisted the poet Denis Davydov when he met Napoleon in 1807. Here again, we're only going back about two hundred years. What is the realistic probability that the contemporary understanding of Hannibal's 218 BC crossing of the Alps on the back of war elephants is remotely accurate? The two primary texts that elucidate this story were both composed decades after it happened, by authors[10] who were not there, with motives that can't be understood. And there's no conspiracy here; this is just how history is generated. We know the story exists and we know how the Second Punic War turned out. To argue that we know—really, truly *know*—much more than that is an impossibly optimistic belief. But this is the elephant-based Hannibal narrative we've always had, and any story contradicting it would be built on the same kind of modern conjecture and ancient text. As far as the world is concerned, it absolutely happened. Even if it didn't happen, it happened.

This is the world that is not there.

---

10   One of these historians, Polybius of Megalopolis, supposedly retraced Hannibal's path himself in order to understand how Hannibal did it. But imagine how difficult this would be, with the limited resources of the era. It might *decrease* the story's accuracy. Much more recently, an international team of microbiologists discovered massive numbers of a microbe belonging to the class Clostridia embedded in the soil of an Alpine pass, the Col de la Traversette, dated to the same period Hannibal would have crossed the Alps. The Clostridia bacterium is a product of horse manure, and the quantity discovered reflects the bowel movements of a huge army of mammals moving through a relatively small area. It's the best evidence that something akin to the classic Hannibal legend happened at this specific place at this specific time. But that's still a long way from knowing what actually transpired 2,200 years ago.

Don't Tell Me What Happens. I'm Recording It.

Television is an art form where the relationship to technology supersedes everything else about it. It's one realm of media where the medium *is* the message, without qualification. TV is not like other forms of consumer entertainment: It's slippier and more dynamic, even when it's dumb. We know people will always read, so we can project the future history of reading by considering the evolution of books. (Reading is a static experience.) We know music will always exist, so we can project a future history of rock 'n' roll by placing it in context with other genres of music. The internal, physiological sensation of hearing a song today is roughly the same as it was in 1901. (The ingestion of sound is a static experience.) The machinery of cinema persistently progresses, but how we watch movies in public—and the communal role cinema occupies, particularly in regard to dating—has remained weirdly unchanged since the fifties. (Sitting in a dark theater with strangers is a static experience.) But this is not the case with television.

Both collectively and individually, the experience of watching TV in 2016 already feels totally disconnected from the experience of watching TV in 1996. I doubt the current structure of television will exist in two hundred fifty years, or even in twenty-five. People will still want cheap escapism, and something will certainly satisfy that desire (in the same way television does now). But whatever that something is won't be anything like the television of today. It might be immersive and virtual (like a *Star Trek*ian holodeck) or it might be mobile and open-sourced (like a universal YouTube, lodged inside our retinas). But it absolutely won't be small groups of people, sitting together in the living room, staring at a two-dimensional thirty-one-inch rectangle for thirty consecutive minutes, consuming linear content packaged by a cable company.

Something will replace television, in the same way television replaced radio: through the process of addition. TV took the audio of radio and added visual images. The next tier of innovation will affix a third component, and that new component will make the previous iteration obsolete. I have no idea what that third element will be. But whatever it is will result in a chronological "freezing" of TV culture. Television will be remembered as a stand-alone medium that isn't part of any larger continuum[1]—the most domi-

---

1 There's a temptation to argue that television *is* part of a continuum, and that it represents the second step in a technological ladder that starts with radio and will continue through whatever mode eventually usurps network TV. There is, certainly, a mechanical lineage (the Paley Center for Media was originally known as the Museum of Television and Radio). But anecdotally, this will never happen. We will not connect the content of television with the content of whatever replaces it. The two experiences will be aesthetically incomparable, in the same way that TV and radio are incomparable. Over time, society simply stopped connecting the content of the radio era with the content of the TV era, even though many performers worked in both platforms and the original three

nant force of the latter twentieth century, but a force tethered to the period of its primacy. And this will make retroactive interpretations of its artistic value particularly complicated.

Here's what I mean: When something fits into a lucid, logical continuum, it's generally remembered for how it (a) reinterprets the entity that influenced its creation, and (b) provides influence for whatever comes next. Take something like skiffle music—a musical genre defined by what it added to early-twentieth-century jazz (rhythmic primitivism) and by those individuals later inspired by it (rock artists of the British Invasion, most notably the Beatles). We think about skiffle outside of itself, as one piece of a multidimensional puzzle. That won't happen with television. It seems more probable that the entrenched memory of television will be like those massive stone statues on Easter Island: monoliths of creative disconnection. Its cultural imprint might be akin to the Apollo space program, a zeitgeist-driving superstructure that (suddenly) mattered more than everything around it, until it (suddenly) didn't matter at all. There won't be any debate over the *importance* of TV, because that has already been assured (if anything, historians might exaggerate its significance). What's hazier

---

networks started as radio outlets; from a consumer perspective, they just *felt* different, even when trafficking in the same milieu. For example, sitcoms were invented for radio. There were situation comedies on radio long before even the richest Americans owned TVs, and that includes a few sitcoms that were conceived on radio and jumped to the tube. But the experience of watching a sitcom was totally alien from the experience of hearing a sitcom. It altered things so much that the second definition became the universal definition. By 1980, using the word "sitcom" to describe anything that wasn't a TV show required explanation. Its origin in radio is irrelevant, and we would never compare *Cheers* or *M*A*S*H* to something like *Fibber McGee and Molly*. They have a mechanical relationship, but not a practical one. They seem entwined only to the specific generation of people who happened to live through the transition.

are the particulars. Which specific TV programs will still matter centuries after the medium itself has been replaced? What TV content will resonate with future generations, even after the technological source of that content has become nonexistent?

These are queries that require a thought experiment.

[2] Let's pretend archaeologists made a bizarre discovery: The ancient Egyptians had television. Now, don't concern yourself with how this would have worked.[2] Just pretend it (somehow) happened, and that the Egyptian relationship to television was remarkably similar to our own. Moreover, this insane archaeological discovery is also insanely complete—we suddenly have access to all the TV shows the Egyptians watched between the years 3500 and 3300 BC. Every frame of this library would be (on some level) interesting. However, some frames would be way more interesting than others. From a sociological vantage point, the most compelling footage would be the national news, closely followed by the local news, closely followed by the commercials. But the least compelling material would be whatever the Egyptians classified as their version of "prestige" television.

The ancient Egyptian *Breaking Bad*, the ancient Egyptian *House of Cards*, the ancient Egyptian rendering of *The Americans* (which

---

2 This, somewhat obviously, requires the mental evasion of certain critical details— the ancient Egyptians didn't have electricity, they didn't invent the camera, and it would still be at least 5,200 years before the birth of Shonda Rhimes. But don't worry about the technical issues. Just assume the TVs ran on solar power and involved the condensation of river water and were sanctioned by Ra.

I suppose would be called *The Egyptians* and involve promiscuous spies from Qatna)—these would be of marginal significance. Why? Because the aesthetic strengths that make sophisticated TV programs superior to their peers do not translate over time. Looking backward, no one would care how good the acting was or how nuanced the plots were. Nobody would really care about the music or the lighting or the mood. These are artful, subjective qualities that matter in the present. What we'd actually want from ancient Egyptian television is a way to look directly into the past, in the same manner we look at Egyptian hieroglyphics without fixating on the color palette or the precision of scale. We'd want to see what their world looked like and how people lived. We would want to understand the experience of subsisting in a certain place during a certain time, from a source that wasn't consciously trying to illustrate those specific traits (since conscious attempts at normalcy inevitably come with bias). What we'd want, ultimately, is "ancillary verisimilitude." We'd want a TV show that provided the most realistic portrait of the society that created it, without the self-aware baggage embedded in any overt attempt at doing so. In this hypothetical scenario, the most accurate depiction of ancient Egypt would come from a fictional product that achieved this goal accidentally, without even trying. Because that's the way it *always* is, with *everything*. True naturalism can only be a product of the unconscious.

So apply this philosophy to ourselves, and to our own version of televised culture: If we consider all possible criteria, what were the most accidentally realistic TV shows of all time? Which American TV programs—if watched by a curious person in a distant future—would latently represent how day-to-day American society actually was?

This is the kind of question even people who think about television for a living don't think about very often. When I asked *The Revolution Was Televised* author Alan Sepinwall, he noted the "kitchen-sink realism" of sitcoms from the seventies (the grimy aesthetics of *Taxi* and the stagnation of *Barney Miller*, a cop show where the cops never left the office). *New Yorker* TV critic Emily Nussbaum suggested a handful of shows where the dialogue captured emotional inarticulation without the crutch of clichés (most notably the mid-nineties teen drama *My So-Called Life*). Still, it's hard to view any of the programs cited by either as vehicles for understanding reality. This is not their fault, though: We're not supposed to think about TV in this way. Television critics who obsess over the authenticity of picayune narrative details are like poetry professors consumed with penmanship. To attack *True Detective* or *Lost* or *Twin Peaks* as "unrealistic" is a willful misinterpretation of the intent. We don't need television to accurately depict literal life, because life can literally be found by stepping outside. Television's only real-time responsibility is to entertain. But that changes as years start to elapse. We don't reinvestigate low culture with the expectation that it will entertain us a second time—the hope is that it will be instructive and revelatory, which sometimes works against the intentions of the creator. Take, for example, a series like *Mad Men*: Here was a show set in the New York advertising world of the 1960s, with a dogged emphasis on precise cultural references and era-specific details. The unspoken goal of *Mad Men* was to depict how the sixties "really" were. And to the present-day *Mad Men* viewer, that's precisely how the show came across. The goal was achieved. But *Mad Men* defines the difference between ancillary verisimilitude and premeditated reconstruction. *Mad Men* cannot show us what life was like in the sixties. *Mad Men* can only show how life in the sixties came to be interpreted in the twenty-first century. Sociologically, *Mad Men* says more about the mind-set of 2007 than it does about the mindset of 1967, in the same way *Gunsmoke* says more about the world of 1970 than the world of 1870. Compared to *The Andy Griffith Show* or *Gilligan's Island*, a mediated construct like *Mad Men* looks infinitely more authentic—but it can't be philosophically authentic, no matter how hard it tries. Its well-considered portrait of the sixties can't be more real than the accidental sixties rooted in any 1964 episode of *My Three Sons*. Because those 1964 accidents are what 1964 actually was.

[**3**] My point is not that we're communally misguided about which TV series are good, or that prestige programming should be ignored because the people who make it are too aware of what they're doing. As a consumer, I'd argue the opposite. But right now, I'm focused on a different type of appreciation. I'm trying to think about TV as a dead medium—not as living art, but as art history (a process further convoluted by the ingrained reflex to *never* think about TV as "art," even when it clearly is). This brand of analysis drives a certain type of person bonkers, because it ignores the conception of taste. Within this discussion, the quality of a program doesn't matter; the assumption is that the future person considering these artifacts won't be remotely concerned with entertainment value. My interest is utility. It's a

formalist assessment, focusing on all the things a (normal) person is not supposed to (normally) be cognizant of while watching any given TV show. Particularly . . .

1. The way the characters talk.
2. The machinations of the world the characters inhabit.
3. The manner in which the show is filmed and presented.
4. The degree to which "realness" is central to the show's ethos.

That first quality is the most palpable and the least quantifiable. If anyone on a TV show employed the stilted, posh, mid-Atlantic accent of stage actors, it would instantly seem preposterous; outside a few notable exceptions, the goal of televised conversation is fashionable naturalism. But vocal delivery is only a fraction of this equation. There's also the issue of word choice: It took decades for screenwriters to realize that no adults have ever walked into a tavern and said, "I'll have a beer," without noting what specific brand of beer they wanted[3] (an interaction between Kyle MacLachlan and Laura Dern in the 1986 theatrical film *Blue Velvet* is the first time I recall seeing the overt recognition of this). What's even

---

3 I should note again that there's also a popular line of thinking that argues against this type of realism. Some screenwriters feel that directly using an explicit example of any non-essential object dates the material and amplifies the significance of something that doesn't really matter to the story; in other words, having a character ask for a specific brand name like "Heineken" (instead of the generic "beer") forces the audience to *notice* the beverage a little too much, which might prompt them to read something into that transaction that detracts from the story. It imposes a meaning onto Heineken as a brand. But remember: If we're looking backward from a distant future, we don't care about the story, anyway. We *want* the scene to be dated.

harder to compute is the relationship between a period's depiction of conversation and the way people of that period were talking in real life. Did the average American father in 1957 truly talk to his kids the way Ward Cleaver talked to Wally and the Beaver? It doesn't seem possible—but it was, in all likelihood, the way 1957 suburban fathers *imagined* they were speaking.

The way characters talk is connected to the second quality, but subtly. I classify "the machinations of the world" as the unspoken, internal rules that govern how characters exist. When these rules are illogical, the fictional world seems false; when the rules are rational, even a sci-fi fantasy realm can seem plausible. Throughout the 1970s, the most common narrative trope on a sitcom like *Three's Company* or *Laverne and Shirley* was "the misunderstanding"—a character infers incorrect information about a different character, and that confusion drives the plot. What always felt unreal about those scenarios was the way no one ever addressed these misunderstandings aloud, even when that was the obvious solution. The flawed machinations of the seventies sitcom universe required all misunderstandings to last exactly twenty-two minutes. But when a show's internal rules are good, the viewer is convinced that they're seeing something close to life. When the rom-com series *Catastrophe* debuted on Amazon, a close friend tried to explain why the program seemed unusually true to him. "This is the first show I can ever remember," he said, "where the characters laugh at each other's jokes in a non-obnoxious way." This seemingly simple idea was, in fact, pretty novel—prior to *Catastrophe*, individuals on sitcoms constantly made hilarious remarks that no one seemed to notice were hilarious. For decades, this was an unspoken, internal rule: No one laughs at anything. So seeing characters laugh naturally at things that were plainly funny was a new level of realness.

The way a TV show is photographed and staged (*this is point number three*) are industrial attributes that take advantage of viewers' preexisting familiarity with the medium: When a fictional drama is filmed like a news documentary, audiences unconsciously absorb the action as extra-authentic (a scene shot from a single mobile perspective, like most of *Friday Night Lights*, always feels closer to reality than scenes captured with three stationary cameras, like most of *How I Met Your Mother*). It's a technical choice that aligns with the fourth criterion, the extent to which the public recognition of authenticity informs the show's success (a realization that didn't happen in earnest until the 1980s, with shows like *Hill Street Blues*). Now, it's possible that—in two hundred fifty years—those last two points may be less meaningful to whoever is excavating these artifacts. Viewers with no relationship to TV won't be fooled by the perspective of the camera, and people living in a different time period won't intuitively sense the relationship between the world they're seeing and the world that was. But these points will still matter a little, because all four qualities are interrelated. They amplify each other. And whatever television program exemplifies these four qualities most successfully will ultimately have the most usefulness to whatever future people end up watching them. For these (yet-to-be-conceived) cultural historians, TV will be a portal into the past. It will be a way to psychically contact the late twentieth century with an intimacy and depth that can only come from visual fiction, without any need for imagination or speculation. It won't be a personal, interpretive experience, like reading a book; it will be like the book is alive.

Nothing will need to be mentally conjured. The semi-ancient world will just be *there*, moving and speaking in front of them, unchanged by the sands of time.

All of which leads to one central question: What TV show will this be?

Removed from context, it's a question that can also be asked like this: What is the realest fake thing we've ever made on purpose?

I'm (slightly, but not really) embarrassed to admit that this is an inquiry I've been thinking about for my entire life, years before I ever had a financial incentive to do so. It is inexplicably hardwired into my brain. For as long as I can remember, whenever I watch *any* scripted TV show, part of my consciousness interrogates its relationship to reality. "Could this happen? Does this look the way it would actually look? Does this work the way it would actually work?" It does not matter if the details are factually impossible—if I'm watching *Game of Thrones*, I can readily accept that dragons exist. Yet I still wonder if the dragons on my TV are behaving in the way I believe real dragons would behave in reality. I still question the veracity of those dragons, and I instinctively analyze the real-world plausibility of a scenario that's patently impossible. This is just the way I am, and I never had to try.

So I am ready for this question.

(And I'd better be, since I appear to be the only person asking it.)

The first candidate to consider—and the easiest candidate to discount—is reality television. As a genre, the social and generational importance of these shows is vastly underrated; they are postmodern picture windows. But they're pretty worthless at demonstrating the one quality they all purport to deliver. Even if we take *The Hills* and *Storage Wars* and *Keeping Up with the Kar-dashians* at face value—that is to say, even if we're willing to accept (or pretend) that these are normal people, behaving naturally in unnatural circumstances—the visual presentation makes no attempt at masking the falseness of the staging or the contrived banality of the conflicts. Nothing on TV looks faker than failed attempts at realism. A show like *The Bachelor* is instantly recognized (by pretty much everyone, including its intended audience) as a prefab version of how such events might theoretically play out in a distant actuality. No television show has ever had a more paradoxical title than MTV's *The Real World*, which proved to be the paradoxical foundation of its success.

Programming that nakedly operates as a subcultural roman à clef actually gets a little closer. The early twenty-first century spawned a glut of these series: *Empire* (a fictionalized portrait of the "urban" music industry) and *Entourage* (a fictionalized portrait of the celebrity industry) were the most successful attempts, but others include *Nashville* (centered on the country music scene), *Ballers* (the post-NFL brain economy), *UnREAL* (the reality of reality TV), and *Silicon Valley* (a satire of the Bay Area tech bubble). None of these programs claim to depict actual events, but all compel viewers to connect characters with the real people who inspired them. The star of *Empire* is some inexact synthesis of Jay Z, Suge Knight, and Berry Gordy. The protagonist in *Entourage* was supposed to be a version of *Entourage* producer Mark Wahlberg, had Wahlberg experienced Leonardo DiCaprio's career. There's a venture capitalist on *Silicon Valley* based (at least partially) on a melding of billionaire Mark Cuban and online entrepreneur Sean Parker. Part of the pleasure these programs provide is an opportunity to make these Xerox associations—and once the connections calcify in viewers' heads, they can effortlessly inject living public figures into fake story lines.[4] That intellectual transfer makes this programming far more watchable than the writing justifies. But this essential process, somewhat ironically, erodes the level of realism. It exaggerates every narrative detail and forces the characters to unload bushels of awkward exposition, simply because casual viewers won't make those subtextual connections without heavy-handed guidance. Beyond a few key exceptions, simulacrum shows are soap operas, marketed as fantasies, geared toward mass audiences who don't want to think very hard about what they're watching. Characters need to invent ways to say, "This is who I'm supposed to be," without saying so directly. Nothing in a simulacrum is accidental, so you end up with the opposite of naturalism: It's bogus inside baseball, designed for outsiders who didn't know anything to begin with. You can't be real by *trying* to be real.

"Aha," you might say to yourself after reading the previous sentence. "If you can't be real by trying to be real, the inverse must be the answer. The path to TV realness must involve trying to be fake on purpose." Well, not quite—although it does get closer. Television shows that make no attempt at tracing reality hold up better over time: the best episodes of *The Twilight Zone*, early Fox experiments like *Herman's Head* and *Get a Life*, the stridently meta *It's*

----

4 When a record producer on *Nashville* ("Liam McGuinnis") was introduced into the story line, he appeared to be directly modeled after musician (and current Nashville resident) Jack White. I now see "Jack White" in every scene involving this character, which is unintentionally hilarious, especially since he constantly does things Jack White would never do, such as have sex with Connie Britton (a.k.a. "Rayna James," who is 60 percent Reba McEntire, 25 percent Sara Evans, and 15 percent Faith Hill).

Garry Shandling's Show, and anything featuring Muppets. If a piece of art openly defines itself as 90 percent fake, whatever remains is legitimized (and it's that final 10 percent that matters most). But a self-aware vehicle like *Community* or *Mr. Show* still collides with the reality-killing property of self-serious programs like *Homeland* or *St. Elsewhere*—premeditated consciousness. The former takes advantage of people's knowledge that TV is not real; the latter does whatever it can to make people forget that this unreality is something they recognize. In both cases, the effort exposes the hand. For this to work, the people creating the TV program can't be thinking about how real (or how unreal) the product seems. They need to be concerned with other issues, so that the realness is just the residue. And this kind of unintentional residue used to build up all the time, before TV decided to get good.

What I'm talking about, in essence, is a disrespected thirty-five-year window of time. The first Golden Age of Television started in the late 1940s and lasted until the demise of *Playhouse 90* in 1960; this was a period when the newness of TV allowed for unprecedented innovations in populist entertainment. The second Golden Age of Television started in the late 1990s (with *The Sopranos* and *Freaks and Geeks* and the mass metabolizing of *Seinfeld*) and is just now starting to fade; this is a period when television was taken as seriously as film and literature. But as a reality hunter with a reality hunger, my thinking occupies the dark years in between. Throughout the 1970s and '80s, watching TV was just what people did when there was nothing else to do. The idea of "appointment television" would have been considered absurd—if you missed a show, you missed it. It was not something to worry about. The family television was simply an appliance—a cathode box with the mentality of a mammary gland, actively converting couch owners into potatoes. To genuinely care about TV certified someone as a dullard, even to the dullards in the band Black Flag. This perception turned television into a pure commodity. The people writing and producing the shows were still smart and creative, but they were far less concerned with aesthetics or mechanics. There was no expectation that audiences would *believe* what they were seeing, so they just tried to entertain people (and to occasionally "confront them" with social issues). From a linguistic standpoint, this allowed for a colossal leap in realism. Particularly with the work of Norman Lear, the creator of long-running, heavily syndicated shows like *All in the Family*, *The Jeffersons*, *Good Times*, and *One Day at a Time*, it became possible for characters on television to use language that vaguely resembled that of actual humanoids. The only problem was that these productions still had the visual falseness of thirty-minute theatrical plays. The sets were constant reminders that this was not life. Archie and Edith Bunker's living room furniture already resembled the museum installation it would eventually become. George Jefferson and Ann Romano[5] seemed more like symbols than citizens. It was not until the late 1980s that the residue really stuck, and most of it stuck to one specific vehicle: *Roseanne*. It wasn't perfect, it wasn't reasonable, and—sometimes—it wasn't

----

5 As I note these characters, I find myself wondering how confusing it must be for readers born in (say) 1995 to contextualize the meaning of TV personalities from TV programs they've never even heard of. But something I've learned from lecturing at colleges is that young people read nonfiction books very differently from the way I once did; they instantaneously Google any cultural reference they don't immediately comprehend. Learning about the life of Ann Romano is no different from learning about the life of Abe Lincoln. Due to Wikipedia, they're both historical figures.

even clever. But *Roseanne* was the most accidentally realistic TV show there ever was.

The premise of *Roseanne* was not complex. Over time, it adopted an unrepentant ideology about gender and oppression. But that was not how it started. It was, in many ways, an inverted mirror of *The Cosby Show*: If *The Cosby Show* was an attempt to show that black families weren't necessarily poor and underprivileged, *Roseanne* was an attempt to show how white families weren't necessarily rich and functional. The show was built around (and subsequently named after) Roseanne Barr, a domineering comedic force from Colorado who did not give a fuck about any vision that wasn't her own. John Goodman was cast as her husband. By the standards of TV, both of these people were wildly overweight. Yet what made *Roseanne* atypical was how rarely those weight issues were discussed. *Roseanne* was the first American TV show comfortable with the statistical reality that most Americans are fat. And it placed these fat people in a messy house, with most of the key interpersonal conversations happening in the kitchen or the garage or the laundry room. These fat people had three non-gorgeous kids, and the kids complained constantly, and two of them were weird and one never smiled. Everything about *Roseanne* looked right. The house looked chaotic and unfinished—it looked like it had been decorated by people who were trying to trick themselves into believing they didn't have a shitty house.

Roseanne ran for nine seasons, and the dialogue changed considerably over that span. The (popular) early years were structurally similar to other sitcoms; the (unpopular) final season was the equivalent of a twenty-four-episode dream sequence that canceled out almost everything that had come before. But there was realness residue from start to finish. Episodes would conclude with jarring, unresolved arguments. Barr was an untrained actress working with veteran performers, so scenes sometimes felt half rehearsed (not improvised, but uncontained by the normal rules of TV). There appeared to be no parameters on what could qualify as a normal conversation: An episode from the eighth season includes a sequence where Barr sits in the passenger seat of a car, reading Bikini Kill lyrics aloud. If these details strike you as immaterial, I understand—when described on paper, examples of ancillary veri-similitude usually sound like minor mistakes or illogical choices. And sometimes, that's what they are—essential flaws that link a false reality to the real one.

So what does this mean? Am I arguing that future generations will watch *Roseanne* and recognize its genius? Am I arguing that they *should* watch it, for reasons our current generation can't fully appreciate? Am I arguing that future generations *might* watch it, and (almost coincidentally) have a better understanding of our contemporary reality, even if they don't realize it?

I don't know.

I really don't. It's possible this debate doesn't even belong in this book, or that it should be its own book. It's a phenomenon with no willful intent and no discernible result. I'm not satisfied with what my conclusion says about the nature of realism. *But I know this matters.* I know there is something critical here we're underestimating, and it has to do with television's ability to make the present tense exist forever, in a way no other medium ever has. It's not disposable, even if we want it to be. And someday, future potatoes will prove this.

Sudden Death (Over Time)

On a frigid evening in February 2010, I was asked to appear at a reading series held in a Brooklyn art gallery. I accepted the invitation. I did not, however, pay much attention to the details of the invite and erroneously assumed this art gallery was located in Manhattan, which meant I was twenty-five minutes late for the opening of an event where I was the opening act. The evening's headliner was writer Malcolm Gladwell, whom I'd met in person maybe five or six times before (and on two of those occasions, we'd discussed the Buffalo Bills[1]). Since I was still crossing the East River in a taxi at the seven p.m. start time, the order of the speakers was flopped. Gladwell graciously spoke first. When I finally arrived, he was almost finished with his piece, a reported essay from *The New Yorker* about why NFL teams are habitually terrible

---

1 Gladwell went to college in Toronto. People from Toronto view the Bills as their local franchise.

at drafting quarterbacks. Upon finishing the reading, he took a handful of questions from the audience, almost all of which were about football. The last question was about the future of the sport. Gladwell's response, at least at the time, seemed preposterous. "In twenty-five years," he said, "no one in America will play football and no one in America will eat red meat." He thanked the crowd and exited the stage.

After a brief intermission, it was my turn to perform. Sensing a mild degree of bewilderment from the audience, I tried to break the ice by making a joke about Gladwell's closing prediction. "There is no way people will not be playing football or eating meat in twenty-five years," I said. "In fact, there is a much higher likelihood that in twenty-five years, I will literally eat the flesh of all the various football players who've died during whatever game I happened to watch that day." Forty people laughed. I then favorably compared the state of Alabama to the island of Samoa. Four people laughed. But here's the pivotal takeaway from that particular night: At the time, my absurdist jokes felt more reasonable than Gladwell's analysis. Predicting that the most popular game in the country would no longer exist in less than two generations made it seem like he didn't really know what he was talking about. But now, of course, everyone talks like Gladwell. In the span of five years, that sentiment has become the conventional intellectual take on the future of football. It is no longer a strange thing to anticipate. Gladwell has grown even more confident: "This is a sport that is living in the past, that has no connection to the realities of the game right now and no connection to the rest of society," I heard him say on a local TV show called *Studio 1.0.* "[The NFL] is completely disconnected to the consequences of the sport that they are engaged in . . . They are off on this nineteenth-century trajectory which is fundamentally out of touch with the rest of us." The show's host asked if he still believed football was destined to die. "I don't see how it doesn't. It will start to shrivel at the high school and college level, and then the pro game will wither on the vine."

It's disorienting how rapidly this perception has normalized, particularly considering a central contradiction no one seems to deny—football is not only the most popular sport in the country, but a sport that is becoming *more* popular, assuming TV ratings can be trusted as a yardstick. It's among the few remnants of the pre-Internet monoculture; it could be convincingly argued that football is more popular in America than every other sport combined. Over 110 million people watched the most recent Super Bowl, but that stat is a predictable outlier—what's more stunning is the 25 million people who regularly watch the NFL draft. Every spring, millions of people spend three days scrutinizing a middle-aged man in a gray suit walking up to a podium to announce the names of people who have not yet signed a contract. Football is so popular that people (myself included) have private conversations about *how many* people would have to die on the field before we'd seriously consider giving it up. Which is the kind of conversation that pushes everyone else toward one of two conclusions:

1. **Football is doomed.** This is the Gladwellian outlook, and it generally goes something like this: The number of on-field concussions continues to increase, as does the medical evidence of how dangerous football truly is. More and more pro players proactively quit (San Francisco

linebacker Chris Borland being the first high-profile example). Retired players start to show signs of mental deficiency at a higher and higher frequency. Perhaps a prominent wide receiver is killed on national television, and his death dominates the national conversation for three months. The issue becomes political, and the president gets involved (much like Teddy Roosevelt did in 1905, the year nineteen college players were killed on football fields). Virtually all parents stop their children from playing youth football, and schools can't afford the insurance liability required for a collision sport of this magnitude. The high school game rapidly disappears, leading to a collapse of the college game. With its feeder system eliminated, the NFL morphs into a sloppy enterprise that's still highly dangerous and prohibitively expensive. Public interest evaporates and a $50 billion bubble spontaneously bursts. Like thirty-two brachiosaurs, NFL teams are too massive to evolve. In less than a generation, the game vanishes. Its market share is split between soccer and basketball.

2. **Football will survive, but not in its current form.** The less incendiary take on football's future suggests that it *will* continue, but in a different shape. It becomes a regional sport, primarily confined to places where football is ingrained in the day-to-day culture (Florida, Texas, etc.). Its fanbase resembles that of contemporary boxing—rich people watching poor people play a game they would never play themselves. The NFL persists through sheer

social pervasiveness—a system that's too big to fail and too economically essential to too many microeconomies. The game itself is altered for safety. "As a natural optimist who loves football, I can only really give one answer to this question, and the answer is yes. I believe that football can and will still have a significant place in American culture in a hundred years," says Michael MacCambridge, author of the comprehensive NFL history *America's Game*. "That said, I suspect it will be a less violent game than it has been in the past. And this would be in line with the changes throughout American spectator sports—and society at large—over the previous century. In the nineteenth century, in baseball, you could throw a runner out on his way to first merely by pegging him in the back with the ball while he was hurrying down the first-base line. That age of bare-knuckles boxing and cockfighting and football as organized mayhem eventually changed to reflect the sensibilities of the modern era. So football will continue to change over the next century, and so will protective football equipment."

Though they empty into dissimilar cul-de-sacs, these two roads share one central quality: a faith in reason. Both the Gladwell model and the MacCambridge model are built on the thesis that logic will dictate the future of sport. Gladwell believes consumers are too reasonable to continue supporting a game that kills people; MacCambridge believes the people who drive football are too reasonable to allow the game to continue killing its participants. Both perspectives place trust in the motives and intelligence of the populace.

But I am less willing to do that.

If forced to gamble on which of these two men will eventually be correct, I would flip a coin. But I find myself wondering if that coin might end up irrationally balancing itself on its side. I can imagine two other possibilities, both of which exist in the margins. The first possibility is that football survives *because* of its explicit violence, and that this discomfiting detail ends up being its twisted salvation. The second possibility is that football will indeed disappear—but not just because of its brutality. It will disappear because *all team sports* are going to disappear, and football will merely be the first.

[2] When does something truly become popular? And I don't mean "popular" in the sense that it succeeds; I mean "popular" in the sense that the specific thing's incontrovertible popularity is the most important thing about it. I mean "popular" in the way Pet Rocks were popular in 1975, or the way *E.T.* was popular in 1982, or the way Oprah Winfrey was popular for most of the nineties.

The answer to this question is both obvious and depressing: Something becomes truly popular when it becomes interesting to those who don't particularly care. You don't create a phenomenon like *E.T.* by appealing to people who love movies. You create a phenomenon like *E.T.* by appealing to people who see one movie a year. And this goal is what the NFL has been working toward since the late 1970s. The hard-core football audience is huge, but not huge enough—the NFL also wants to lasso those who can't name any player whose wife doesn't get mentioned in *Us Weekly*.

They want people who watch three games a season to join their office fantasy league. They want informal sports fans to feel like they *must* follow pro football, lest they be seen as people who don't like sports at all. You can't perpetuate a $7 billion industry without aggressively motivating the vaguely unmotivated. Yet this level of social saturation is precisely what places football on the precipice. There are many athletic activities more dangerous than football—bull riding, BASE jumping, auto racing. It has been alleged that seventy-one of the first seventy-five people who pioneered the wingsuit died during the testing process. Every year, multiple people perish climbing Mount Everest (in April of 2014, sixteen Sherpas were killed *on the same day*). But the difference with football is the ethical compliance, particularly for casual spectators with little emotional investment. The audience for the Brickyard 400 is a marginalized audience (they all know what happens when cars crash into walls at 140 mph). The audience for Cheyenne Frontier Days is a marginalized audience (they all know what happens when a 2,200-pound bull lands on a cowboy's neck). These are fully invested fans who aren't alarmed or confused by the inherent dangers of their niche obsession. They know what they're getting into. No UFC fan is shocked by the sight of a man knocked unconscious. Football, however, appeals to a swath of humanity many magnitudes larger. It attracts people who haven't necessarily considered the ramifications of what they're witnessing—people who think they're relaxing at home on a Sunday afternoon, nonchalantly watching the same low-stakes distraction as everyone else. So when this type of person is suddenly confronted with the realization that what he is watching might be killing the people who participate—or if he was to actually *see* a player killed on the field, which seems increasingly inevitable—he is overcome with guilt and discomfort (and bewilderment over how he's supposed to feel about economically supporting a game that mildly terrifies him). The sheer scale of football's popularity likewise creates an opportunity for media grandstanding—self-righteous pundits denounce football the same way histrionic gate-keepers denounced booze in 1919 and *Dungeons & Dragons* in 1985. Over time, this fusion of public discomfort and media theatrics generates a political meaning. It now "means something" to support football. Those who self-identify as enlightened believe it means something tragic. And in ten years, that sentiment might reflect most of the US population.

But it won't represent *all* of the population.

It will never represent all of the population, even if it becomes the dominant way to think and feel. And that will make it unkill-able. When any idea becomes symbolically dominant, those who dislike the idea will artificially inflate the necessity of whatever it opposes. (Second Amendment purists do this all the time.) This is why I can imagine a world where football continues to thrive—not in spite of its violence, but because of it. And not in some latent, unspoken context—openly, and without apology.

In the present moment, football operates as two parallel silos, both of which are shooting skyward and gaining momentum. One silo reflects the overall popularity of the sport, which increases every year. The other silo houses the belief that the game is morally reprehensible, a sentiment that swells every day. Somehow, these two silos never collide. But let's assume such a collision eventually happens, and the silo of popularity collapses on impact. It stops rocketing upward and is obliterated into a pile of bricks.

That brick pile will be titanic, and it won't disappear. Neither will the people who built that silo, or those who lived inside it, or those who grew up worshipping its architecture. So they will use those bricks as weapons. They will throw them at the other silo. And since the game will no longer appeal to the casual fan, certain innate problems will turn into strengths.

A few months after being hired as head football coach at the University of Michigan, Jim Harbaugh was profiled on the HBO magazine show *Real Sports*. It was a wildly entertaining segment, heavily slanted toward the intellection that Harbaugh is a lunatic. One of the last things Harbaugh said in the interview was this: "I love football. Love it. Love it. I think it's the last bastion of hope for toughness in America in men, in males." Immediately following the segment, the reporter (Andrea Kremer) sat down with *Real Sports* host Bryant Gumbel to anecdotally unpack the story we'd all just watched. Gumbel expressed shock over Harbaugh's final sentiment. To anyone working in the media (or even to anyone who cares about the media), Harbaugh's position seemed sexist and ultra-reactionary, so much so that Rush Limbaugh felt the need to support it on his radio show.

This is what happens when any populist, uncomfortable thought is expressed on television.

There's an embedded assumption within all arguments regarding the doomed nature of football. The assumption is that the game is even more violent and damaging than it superficially appears, and that as more people realize this (and/or refuse to deny the medical evidence verifying that damage), the game's fan support will disappear. The mistake made by those advocating this position is their certitude that this perspective is self-evident. It's not. These advocates remind me of an apocryphal quote attributed to film critic Pauline Kael after the 1972 presidential election: "How could Nixon have won? I don't know one person who voted for him." Now, Kael never actually said this.[2] But that erroneous quote survives as the best shorthand example for why smart people tend to be wrong as often as their not-so-smart peers—they work from the flawed premise that their worldview is standard. The contemporary stance on football's risk *feels* unilateral, because nobody goes around saying, "Modern life is not violent enough." Yet this sentiment quietly exists. And what those who believe it say instead is, "I love football. It's the last bastion of hope for toughness in America." It's not difficult to imagine a future where the semantic distance between those statements is nonexistent. And if that happens, football will change from a popular leisure pastime to an unpopular political necessity.

When discussing football's future, the gut reaction is to try to reconcile its current condition with whatever we imagine the future will be like. At present, football is a problematic monolith, and it seems unlikely that such monolithic status can be sustained over time. But you don't need to remain monolithic if your core constituency cares more deeply than those who want the monolith destroyed. Football could lose 75 percent of its audience and matter just as much as it does now, assuming the people who stick with the game view it as a sanctuary from a modern world they distrust. Over time, it could really, *really* "mean something" to love foot-

---

2 What she actually said was: "I live in a rather special world. I only know one person who voted for Nixon. Where they are I don't know. They're outside my ken. But sometimes when I'm in a theater I can feel them."

ball, in a context that isn't related to sports at all. It could be a signifier for an idea that can't be otherwise expressed—the belief that removing physicality from the public sphere does not remove it from reality, and that attempts to do so weaken the republic. Football could become a dead game to the casual sports fan without losing a fraction of its cultural influence. It could become the only way for a certain kind of person to safely access the kind of controlled violence he sees as a critical part of life.

"But look what happened to boxing," people will say (and these people sometimes include me). "Boxing was the biggest sport in America during the 1920s, and now it exists on the fringes of society. It was just too brutal." Yet when Floyd Mayweather fought Manny Pacquiao in May of 2015, the fight grossed $400 million, and the main complaint from spectators was that the fight was not brutal *enough*. Because it operates on a much smaller scale, boxing is—inside its own crooked version of reality—flourishing. It doesn't seem like it, because the average person doesn't care. But boxing doesn't need average people. It's not really a sport anymore. It's a mildly perverse masculine novelty, and that's enough to keep it relevant. It must also be noted that boxing's wounds were mostly self-inflicted. Its internal corruption was more damaging than its veneration of violence, and much of its fanbase left of their own accord. Conversely, football is experiencing a different type of crisis—there is a sense that the game is being *taken* from fans, and mostly by snooty strangers who never liked the sport in the first place. It will come to be seen as the persecution of a culture. This makes football akin to the Confederate flag, or Christmas decorations in public spaces, or taxpayer-supported art depicting

Jesus in a tank of urine—something that becomes intractable precisely *because* so many people want to see it eliminated. The game's violence would save it, and it would never go away.

[**3**] But then—sometimes—I think something else.

[**4**] During the first week of 2015, I interviewed Los Angeles Lakers guard Kobe Bryant in a pancake house. It was a short conversation, but we covered a lot of ground—his lack of close friends, the rape accusations levied against him in 2003, his self-perceived similarities to Mozart. It was the best interview experience I'd ever had with an athlete. At one point, we were talking about film, and I asked Kobe if he'd seen the movie *Whiplash*. "Of course," he said. "That's me." The trajectory of the conversation switched after he said this, so I was never able to ask a follow-up; I was never able to ask if he meant that he saw himself as the film's protagonist, its antagonist, or a human incarnation of the entire movie. All three possibilities seemed plausible.

Whiplash is a movie about conservatory jazz, but it's really a sports movie. It's about a teenage drumming prodigy (Miles Teller) who will do whatever it takes to be great, even though he's never really considered what "greatness" signifies. He becomes the pupil of an esteemed, sociopathic jazz instructor (J. K. Simmons) who proceeds to verbally and physically abuse him, relentlessly manipulating his emotions. The character Simmons embodies believes this cruelty is the only true path to genius. "There are no

two words in the English language more harmful than 'good job,'"
he says without discernible emotion. What sets this film apart is
its unexpected conclusion: *The abuse works.* Simmons's unethical,
unacceptable mistreatment of Teller is precisely what pushes him
to transcendence. He is, essentially, pounded into greatness.

The broad response to *Whiplash* was positive. It's a good movie—
there are a few unrealistic twists, but the acting is excellent (Simmons won an Academy Award) and the emotional resonance is hard
to deny. It was well reviewed and made decent money. Yet the more
political, more sophisticated takes on *Whiplash* inevitably implied
that something about this movie was immoral, in a deeper context
unrelated to film. *Whiplash* was entertaining, these critics would
always concede, but it got something wrong: It got jazz wrong, or
it got race wrong, or it latently supported the patriarchy, or it glorified masochism. But I suspect all of those critiques were veiled
attempts at expressing discomfort with the movie's bedrock theme,
a notion that has been entirely eradicated from the popular culture.
Only Richard Brody of *The New Yorker* came close to saying this
directly: "To justify his methods," he writes, "[Simmons] tells
[Teller] that the worst thing you can tell a young artist is 'Good
job,' because self-satisfaction and complacency are the enemies of
artistic progress . . . and it's utter, despicable nonsense. There's
nothing wrong with 'Good job,' because a real artist won't be
gulled or lulled into self-satisfaction by it: real artists are hard on
themselves, curious to learn what they don't know and to push
themselves ahead."

Socially, this is absolutely the way we have been conditioned to
think. The idea that greatness is generated through pain and
adversity and fear is not just an unpopular position—when applied

to the lives of young people, it's practically a criminal act. The modern goal is to *remove* those things from whatever extracurricular pursuit any young person is pursuing. Now, the logic behind this is hard to criticize: What is the value of a hobby that makes a kid unhappy? The response, I suppose, is that someday that kid will be an adult (and scenarios involving adversity and fear won't be optional). But I'm not interested in the argument over whether this is positive or negative. I'm simply wondering if the overall state of society is—very slowly, and almost imperceptibly—moving toward a collective condition where team sports don't have a place. In other words, a distant future where football disappears, followed by every other sport with vaguely similar values. Which, to varying degrees, is every team sport there is.

A few days before Super Bowl XLIX, the public radio show *Radiolab* produced an episode on football,[3] specifically its origin and its troubling appeal (they essentially billed it as a football show for people who don't like football, which is how they see their audience). Midway through the episode, the show's producers try to mathematically verify if youth participation in football is decreasing as much as we suspect. It is. But the specificity of that stat is deceiving: It turns out youth participation is down for all major sports—football, basketball, baseball, and even soccer (the so-called sport of the future). Around the same time, *The Wall Street Journal* ran a similar story with similar statistics: For all kids between six and eighteen (boys and girls alike), overall participa-

----

3 I should note that I was involved with this episode. But my involvement was negligible.

tion in team sports was down 4 percent. Surprisingly, basketball took a bigger hit than football.

As part of their investigation, the *Radiolab* staff contacted a cross-section of youth football coaches and asked why this is happening. The producers mildly scoffed at the coaches' answers, all of which were eerily similar: video games. "The bottom line is that—today—if the kid doesn't like the score, he just hits restart. He starts the game over." This is a quote from a youth coach in Louisiana, but it was mirrored by almost every coach *Radiolab* encountered. On the surface, it seemed like the reactionary complaint of a Luddite. But sometimes the reactionaries are right. It's wholly possible that the nature of electronic gaming has instilled an expectation of success in young people that makes physical sports less desirable. There's also the possibility that video games are more inclusive, that they give the child more control, and that they're simply easier for kids who lack natural physical gifts. All of which point to an incontestable conclusion: Compared to traditional athletics, video game culture is much closer to the (allegedly) enlightened world we (supposedly) want to inhabit.

Should physical differences matter more than intellectual differences? Should the ability to intimidate another person be rewarded? Is it acceptable to scream at a person in order to shape his behavior? Should masculinity, in any context, be prioritized? The growing consensus regarding all of these questions is no. Yet these are ingrained aspects of competitive sports, all the way back to Sparta. A key reason college football came into existence in the late nineteenth century was that veterans who'd fought in the Civil War feared the next generation of men would be soft and ill prepared for the building of a republic ("We gotta give these boys something to do," these veterans believed. "Hell, they'll probably go through life without killing *anyone!*"). We inject sports with meaning because *they are supposed to mean something.* So what happens when the things they signify are no longer desirable traits? It would mean the only value sports offer is their value as an aerobic entertainment commodity. And that would make it the equivalent of a fad, with the inherently finite life span all fads possess.

In 2014, the NCAA implemented a playoff system for major college football. They did not, however, end the traditional bowl system—if you include the two semifinal games and the championship, there are still around forty bowl games played throughout December and January. What emerged from this structure was a fascinating trend: The only people interested in these games were the people watching on television. The Camellia Bowl pitted Bowling Green against South Alabama. The game was played in the state of Alabama, less than six hours from the South Alabama campus. Somehow, it drew just 20,256 fans. But the TV audience was relatively huge—around 1.2 million viewers. The gap for the Famous Idaho Potato Bowl was even greater—the human attendance was under 18,000 while the TV audience approached 1.5 million. This prompted *USA Today* to examine the bizarre possibility of future bowl games being played inside gigantic television studios, devoid of crowds. Crazy as that may sound, there would be some real practicality to this. With no concern for a live audience, the entire event could be constructed to maximize the TV experience. The whole facility could serve as a camera, and the visuals would be unprecedented. But this kind of fantastical speculation speaks to a broader change in how sports are now perceived. It reframes football as a simulation, not that far removed from a movie. The sole purpose of the event would be to fill a three-hour window of programming on ESPN2, and—if a better, cheaper alternative could be aired in its place—the game would have no purpose at all. Yes, the players would still be real. Yes, the hitting would still hurt. But if all this is merely a distraction to stare at on a pixelated screen, why would the human element remain essential? Robot players would work just as well. CGI players would work even better. It could *literally* be a video game, controlled and manipulated by a computer. Then we wouldn't have any problems at all. It would just be a TV show that provides an opportunity for gambling.

This, obviously, is not something that could (or would) happen overnight. It would take multiple decades and multiple genera-tions, and it would require our current socioeconomic arc to remain unchanged (which, as I've now latently stated countless times, almost never happens). It also denies the long-held assump-tion that physical games are a natural manifestation for a species that is fundamentally competitive, and that team sports are simply adult versions of the same impulse that prompts any two five-year-olds to race across the playground in order to see who's faster. When I mentioned this theory to a friend who works for ESPN, he thought about it for a long time before saying, "I guess I just can't imagine a world where sports don't exist. It would seem like a totally different world." Well, he's right. It would be a totally different world. But different worlds are created all the time, and the world we're currently building does not reasonably intersect with the darker realities of team sports. We want a pain-free world where everyone is the same, even if they are not. That can't hap-pen if we're still keeping score.

The Case Against Freedom

My existence is split into two unequal, asymmetrical halves. The first half was when I lived in North Dakota, where I was an interesting version of a normal person. That lasted twenty-six years. The second half started when I moved to New York, where I became an uninteresting version of an abnormal person. That's lasted thirteen years. But there's also an intermission I barely remember, even though it was the most politically edifying stage of my life—the four years in between, when I lived in Akron, Ohio.

Very little transpired during this period, or at least very little that directly involved me. I wrote a book, but I didn't believe it would be published, even after I signed the contract. I told people I loved my job at the newspaper, and I don't think I was necessarily lying. But if that was true, why did I hate going to work? I guess that's why they call it work. My free time was spent drinking, sometimes with others but often alone. I was single and devoid of prospects, though I don't recall any feelings of loneliness; on at least three evenings, I sat on my balcony and watched a hedgehog eat apples, an experience more satisfying than going on dates and talking to other forlorn strangers about how dating is hard. Nothing was happening in my life, which provided me the luxury of thinking about life and politics at the same time, almost as if they had an actual relationship.

Ohio is a wonderful place to ponder the state of American democracy, because you're constantly being reminded that America is where you are. Ohio is a scale model of the entire country, jammed into 43,000 square miles. Cleveland views itself as the intellectual East (its citizens believe they have a rivalry with Boston and unironically classify the banks of Lake Erie as the North Coast). Cincinnati is the actual South (they fly Confederate flags and eat weird food). Dayton is the Midwest. Toledo is Pittsburgh, before Pittsburgh was nice. Columbus is a low-altitude Denver, minus the New World Order airport. Ohio experiences all possible US weather, sometimes simultaneously. About 13.7 percent of Ohio's population is black, a percentage that mirrors the national percentage of 13.2. The state has spawned eight presidents, three of whom were absurdly unlucky—one died from standing in the rain, another was killed by an anarchist, and a third was (probably) poisoned by his wife. But more essential than the politicians it produces is what Ohio dictates: More than any other state, Ohio decides who sleeps in the White House. The variance of its social construction makes it the only major population center that always feels completely up for grabs. In every presidential race since the Great Depression, the candidate who carried Ohio has lost only once (in 1960, when Nixon hammered Kennedy because Sinatra didn't know anyone in Youngstown). This electoral phenomenon is widely known and endlessly cited, so living in Ohio during an election cycle is madness. It feels like the media is talking directly at you, all the time. Your vote is so (theoretically) valuable that you forget it's (statistically) irrelevant. It sometimes feels like you are actually running for office yourself, and day-to-day life is just an unusually effective attack ad.

One of the years I lived in Akron was the year 2000. Technically, that was sixteen years ago. But those sixteen years might as well be 160, and here's proof: When I wasn't watching the hedgehog from my balcony, I was watching MTV, and they still occasionally played music. The video that seemed most pertinent at the time was "Testify" by Rage Against the Machine, directed by Michael Moore. Now, I was twenty-eight years old, so I considered myself too mature to take Rage Against the Machine seriously (that seemed like something you did when you were nineteen) and too cool to like their music as music (that seemed like something you did when you were twenty-seven). But I was still dumb enough to trust Michael Moore, so I liked this video. The premise was that George W. Bush and Al Gore were the same person, controlled by the same puppet masters and working for the same interests. We see a clip of Bush expressing support for the death penalty, followed by a clip of Gore saying the exact same thing. Bush extols the virtues of free trade, mirrored by Gore praising free trade. Bush is seen dancing with balloons and Gore is captured in a conga line, and then RATM jams econo in a wood-paneled studio (to a song that is, in retrospect, propulsive and committed, taken from an album I probably underrated). We get a supercut of newsmakers in quick succession—Sonny Bono, Ken Starr, the pope, Bill Clinton—with the ingrained implication that they are all complicit in some big-money boondoggle, and that all politicians and parties are fundamentally interchangeable. It ended with a message from Ralph Nader.

Part of the reason I appreciated this video was that I agreed with it. The other part was that the message seemed so self-evidently true that I couldn't believe a group as politically impractical as Rage Against the Machine was the band making it ("Tom Morello is finally embracing pragmatism," I pragmatically assumed). I stayed up until three a.m. on November 8, watching the results of an election that was closer than I ever imagined possible. Bush won Ohio by about 165,000 votes. Gore lost his home state of Tennessee and was upset in New Hampshire, where Nader got 4 percent of the ballots. Florida was called for Bush at 2:17 a.m., providing him a victory much of the country did not accept as legitimate. I watched the whole event like it was a well-played Olympic hockey game between Norway and Finland. I loved it with emotional and cerebral distance, for totally apolitical reasons. The ultimate outcome didn't bother me, because—like Michael Moore and Zack de la Rocha—I naïvely viewed these men as transposable. Most Americans did, as is illustrated by the fact that no one seemed particularly outraged when the Supreme Court upheld Bush's victory, except for those performative armchair revolutionaries who express reflexive outrage over everything. I don't remember any windows getting shattered or banks being burned.

Obviously, no one thinks like this now. In fact, they don't even think that this was how they thought at the time: Huge swaths of the populace have retroactively convinced themselves that their reaction to the 2000 election was far more extreme than all evidence suggests. When Bush took office in January, it felt perfunctory. That September, the world changed completely. America adopted a level of political polarization that had not existed since the Reconstruction, which now feels like the normal way to think about society. This, I grant, is no profound revelation: The world evolves, so perspectives evolve with it. Two US cities experienced a traumatic event, and that event cascaded into smaller, unrelated events. But just because something can be explained doesn't mean it's simple. Sixteen years ago, it was reasonable to believe there was no meaningful difference between Democratic leadership and Republican leadership. That ended up being wrong. But did it *become* wrong, or was it already wrong in 1999? And if this kind of partisan ambivalence eventually returns to prominence—and it almost certainly will—does our current period of polarization become an aberration? Are we actually wrong *now*?

Let me get back to that hedgehog: The view from my Akron apartment[1] faced the back of the building. There was an apple tree in the yard, and the (comically obese) hedgehog would sit underneath its branches and longingly stare at the low-hanging fruit. It often seemed like he was torturing himself, because there was no way a hedgehog of his ample girth could reach an apple two feet above his head. Yet every time he did this, he knew what he was doing. Every time, or at least every time I happened to be watching, an apple would eventually fall to the ground, and he would waddle over and eat it. He was a brilliant goddamn hedgehog. I couldn't stop thinking about it. When I went on dates—and

----

1 1332 Weathervane Lane, just in case somebody out there is writing my unauthorized biography and is using this book as source material.

maybe this explains why I was single—I would always talk about this hedgehog, inevitably noting a platitude that often applies to politics. *The clever fox knows many things*, states the proverb, *but the old hedgehog knows one big thing.* "I finally understand what that means," I'd tell the confused woman sitting across from me. "The old hedgehog knows that gravity applies to fruit." This banter, I must admit, did not lead to any canoodling (although most women did laugh, and one literally said, "You sure know a lot about hedgehogs," which I almost count as a common-law marriage). It did, however, lead to a lot of casual discussion about what this phrase is supposed to mean. The origin of fox vs. hedgehog is Greek, but it was popularized by the British essayist Isaiah Berlin (note: These were *not* details I knew in 2000). In a plain sense, the adage simply means that some people know a little about many subjects while other people know a lot about one subject. Taken at face value, it seems like the former quality should be preferable to the latter— yet we know this is not true, due to the inclusion of the word "but." The fox knows a lot, *but* the hedgehog knows one singular thing that obviously matters more. So what is that singular thing? Well, maybe this: The fox knows all the facts, and the fox can place those facts into a logical context. The fox can see how history and politics intertwine, and he can knit them into a nonfiction novel that makes narrative sense. But the fox can't see the future, so he assumes it does not exist. The fox is a naïve realist who believes the complicated novel he has constructed is almost complete. Meanwhile, the hedgehog constructs nothing. He just reads over the fox's shoulder. But he understands something about the manuscript that the fox can't comprehend—this book will never be finished. The fox thinks he's at the end, but he hasn't even reached the middle. What the fox views as conclusions are only plot mechanics, which means they'll eventually represent the opposite of whatever they seem to suggest.

This is the difference between the fox and the hedgehog. Both creatures know that storytelling is everything, and that the only way modern people can understand history and politics is through the machinations of a story. But only the hedgehog knows that storytelling is secretly the problem, which is why the fox is constantly wrong.

[2] "History is the autobiography of a madman," wrote Alexander Herzen, a nineteenth-century Russian who helped define socialism and agrarian populism. Of course, I did not discover this slogan by reading about socialist farmers. I saw it on a promotional T-shirt. The shirt promoted *Hardcore History*, a podcast conducted by a man living in Oregon named Dan Carlin. Unlike most podcasts, *Hardcore History* is not a conversation or an interview or a comedic debate—it's just one guy sitting in a studio, talking about history. And Carlin talks a long time: His lecture on World War I clocks in at over four hours. He doesn't classify himself as a historian, because he doesn't have a PhD. ("There's a real divide between historians and non-historians," he says. "I don't want historians to think that I'm a historian, if you know what I mean.") His mother, retired actress Lynn Carlin, is still more famous than he is.[2] But his podcast is fascinating, mostly due to

----

2 She was nominated for an Academy Award for her performance in the John Cassavetes film *Faces*.

Carlin's knowledge but also because of his perspective. If my goal with this book is to think about the present as if it were the distant past, the goal of Carlin's podcast is to think about the distant past as if it were the present. When he talks about historical periods that seem retrospectively unhinged—the Red Scare, the era of Attila the Hun, the administration of Teddy Roosevelt—he resists the urge to view these events as insane aberrations that could never exist in modernity. Instead, he places himself inside the life of long-dead people he's never met and tries to imagine how the world must have appeared to them, at that time and in that place. Which, he concedes, is antithetical to how serious history is now conducted.

"If someone pursued history at Harvard University fifty years ago, it would have been clumped in with the humanities, mixed in with religion and law and language and art and those kinds of subjects," Carlin says. "But if you did this today, it's much more likely to be mixed in with the soft sciences, with archaeology and anthropology and those kinds of things. The good part about that change is that historians are much more diligent about facts than they used to be, and much more careful and much more quantified, and they're likely to talk about things like radiocarbon dating. They sound more like archaeologists. But the downside is—when you're talking about stories that involve human beings—there's a lot of it that's just not quantifiable."

What Carlin is describing, really, is a dispute over the way true stories *should* be told. And this is important, because there really isn't a second option. Storytelling's relationship to history is a little like interviewing's relationship to journalism: a flawed process without a better alternative. We are socially conditioned to understand the universe through storytelling, and—even if we weren't—there's neurological evidence that the left hemisphere of our brain automatically organizes information into an explainable, reassuring narrative.[3] This is how the world will be understood, even if we desire otherwise. So which mode of storytelling is preferable? Is it better to strictly rely on verifiable facts, even if that makes the story inherently incomplete? Or is it better to conscientiously interpret events, which often turns history into an informed opinion? According to Carlin, the former methodology is becoming increasingly dominant. Barring an unforeseeable academic reversal, one can infer that this fact-oriented slant will only gain momentum. It will eventually be the only way future historians consider the present era of America. And that will paint a much different portrait from the interpretive America we're actually experiencing.

Near the end of our phone conversation, Carlin and I start talking about Ronald Reagan. "I don't know what your views are, Chuck, but I lived through that period," says the fifty-year-old Carlin. "I don't understand the hero worship at all. I can't get my mind around it." We then run through the various problems with Reagan's presidential tenure, namely the lowering of the top marginal income tax on the super-rich from 70 percent to 28 percent and (what Carlin considers) the myth of Reagan's destruction of

---

3 "I think the human as a storytelling animal, as some people put it, is because this [left hemisphere] system is continually trying to keep the story coherent, even though these actions may be coming outside of conscious awareness," University of California psychology professor Michael Gazzaniga said in a 2011 interview with Jason Gots. "Why does the human always seem to like fiction? Could it be that it prepares us for unexpected things that happen in our life, because we've already thought about them in our fantasy world?"

the Soviet Union. "The reason the Soviet Union fell was that it was a system designed on an early-twentieth-century model that could not incorporate the changes necessary for the late twentieth century," he explains. "The idea that Reagan somehow foresaw that is, to me, insane." These points, along with his disempowering of labor unions and the deregulation of business, tend to be the tangible aspects of Reagan's presidency most often noted by presidential scholars. He was, factually, a bad president. But this contradicts something obvious. "I think that if you polled a bunch of random Americans," concedes Carlin, "a significant number would think Reagan belongs on Mount Rushmore." Even as a decomposed corpse, Reagan remains an extremely popular leader, at least among those who liked him when he was alive. His 1984 win over Walter Mondale was the most lopsided landslide in electoral history, and he exited office with an approval rating of 63 percent.[4] He was the ultra-hedgehog, obsessed with only one truth: If people feel optimistic about where they live, details don't matter. But here's the thing—you need to have an active, living memory of Reagan for any of this to seem plausible. You need to personally remember that the 1980s felt prosperous, even when they weren't. Every extension of mainstream popular culture expressed this. The 1980s felt prosperous *even if you were poor.* Somewhat ironically, Carlin can't reconcile Reagan's legacy, because he has distanced himself from his own memory. He's unconsciously applied

---

4 By comparison, Lyndon Johnson left office with an approval rating of just 49 percent (according to the University of California's American Presidency Project). Reagan's approval rating of 63 percent is especially remarkable when you consider that only 32 percent of Americans polled by Gallup in 1988 classified themselves as Republicans.

a fact-based perception, just like those (currently unborn) historians who will dictate reality in the year 2222. Those historians will look back at the 1980s and presume the US populace must have suffered some kind of mass delusion, prompting them to self-destructively lionize a president who—factually—made the country worse. Within the minds of those historiographers, Reagan will be defined as an objectively bad president . . . except, of course, for that eight-year period when he actually *was* president, when he was beloved and unbeatable and so emotionally persuasive that—twenty-five years after he left office—his most ardent disciples sincerely suggested his face be carved into a South Dakota mountain. And that will make no narrative sense, except to Herzen's self-published madman.

[3] These illustrative examples, however, are still relegated to the pot of small spuds. The election of 2000 was less than a generation ago (as I type this sentence, those born the night it happened still can't vote). Reagan's success or failure is part of history, but it's still *recent* history—he will be classified, at least for the next twenty-five or so years, as a modern president, subject to the push and pull of many of the same people who pushed and pulled when he was sitting in the Oval Office. And even when all those pundits are finally gone, Reagan's merits will continue to incrementally rise and incrementally fall, simply because he held the one job that is re-ranked and re-imagined every single year. The way we think about presidential history is shifting sand; it would be like re-ranking the top twenty college football teams from the 1971 season every new September and having the sequential

order (somehow) never be the same. When I was in college, everyone told me the worst president of all time was Ulysses S. Grant. But we now consider Grant to be merely subpar. The preferred answer to that question has become James Buchanan. On the final day of 2014, *U.S. News & World Report* classified Grant as only the seventh-worst president of all time, almost as good as William Henry Harrison (who was president for only thirty-one days). I have no idea how this happened. If Grant can manage to stay dead, he might become halfway decent. He could overtake Grover Cleveland!

When we elect the wrong president (or if we remember that president inappropriately), certain things happen. But nothing that can't be undone. If Buchanan truly was the worst president, his failure has had about as much impact on contemporary society as the cancellation of *Two and a Half Men*. Big potatoes don't dwell on personalities. From a political science perspective, they dwell on ideas—towering ideas that could never be changed, regardless of the arguments against them. These are things like the concept of privately owned property, freedom of speech, and voting. These are elements so imbued in the fabric of American civilization that we would never seriously debate their worth in a non-academic setting (and even then, only as a thought experiment). Yet if we are wrong about *these* ideas—if we are wrong about the value of our most principal values—the cost will eventually be cataclysmic. And we will just have to wait for that unstoppable cataclysm to transpire, the way the West Coast waits for earthquakes.

Every few months, something happens in the culture that prompts people to believe America is doomed. Maybe a presidential candidate suggests the pyramids were built to store wheat; maybe

Miley Cyrus licks someone's face at the Video Music Awards; maybe a student at Yale insists her college is not supposed to be an intellectual space, based on a fear of hypothetical Halloween costumes. The story becomes an allegory, and unoriginal idiots on the local news and the Internet inevitably suggest that this fleeting event is a sign that the United States is experiencing its own version of the fall of the Roman Empire. That's always the comparison. The collapse of Rome has been something alarmists have loved and worried about since 1776, the year British historian Edward Gibbon published *The History of the Decline and Fall of the Roman Empire*. That was, probably coincidentally, the same year the US declared its independence. What makes the United States so interesting and (arguably) "exceptional" is that it's a superpower that did not happen accidentally. It did not evolve out of a preexisting system that had been the only system its founders could ever remember; it was planned and strategized from scratch, and it was built to last. Just about everyone agrees the founding fathers did a remarkably good job, considering the impossibility of the goal. But the key word here is "impossibility." There is simply no way a person from that era— even a person as conscientious as James Madison—could reasonably anticipate how the world would change in the coming two hundred years (and certainly not how it would continue to change over the next two hundred following those, since we can't even do that now, from our position in the middle). This logic leads to a strange question: If and when the United States does ultimately collapse, will that breakdown be a consequence of the Constitution itself? If it can be reasonably argued that it's impossible to create a document that can withstand the evolution of any society for five hundred or a thousand or five thousand years, doesn't that mean present-day America's pathological adherence to the document we happened to inherit will eventually wreck everything?

It's a question people will answer unequivocally only if their answer is no.

If their answer is yes, the response entails a metric shitload of weaselly qualifications. Criticizing the Constitution is a little like criticizing a war hero—you always need to open with a compliment. Attacking the Constitution is attacking America, which means the only people who will do it openly are so radicalized that every subsequent opinion they offer is classified as extremist. When the Constitution is criticized, the disapproval is more often with how the courts have interpreted its language. But if you doggedly ask a person who has studied the Constitution about its flaws, that person will usually concede that the greatest strength of any document is inherently tied to its flaws. Take someone like Jay D. Wexler, for example. Wexler is a law professor at Boston University who wrote a book titled *The Odd Clauses*, an examination of the Constitution through ten of its most bizarre provisions. His interest in its peculiarities is an extension of his appreciation for the document's integrity as a whole. He's fascinated by ideas like the separation of powers, inserted by the founders as a barrier against their ultimate fear, tyranny. He will directly exclaim, "I love the separation of powers!" which is a weird thing to exclaim. But he also realizes this trifurcation comes with a cost.

"One can imagine how the sluggishness and potential for gridlock that such a system creates might actually be our undoing—perhaps because of some single major incident that the government cannot respond to adequately. But more likely because it slowly, quietly, in ways that may be hard to identify, weakens our society and culture and economy, rendering the nation unable to sustain itself and rise to the challenges of the future," says Wexler. "States and localities play the most significant role in shaping the education of children, which is great—except in those states that water down science education to placate creationists. The Supreme Court can strike down laws that it thinks violate the Constitution, which is great—except when it invalidates campaign finance laws that are designed to make our political system fair. Both houses of Congress have to agree to pass legislation, which is great—except when one house holds the entire country hostage by refusing to pass a budget. And if in some future, far-off day we find ourselves no longer a superpower, we may look back and say that this was the result of a constitutional structure that made it overly difficult to implement wise social and economic policy. Now, I don't know if the criticism will be justified. I'm just glad that I'll be dead by then."

Wexler notes a few constitutional weaknesses, some hypothetical and dramatic (e.g., what if the obstacles created to make it difficult for a president to declare war allow an enemy to annihilate us with nuclear weapons while we debate the danger) and some that may have outlived their logical practicality without any significant downside (e.g., California and Rhode Island having equal representation in the Senate, regardless of population). But like virtually every world citizen who's not a member of ISIS, he has a hard time imagining how the most beloved constitutional details—the Bill of Rights and the visions of unalienable freedom—could ever be perceived as an Achilles' heel, even if they somehow were.

"I'd distinguish the parts of the Constitution that we talk about most—the liberty and equality protections and the Fourteenth Amendment—from the parts of the Constitution that create the structure of the government. I think it's more likely that if we look back with regret at our dedication to the Constitution, it will be with respect to the structural provisions, rather than the liberty and equality ones. The liberty and equality provisions of the Constitution are worded so vaguely that whatever hypothetical blame we might place on them in any faraway future will more likely be aimed at the Supreme Court's interpretation of the provisions, as opposed to the provisions themselves," Wexler says. "Now, what if because of these provisions, someone gets away with urging or instructing someone else to blow up the White House, thus instigating a chain of events that leads to a nation-destroying insurrection? Or someone who is arrested without being given the proper Miranda warnings goes free and then blows up the White House? Are we really going to blame the First Amendment or the Fourth Amendment for those catastrophes? If people end up blaming anyone or anything having to do with these provisions—and that itself is a really big *if*—I think people would blame the Supreme Court and the opinions which gave those amendments the specific content that, when applied, turned out to be disastrous. Earl Warren, rather than James Madison, would turn out to be the real culprit."

Wexler's distinction is almost certainly correct. There are a handful of sacrosanct principles within the Constitution that would never be *directly* blamed for anything that happens, based on the logic that the principles themselves are so unassailable that any subsequent problem must be a manifestation of someone applying those principles incorrectly. In this regard, I'm no different from anyone else. My natural inclination, for most of my life, was to believe that nothing is more important than freedom. I tried very hard to convince myself that my favorite writer was John Locke. My guts still feel that way, and so does much of my mind. But there's a persuasive sliver of my brain that quietly wonders, "Why do I believe this so much?" I fear it might be because I've never allowed myself to question certain things that seem too obvious to question.

"Are we really going to blame the First Amendment?" Wexler asked rhetorically, and he might as well have tacked on the prepositional phrase *for anything*. And of course the answer is no. There is no amendment more beloved, and it's the single most American sentiment that can be expressed. Yet its function is highly specific. It stops the government from limiting a person or an organization's freedom of expression (and that's critical, particularly if you want to launch an especially self-righteous alt weekly or an exceptionally lucrative church or the rap group N.W.A). But in a capitalistic society, it doesn't have much application within any scenario where the government doesn't have a vested interest in what's being expressed. If someone publishes an essay or tells a joke or performs a play that forwards a problematic idea, the US government generally wouldn't try to stop that person from doing so, even if they could. If the expression doesn't involve national security, the government generally doesn't give a shit. But if enough vocal consumers are personally offended, they can silence that artist just as effectively. They can petition advertisers and marginalize the artist's reception and economically remove that individual from whatever platform he or she happens to utilize,

simply because there are no expression-based platforms that don't
have an economic underpinning. It's one of those situations where
the practical manifestation is the opposite of the technical intention: As Americans, we tend to look down on European countries
that impose legal limitations on speech—yet as long as speakers in
those countries stay within the specified boundaries, discourse is
allowed relatively unfettered (even when it's unpopular). In the
US, there are absolutely no speech boundaries imposed by the
government, so the citizenry creates its own limitations, based on
the arbitrary values of whichever activist group is most successful
at inflicting its worldview upon an economically fragile public
sphere. As a consequence, the United States is a safe place for those
who want to criticize the government but a dangerous place for
those who want to advance unpopular thoughts about any other
subject that could be deemed insulting or discomfiting.

Some would argue that this trade-off is worth it. Time may
prove otherwise.

[4] The Declaration of Independence predates the Constitution by eleven years and doesn't have any legislative
power. Still, it's central to everything we think about the US, particularly one sentence from its second paragraph that many Americans assume is actually in the Constitution itself: "We hold these
truths to be self-evident, that all men are created equal, that they
are endowed by their Creator with certain unalienable Rights, that
among these are Life, Liberty, and the Pursuit of Happiness."
Now, there are surface details of this passage that people have

always quibbled with: the use of the word "men" instead of "people," the fact that the man who wrote these words owned slaves, the fact that the language inserts God into a situation that doesn't seem particularly religious, and that Thomas Jefferson's genius did not keep him from capitalizing non-proper nouns. But these problems (except maybe the slave part) are easily deflected by the recognition of the era. The overall premise—tweaked to fit modernity—is still embraced as "self-evident."

Even though this is not remotely true, in practice *or* theory.

Pointing out how it's not true in practice is so easy it doesn't even require examples; all you need to do is look at the socioeconomic experiences of American citizens from varying races and opposing genders. But it's not even true with people whose experiences are roughly identical. Take any two white males raised in the same income bracket in the same section of the same city, and assume they receive the same treatment from law enforcement and financial institutions and prospective employers. They're still not equal. One of these people will be smarter than the other. One will be more physically attractive. One will be predisposed to work harder and care more. Even in a pure meritocracy, they would experience differing levels of happiness. "It is not the case that we are born equal and that the conditions of life make our lives unequal," writes Karl Ove Knausgaard in his nonfiction novel *My Struggle: Book 2*. "It is the opposite, we are born unequal, and the conditions of life make us more equal." The apparent unfairness of reality can't be blamed on our inability to embody this "self-evident" principle. The world would be just as unfair if we did.

I realize there's a natural response to the previous statement, and it's the same response I would have given fifteen years ago: "This is a conscious misreading of the message. Jefferson is not claiming that all men are *literally* equal. He's arguing that all men deserve equal protection under the law, and that they are to be treated *as if* they are equal." Which, of course, I agree with (because who wouldn't). But this technical application is not the way the principle is considered. It's mostly considered symbolically, which means it's illusionary. That's the problem. I sometimes wonder if the pillars of American political culture are really just a collection of shared illusions that will either (a) eventually be disbelieved or (b) collapse beneath the weight of their own unreality. And that would certainly be the end of everything (or at least something that will *feel* like everything to those who live through the collapse).

The men and women who forged this nation were straight-up maniacs about freedom. It was just about the only thing they cared about, so they jammed it into everything. This is understandable, as they were breaking away from a monarchy. But it's also a little bonkers, since one of the things they desired most desperately was freedom of religion, based on the premise that Europe wasn't religious *enough* and that they needed the freedom to live by nonsecular laws that were more restrictive than that of any government, including provisions for the burning of suspected witches. The founding fathers saw themselves as old hedgehogs, and the one big thing they knew was that nothing mattered more than liberty. They were of the opinion that a man cannot be happy if he is not wholly free from tyranny, a sentiment that is still believed by almost every American citizen.

But how, exactly, do we know this?

It wasn't always this way. For a long time, many smart people—Plato, most famously in *The Republic*—did not automatically think like this.

"During the wars between Athens and Sparta, there were a lot of people questioning if the idea of democracy in Athens made much sense," says Carlin. "These were guys who came in right after the Roman Republic fell who were basically wiping their brow and saying, 'Thank god that whole experiment with people running things is over, look where that took us.' These are thoughts conditioned by what we remember. When we talk about one-man rule—some kind of dictatorship or empire or whatever—look at the examples recent history has given us. They're not exactly shining examples of how it might work out well, whether it's a Hitler or a Stalin or whoever, so we don't have any good examples [of how this could successfully operate]. But in the ancient world, they often had bad examples of democracy. Some of those guys looked at democracies the way we look at failed dictatorships. And yet, had we had, in the 1930s or 1940s, some dictatorship that was run by a real benevolent, benign person who did a really good job and things were great—and let's throw out the obvious problem of succession, of potentially getting a bad guy after the good guy—we might have a different view of all that."

This notion, I must concede, is a weird thing to think about, and an even weirder thing to type. It almost feels like I'm arguing, "Democracy is imperfect, so let's experiment with a little light fascism." But I also realize my discomfort with such thoughts is a translucent sign of *deep* potential wrongness—so deep that I can't even think about it without my unconscious trying to convince me otherwise. The Western world (and the US in particular) has invested so much of its identity into the conception of democracy that we're expected to unconditionally support anything that comes with it. Voting, for example. Everyone who wants to vote should absolutely do so, and I would never instruct anyone to do otherwise. But it's bizarre how angry voters get at non-voters. "It's your civic responsibility," they will say. Although the purpose of voting is to uphold a free society, so one might respond that a free society would not demand people to participate in an optional civic activity. "But your vote matters," they argue. Well, it is counted, usually. That's true (usually). But believing your one vote makes a meaningful difference reflects unfathomable egotism. Even if you'd illegally voted twenty times in the single tightest Florida county during that aforementioned 2000 presidential election, the outcome would have been unchanged. "But what if everybody thought that way," they inevitably counter. This is the stupidest of arguments—if the nation's political behavior were based on the actions of one random person, *of course* that person would vote, in the same way that random person would never jaywalk if his or her personal actions dictated the behavior of society as a whole. But that is not how the world works. "Okay, fine. But if you don't vote, you can't complain." Actually, the opposite is true—if you participate in democracy, you're validating the democratic process (and therefore the outcome). You can't complain *if* you vote. "People in other countries risk their life for the right to vote." Well, what can I say? That's a noble act, but not necessarily a good decision.

What's so strange about these non-persuasive techniques is that—were they somehow successful—they would dilute the overall value of voting, including the ballot of the person making the argument. If you want to amplify the value of your vote, the key is convincing other voters to stay home. But nobody does this, unless they're actively trying to fix an election. For any lone individual, voting is a symbolic act that retains its illusionary power from everyone else agreeing that it's indispensable. This is why voters want other people to vote, even if those other people are uninformed and lazy and completely unengaged with politics. This is also why, when my son watches his first election on TV, I'll tell him that voting is a crucial, profound extension of the American experience, for all the bad reasons he'll be socially conditioned to accept (until, of course, he doesn't).

[**5**] I am of the opinion that Barack Obama has been the greatest president of my lifetime, and by a relatively wide margin. This, I realize, is not a universally held position, and not just among the people who still think he was born in Kenya. With a year remaining in Obama's tenure, *New York* magazine polled fifty-three historians about his legacy, most of whom gave him lukewarm reviews. Several pointed to his inability to unite the country. Others lauded ObamaCare while criticizing his expansion of the Oval Office itself. But those critiques remind me of someone looking at the career of Hank Aaron and focusing on his throwing arm and base running. It's not merely that Obama was the first black president. It's that he broke this barrier with such deftness and sagacity that it instantaneously seemed insane no black person had ever been elected president before. In fact, he broke the barrier so fluidly that a few of the polled historians suggested his blackness will eventually be a footnote to his presidency,

in the same way that John F. Kennedy's Catholicism has become a factoid referenced only by Catholics. That seems like a questionable analogy to me (and I say that as someone who's built a career on questionable analogies). The finer points of Obama's administration will wash away, but his central achievement—his straightforward aptitude at overcoming the systematic racism that previously made his existence impossible—will loom over everything else. To me, this seems obvious.

I'm very much a One Big Thing kind of guy, though, and especially with presidents. If I'm arguing about the greatest president of all time, it always comes down to Washington vs. Lincoln, and those in the Lincoln camp inevitably point to his freeing of the slaves—which, I will grant, is the definition of a One Big Thing move. But I would traditionally counter that Washington's One Big Thing mattered more, and it actually involved something he *didn't* do: He declined the opportunity to become king, thus making the office of president more important than any person who would ever hold it. This, as it turns out, never really happened. There is no evidence that Washington was ever given the chance to become king, and—considering how much he and his peers despised the mere possibility of tyranny—it's hard to imagine this offer was ever on the table. It is, I suppose, the kind of act that *seems* like something Washington would have done, in the same way he seems like the kind of fellow who wouldn't deny that he iced a cherry tree for no reason. Washington's kingship denial falls into the category of a "utility myth"—a story that supports whatever political position the storyteller happens to hold, since no one disagrees with the myth's core message (i.e., that there are no problems with the *design* of our government, even if that design allows certain people to miss the point). You see the application of other utility myths during any moment of national controversy. Someone will say or do something that offends a group of people, so the offended group will argue that the act was unpatriotic and harmful to democracy. In response, the offending individual will say, "Actually, I'm doing this *because* I'm patriotic and *because* I'm upholding democracy. You're unpatriotic for trying to stop me." Round and round this goes, with both sides claiming to occupy the spiritual center of the same philosophy, never considering the possibility that the (potentially real) value of their viewpoint hinges on the prospect that patriotism is not absurd and democracy is not simply the system some wig-wearing eighteenth-century freedom junkies happened to select.

Here again, I must reiterate that *I am like this, too.* When I claim that Obama is the finest president of my lifetime, I'm using criteria I've absorbed without trying, all of which are defined by my unconscious assumption that the purest manifestation of representative democracy would be the best scenario for the country and the world. This is, in fact, what I believe. But I don't know why I believe this, outside of the realization that I can't really control my own thoughts and feelings. When I see a quote from Plato that condescendingly classifies democracy as "charming" and suggests democracy dispenses "a sort of equality to equals and unequaled alike," my knee-jerk reaction is to see this as troubling and unenlightened. But Plato is merely arguing that democracy is a nice idea that tries to impose the fantasy of fairness upon an organically unfair social order. I'm not sure how anyone could disagree with that, myself included. But if you're really into the idea of democracy, this is something you reject out of hand.

On those rare occasions when the Constitution is criticized in a non-academic setting, the criticisms are pointed. It's often argued, for example, that the Second Amendment is antiquated[5] and has no logical relationship to the original need to own a musket in order to form a militia, or that the Fourteenth Amendment's extension of personhood to corporations has been manipulated for oppressive purposes.[6] The complaints suggest we tweak the existing document with the intent of reinforcing the document's sovereignty within the present moment (because the present is where we are, and no one would ever suggest starting over from scratch). But sometimes I think about America from a different vantage point. I imagine America as a chapter in a book, centuries after the country has collapsed, encapsulated by the casual language we use when describing the foreboding failure of the Spanish Armada in 1588. And what I imagine is a description like this: The invention of a country is described. This country was based on a document, and the document was unassailable. The document could be altered, but alterations were so difficult that it happened only seventeen times in two hundred years (and one of those changes merely retracted a previous alteration). The document was less than five thousand words but applied unilaterally, even as the country dramatically increased its size and population and even though urban citizens in rarefied parts of the country had nothing in common with rural citizens living thousands of miles away. The document's prime directives were liberty and representation, even when 5 percent of the country's population legally controlled

----

5 Which is obviously true.

6 Which is obviously true.

65 percent of the wealth. But everyone loved this document, because it was concise and well composed and presented a possible utopia where everyone was the same. It was so beloved that the citizens of this country decided they would stick with it no matter what happened or what changed, and the premise of discounting (or even questioning) its greatness became so verboten that any political candidate who did so would have no chance to be elected to any office above city alderman. The populace decided to use this same document forever, inflexibly and without apprehension, even if the country lasted for two thousand years.

Viewed retrospectively, it would not seem stunning that this did not work out.

Now, do I have a better alternative here? I do not. If George Washington truly had been offered the chance to be king, I am not of the opinion that life would be better had we handed him the crown, since that would mean we'd currently be governed by some rich guy in Virginia who happens to be his distant nephew. It often seems like a genteel oligarchy would make the most theoretical sense, but the fact that this never works in practice (and the fact that they never remain genteel) contradicts that notion. Sometimes I fantasize about the US head of state as a super-lazy, super-moral libertarian despot and think, "That would certainly make everything easier," even though I can't think of one person who'd qualify, except maybe Willie Nelson. I'm not looking to overthrow anybody. The first moment someone calls for a revolution is usually the last moment I take them seriously. I'm not Mr. Robot. And I'm not saying we're "wrong" for caring about the Constitution or separating the powers of government or enforcing an illusion of equality through the untrue story of how democracy works. I'm just working through my central hedgehog thought, which is this: The ultimate failure of the United States will probably not derive from the problems we see or the conflicts we wage. It will more likely derive from our uncompromising belief in the things we consider unimpeachable and idealized and beautiful. Because every strength is a weakness, if given enough time.

But What If We're Right?

When John Horgan published his book *The End of Science* in 1996, he'd been a staff writer for *Scientific American* for ten years. A year later, he was fired from the magazine. According to Horgan, his employers suggested his book had caused a downturn in advertising revenue. This claim seems implausible, until you hear Horgan's own description of what his book proposed.

"My argument in *The End of Science* is that science is a victim of its own success," he tells me from his home in Hoboken. "Science discovers certain things, and then it has to go on to the next thing. So we have heliocentrism and the discovery of gravity and the fundamental forces, atoms and electrons and all that shit, evolution, and DNA-based genetics. But then we get to the frontier of science, where there is still a lot left to discover. And some of those things we may never discover. And a lot of the things we are going to discover are just elaborations on what we discovered in the past. They're not that exciting. My belief is that the prospect for really surprising insights into nature is over, and the hope for future revolutionary discoveries is pretty much done. I became a science journalist because I thought science was the coolest thing that humans have ever done. So if you believe the most important thing about life is the pursuit of knowledge, what does it mean if that's over?"

It's now been twenty years since the release of *The End of Science*. Horgan has written four additional books and serves as the director of the Center for Science Writings at the Stevens Institute of Technology (he's also, somewhat interestingly, returned to *Scientific American* as a blogger). The central premise of his book—that the big questions about the natural world have been mostly solved, and that the really big questions that remain are probably impossible to answer—is still marginalized as either cynical or pragmatic, depending on the reader's point of reference. But nothing has happened since 1996 to prove Horgan wrong, unless you count finding water on Mars. Granted, twenty years is not that long, particularly if you're a scientist. Still, it's remarkable how unchanged the conversational landscape has remained. Horgan's most compelling interview in *The End of Science* was with the relatively reclusive Edward Witten, a Princeton professor broadly viewed as the greatest living theoretical physicist (or at least the "smartest," according to a 2004 issue of *Time* magazine). One of the first things Witten noted in that interview was that Horgan had been journalistically irresponsible for writing a profile on Thomas Kuhn, with Witten employing much of the same logic Neil deGrasse Tyson used when he criticized Kuhn in our 2014 conversation for this book.

Now, there's at least one significant difference between those two interviews: I was asking if it's possible that science might be wrong. Horgan was proposing science has been so overwhelmingly right that all that remains are tertiary details. Still, both tracts present the potential for an awkward realization. If the answer to my question is no (or if the answer to Horgan's question is yes), society is faced with a strange new scenario: the possibility that our current view of reality *is* the final view of reality, and that what we believe today is what we will believe forever.

"One of the exercises I always give my [Stevens Institute] students is an essay assignment," Horgan says. "The question is posed like this: 'Will there be a time in our future when our current theories seem as dumb as Aristotle's theories appear to us now?' And the students are always divided. Many of them have already been infected by postmodernism and believe that knowledge is socially constructed, and they believe we'll have intellectual revolutions forever. You even hear that kind of rhetoric from mainstream science popularizers, who are always talking about science as this endless frontier. And I just think that's childish. It's like thinking that our exploration of the Earth is still open-ended, and that we might still find the lost city of Atlantis or dinosaurs living in the center of the planet. The more we discover, the less there is to discover later. Now, to a lot of people, that sounds like a naïve way to think about science. There was a time when it once seemed naïve to me. But it's really just a consequence of the success of science itself. Our era is in no way comparable to Aristotle's era."

What Horgan proposes is mildly contradictory; it compliments and criticizes science at the same time. He is, like Witten and Tyson, blasting Kuhn's relativist philosophy and insisting that some knowledge is real and undeniable. But he's also saying the acquisition of such knowledge is inherently limited, and we've essentially reached that limit, and that a great deal of modern scientific inquiry is just a form of careerism that doesn't move the cerebral dial (this is a little like what Kuhn referred to as "normal science," but without the paradigm shift). "Science will follow the path already trodden by literature, art, music, philosophy," Horgan writes. "It will become more introspective, subjective, diffuse, and obsessed with its own methods." In essence, it will become a perpetual argument over a non-negotiable reality. And like all speculative realities, it seems like this could be amazingly good or amazingly bad.

"By the time I finally finished writing *The End of Science*, I'd concluded that people don't give a shit about science," Horgan says. "They don't give a shit about quantum mechanics or the Big Bang. As a mass society, our interest in those subjects is trivial. People are much more interested in making money, finding love, and attaining status and prestige. So I'm not really sure if a post-science world would be any different than the world of today."

Neutrality: the craziest of all possible outcomes.

[2] When I spoke with Horgan, he'd recently completed his (considerably less controversial) fifth book, *The End of War*, a treatise arguing against the assumption that war is an inescapable component of human nature. The embryo for this idea came from a conversation he'd had two decades prior, conducted while working on *The End of Science*. It was an interview with Francis Fukuyama, the political scientist best known for his 1989 essay "The End of History?" The title of the essay is deceptive, since Fukuyama was mostly asserting that liberal capitalist democracies were going to take over the world. It was an economic argument

that (thus far) has not happened. But what specifically appalled Horgan was Fukuyama's assertion about how a problem-free society would operate. Fukuyama believed that once mankind eliminated all its problems, it would start waging wars against itself for no reason, almost out of boredom. "That kind of thinking comes from a kind of crude determinism," Horgan insists. "It's the belief that what has always been in the past must always be in the future. To me, that's a foolish position."

The level to which you agree with Horgan on this point reflects your level of optimism about human nature (and Horgan freely admits some of his ideas could be classified as "traditionally hippie-ish"). But it can be securely argued that Fukuyama's perspective is much more common, particularly among the kind of people who produce dystopic sci-fi movies. Whether it's *Avengers: Age of Ultron*, *The Matrix*, the entire *Terminator* franchise, or even a film as technologically primitive as *War Games*, a predictable theme inexorably emerges: The moment machines become self-aware, they will try to destroy people. What's latently disturbing about this plot device is the cynicism of the logic. Our assumption is that computers will only act rationally. If the ensuing assumption is that human-built machines would immediately try to kill all the humans, it means that doing so must be the most rational decision possible. And since this plot device was created by humans, the creators must fractionally believe this, too.

On the other end of this speculatory scale—or on the same end, if you're an especially gloomy motherfucker—are proponents of the Singularity, a techno-social evolution so unimaginable that attempting to visualize what it would be like is almost a waste of time. The Singularity is a hypothetical super-jump in the field of artificial intelligence, rendering our reliance on "biological intelligence" obsolete, pushing us into a shared technological realm so advanced that it will be unrecognizable from the world of today. The best-known advocate of this proposition, futurist Ray Kurzweil, suggests that this could happen as soon as the year 2045, based on an exponential growth model. But that is hard to accept. Everyone agrees that Kurzweil is a genius and that his model makes mathematical sense, but no man truly believes this is going to happen in his own lifetime (sans a handful of people who are already living their lives very, very, very differently). It must also be noted that Kurzweil initially claimed this event was coming in 2028, so the inception of the Singularity might be a little like the release of *Chinese Democracy*.

Even compared with Bostrom's simulation hypothesis or the Phantom Time conspiracy, the premise of the Singularity is so daunting that it can't reasonably be considered without framing it as an impossibility. The theory's most startling detail involves the option of mapping and downloading the complete content of a human brain onto a collective server, thus achieving universal immortality—we could all live forever, inside a mass virtual universe, without the limitations of our physical bodies (Kurzweil openly aspires to create an avatar of his long-dead father, using scraps of the deceased patriarch's DNA and exhaustive notes about his father's life). The parts of our brain that generate visceral sensations could be digitally manipulated to make it feel exactly as if we were still alive. This, quite obviously, generates unfathomable theological and metaphysical quandaries. But even its most practical aspects are convoluted and open-ended. If we download the totality of our minds onto the Internet, they—*we*—would effectively become the Internet itself. Our brain avatars could automatically access all the information that exists in the virtual world, so we would all know everything there is to know.

But I suppose we have a manual version of this already.

[3] I was born in 1972, and—because I ended up working in the media—I feel exceedingly fortunate about the timing of that event. It allowed me to have an experience that is not exactly unique, but that will never again be replicated: I started my professional career in a world where there was (essentially) no Internet at all, and I'll end my professional career in a world where the Internet will be (essentially) the only thing that exists. When I showed up for my first day of newspaper work in the summer of '94, there was no Internet in the building, along with an institutional belief that this would be a stupid thing to want. If I aspired to send an e-mail, I had to go to the public library across the street and wait for the one computer that was connected to a modem (and even that wasn't an option until 1995). From a journalistic perspective, the functional disparity between that bygone era and the one we now inhabit is vast and quirky—I sometimes made more phone calls in one morning than I currently make in two months. But those evolving practicalities were things we noticed as they occurred. The amplification of available information and the increase in communication speed was obvious to everyone. We talked about it constantly. What was harder to recognize was how the Internet slowly reinvented the way people thought about everything, including those things that have no relationship to the Internet whatsoever.

In his autobiography *Chronicles*, Bob Dylan (kind of) explains his motivation for performing extremely long songs like "Tom Joad," a track with sixteen verses. His reasoning was that it's simply enriching to memorize complicated things. Born in 1941, Dylan valued rote memorization, a proficiency that had been mostly eliminated by the time I attended grade school in the eighties (the only long passages I was forced to memorize verbatim were the preamble to the Constitution, the Gettysburg Address, and a whole bunch of prayers). Still, for the first twenty-five years of my life, the concept of intelligence was intimately connected to broad-spectrum memory. If I was having an argument with a much older person about the 1970 Kent State shootings, I'd generally have to defer to her analysis, based on the justifiable fact that she was alive when it occurred and I was not. My only alternative was to read a bunch of books (or maybe watch a documentary) about the shooting and consciously retain whatever I learned from that research, since I wouldn't be able to easily access the data again. It was also assumed that—anecdotally, speaking off the cuff—neither party would be 100 percent correct about every arcane detail of the shooting, but that certain key details mattered more than others. So a smart person had a generalized, autodidactic, imperfect sense of history. And there was a circular logic to this: The importance of any given memory was validated by the fact that someone remembered it at all.

But then the Internet started to collect and index everything, including opinions and reviews and other subjective non-facts. This happened Hemingway-style: gradually (I wrote most of my first book in 1999 and the Internet was no help at all) and then suddenly (that book somehow had its own Wikipedia page by

2005). During the last half of the nineties, the Internet still felt highly segregated—to a mainstream consumer, it was hard to see the ideological relationship between limitless porn and fantasy football and Napster and the eradication of travel agents. What unified that diaspora was the rise of blogging, spawning what's now recognized as the "voice" of the Internet. Yet that voice is only half the equation; the other half is the mentality that came along with it. The first successful groundswell of bloggers came from multiple social classes and multiple subcultures. As a collective, they were impossible to define. But they did have one undeniable thing in common: They were, almost by definition, early adopters of technology. They were into the Internet before most people cared what it was. And in most cases, this interest in early adoption was not restricted to computers. These were the kind of people who liked grunge music in 1989. These were the kind of people who subscribed to *Ray Gun* magazine and made a point of mentioning how they started watching *Seinfeld* when it was called *The Seinfeld Chronicles*. These were the kind of people who wore a Premier League jersey to the theatrical premiere of *Donnie Darko*. These are consumers who self-identify as being the first person to know about something (often for the sake of coolness, but just as often because that's the shit they're legitimately into). It's integral to their sensibility. And the rippling ramifications of that sensibility are huge.

For a time in the early 2000s, there was a belief that bloggers would become the next wave of authors, and many big-money blogger-to-author book deals were signed. Besides a handful of notable exceptions, this rarely worked, commercially or critically. The problem was not a lack of talent; the problem was that writing a blog and writing a book have almost no psychological relationship. They both involve a lot of typing, but that's about as far as it goes. A sentence in a book is written a year before it's published, with the express intent that it will still make sense twenty years later. A sentence on the Internet is designed to last one day, usually the same day it's written. The next morning, it's overwritten again (by multiple writers). The Internet experience is not even that similar to daily newspaper writing, because there's no physical artifact to demarcate the significance of the original moment.[1] Yet this limitation is not a failure. It proved to be an advantage. It naturally aligns with the early-adoption sensibility that informs everything else. Even when the Internet appears to be nostalgically churning through the cultural past, it's still hunting for "old newness." A familiar video clip from 1986 does not possess virility; what the medium desires is an obscure clip from 1985 that recontextualizes the familiar one. The result is a perpetual sense of *now*. It's a continual merging of the past with the present, all jammed into the same fixed perspective. This makes it seem like our current, temporary views have always existed, and that what we believe today is what people have always believed. There is no longer any distance between what we used to think and what we currently think, because our evolving vision of reality does not extend beyond yesterday.

And this, somewhat nonsensically, is how we might be right: All we need to do is convince ourselves we always were. And now there's a machine that makes that easy.

---

1 The *Chicago Daily Tribune* was not able to republish its most famous headline as "~~Dewey Defeats Truman~~." They just had to live with it.

$\begin{bmatrix} 4 \end{bmatrix}$ "I am often wrong," wrote satirist and critic H. L. Mencken, a statement that would seem more disarming were it not for the fact that Mencken so often opened his quotations by suggesting his forthcoming thoughts were worthless. "My prejudices are innumerable, and often idiotic. My aim is not to determine facts, but to function freely and pleasantly."

I get this. I understand what he's getting at, and sometimes I relate to it: Since our interior thoughts are (ultimately) arbitrary and meaningless, we might as well think whatever we prefer thinking. This was especially important to a guy like Mencken, who was against US participation in World War II and hated Franklin Roosevelt. He was quite willing to concede that his most intensely held opinions weren't based on factual data, so trying to determine what the factual data actually was would only make him depressed. It's a worldview that—even if expressed as sarcasm—would be extremely unpopular today. But it's quietly become the most natural way to think about everything, due to one sweeping technological evolution: We now have immediate access to *all possible facts*. Which is almost the same as having none at all.

Back in the landlocked eighties, Dave Barry offhandedly wrote something pretty insightful about the nature of revisionism. He noted how—as a fifth-grader—he was told that the cause of the Civil War was slavery. Upon entering high school, he was told that the cause was not slavery, but economic factors. At college, he learned that it was not economic factors but acculturalized regionalism. But if Barry had gone to graduate school, the answer to what caused the Civil War would (once again) be slavery.[2] Now, the Civil War is the most critical event in American history, and race is the defining conflict of this country. It still feels very much alive, so it's not surprising that teachers and historians want to think about it on disparate micro and macro levels, even if the realest answer is the simplest answer. But the Internet allows us to do this with everything, regardless of a subject's significance. It can happen so rapidly that there's no sense the argument has even evolved, which generates an illusion of consistency.

I've been writing this book during a period when many retired eighties-era pro wrestlers have died—the Ultimate Warrior, Dusty Rhodes, Rowdy Roddy Piper, etc. The outpouring of media recognition regarding these deaths has been significant. The obituaries frame these men as legends, and perhaps that's how they deserve to be framed. But what's been weird about this coverage is the unspoken viewpoint. Logically, it seems like a remembrance of Dusty Rhodes should include some version of the following: "We didn't think this guy was important, but he was. Culturally, we were wrong about pro wrestling." Because during the 1980s, almost no one thought pro wrestling mattered at all. Even the teenage males who loved it rarely took it seriously. But this is not

---

2 Part of what I like about Barry's description of Civil War revisionism is how it accidentally mirrors the elliptical path of his own career. When he was a working newspaper columnist at *The Miami Herald* in the 1980s, Barry was considered a comedic genius. He won a Pulitzer Prize. But soon after winning that award, he was viewed as considerably less funny. When CBS made a TV show about his life in the mid-nineties, his writing started to seem forced and unoriginal. His literary style is now marginalized as the problematic template for all derivative newspaper columnists who aspire to be wacky and deep at the same time. Yet when Barry dies, he will be universally (and justifiably) remembered as a comedic genius, just as he was when he started.

how these remembrances were delivered. Instead, the unspoken viewpoint was *of course* these people were important, and *of course* we all accept and understand this, and *of course* there is nothing remotely strange about remembering Dusty Rhodes as a formative critic of Reagan-era capitalism. Somebody once believed this, which means it was possible for anyone to have believed this, which means everyone can retroactively adopt this view as what they've always understood to be true. No one was ever wrong about wrestling. We were always right about it. In 1976, Renata Adler wrote the experimental novel *Speedboat*. It went out of print. When it was re-released in 2013, *Speedboat* was consumed and adopted as "old newness" ("Millennials, Meet Renata Adler," demanded a headline in *The New Republic*). In a span of two years, Adler completely reentered the critical dialogue, almost as if she had been there the whole time. The thirty-plus years this book was ignored no longer exist. Technologically, 1976 and 2013 exist in the same moment.

There's a common philosophical debate about the nature of time. One side of the debate argues that time is happening in a linear fashion. This is easy to understand. The other side argues that all time is happening at once. This is difficult to comprehend. But replace the word "time" with "history," and that phenomenon can be visualized on the Internet. If we think about the trajectory of anything—art, science, sports, politics—not as a river but as an endless, shallow ocean, there is no place for collective wrongness. All feasible ideas and every possible narrative exist together, and each new societal generation can scoop out a bucket of whatever antecedent is necessary to support their contemporary conclusions. When explained in one sentence, that prospect seems a little terrible. But maybe that's just because my view of reality is limited to river-based thinking.

I've slowly become an admirer of Edward Snowden, the former government employee who leaked thousands of classified documents and now lives in exile. I was initially skeptical of Snowden, until I saw the documentary *Citizenfour*. Granted, *Citizenfour* is a non-objective telling of his story, produced by the journalists Snowden was aligned with. It could be classified as a propaganda film. But it's impossible to watch Snowden speak without trusting the sincerity of his motives and the tenacity of his central argument. I believe Snowden more than I believe the government. He does, however, make one statement in *Citizenfour* that seems preposterous and wrong: While discussing the alleged greatness of the early (pre-surveillance) Internet, he notes that a child in one part of the world could have an anonymous discussion with a verified expert in another part of the world and "be granted the same respect for their ideas." To me, that does not sound like a benefit. That sounds like a waste of time and energy, at least for the verified expert. The concept of some eleven-year-old in Poland facelessly debating Edward Witten on an equal platform, just because there's a machine that makes this possible, seems about as reasonable as letting dogs vote. But I suppose that's because I still can't accept the possibility of Witten being totally wrong, no matter how hard I try. I mean, if we found records of an eleven-year-old girl from 340 BC who contacted Aristotle and told him his idea about a rock wanting to sit on the ground was irrational bullshit, we'd name a college after her.

Only the Penitent Man Shall Pass

A large group of people are eating and drinking. They're together, but not *really* together. Some of the people know each other well and others are almost strangers; instead of one mass conversation, there are little pockets of conversations, sprinkled throughout the table. I am at this table. What I am talking about is unimportant, or—more accurately—will need to be classified as "unimportant," as I will not be able to remember what it was when I awake in the morning. But it must be some topic where I'm expressing doubt over something assumed to be self-evident, or a subject where the least plausible scenario is the most interesting scenario, or a hypothetical crisis that's dependent on the actualization of something insane. I say this because someone at the table (whom I've met only once before) eventually joins my semi-private conversation and says, "It must be terrifying to think the world is actually like that."

"What do you mean?" I ask. My memory of what she says next is sketchy, but it's something along the lines of: It must be terrifying to view the world from the perspective that most people are wrong, and to think that every standard belief is a form of dogma, and to assume that reality is not real. Her analysis is delivered in a completely non-adversarial tone; it is polite, almost like she is authentically concerned for my overall well-being. My response is something like "Well, I don't really think like that," because I don't think I think the way she thinks I think. But maybe I do. And I get what she's driving at, and I realize that—from her vantage point—any sense of wide-scale skepticism about the seemingly obvious would be a terrifying way to live.

There's an accepted line of reasoning that keeps the average person from losing his or her mind. It's an automatic mental reflex. The first part of the reasoning involves a soft acceptance of the impossible: our recognition that the specific future is unknowable and that certain questions about the universe will never be answered, perhaps because those answers do not exist. The second part involves a hard acceptance of limited truths: a concession that we can reliably agree on most statements that are technically unprovable, regardless of whether these statements are objective ("The US government did not plan the 9/11 attacks"), subjective ("Fyodor Dostoyevsky is a better novelist than Jacqueline Susann"), or idealistic ("Murder is worse than stealing, which is worse than lying, which is worse than sloth"). It's a little like the way we're biologically programmed to trust our friends and family more than we trust strangers, even if our own past experience suggests we should do otherwise. We can't unconditionally trust the motives of people we don't know, so we project a heightened sense of security upon those we do, even if common sense suggests we should do the opposite. If 90 percent of life is inscrutable, we need to embrace the 10 percent that seems forthright, lest we feel like life is a cruel, unmanageable joke. This is the root of naïve realism. It's not so much an intellectual failing as an emotional sanctuary from existential despair.

It is not, however, necessary.

Is there a danger (or maybe a stupidity) in refusing to accept certain espoused truths are, in fact, straightforwardly true? Yes—if you take such thinking to the absolute extreme. It would be pretty idiotic if I never left my apartment building, based on the remote mathematical possibility that a Komodo dragon might be sitting in the lobby. If my new postman tells me his name is Toby, I don't ask for state-issued identification. But I think there's a greater detriment with our escalating progression toward the opposite extremity—the increasingly common ideology that assures people they're right about what they believe. And note that I used the word "detriment." I did not use the word "danger," because I don't think the notion of people living under the misguided premise that they're right is often *dangerous*. Most day-to-day issues are minor, the passage of time will dictate who was right and who was wrong, and the future will sort out the past. It is, however, *socially detrimental*. It hijacks conversation and aborts ideas. It engenders a delusion of simplicity that benefits people with inflexible minds. It makes the experience of living in a society slightly worse than it should be.

If you write a book about the possibility of collective wrongness in the present day, there are certain questions people ask you the moment you explain what you're doing. Chief among these is, "Are you going to write about climate change?" Now, I elected not to do this, for multiple reasons. The main reason is that the Earth's climate *is* changing, in a documented sense, and that there *is* exponentially more carbon in the atmosphere than at any time in man's history, and that the rise of CO_2 closely corresponds with the rise of global industrialization. Temperature readings and air measurements are not speculative issues. But the more insidious reason I chose not to do this is that I knew doing so would automatically nullify the possibility of writing about any non-polemic ideas even vaguely related to this topic. It would just become a partisan, allegorical battle over what it means to accept (or deny) the central concept of global warming. This is one of those issues where—at least in any public forum—there are only two sides: This is happening and it's going to destroy us (and isn't it crazy that some people still disagree with that), or this is not happening and there is nothing to worry about (and isn't it crazy how people will just believe whatever they're told). There is no intellectual room for the third rail, even if that rail is probably closer to what most people quietly assume: that this is happening, but we're slightly overestimating—or dramatically underestimating—the real consequence. In other words, the climate of the Earth is changing, so life on Earth will change with it. Population centers will shift toward the poles. Instead of getting wheat from Kansas, it will come from Manitoba. The oceans will incrementally rise and engulf the southern tip of Manhattan, so people will incrementally migrate to Syracuse and Albany. The average yearly temperature of London (45 degrees Fahrenheit) might eventually approach the average yearly temperature of Cairo (70.5 degrees), but British society will find a way to subsist within those barren conditions. Or perhaps even the pessimists are too optimistic; perhaps it's already too late, the damage is irrevocable, and humankind's time is finite. The international community has spent the last two decades collectively fixated on reducing carbon emissions, but the percentage of carbon in the atmosphere still continues to increase. Maybe we've already entered the so-called Sixth Extinction and there is no way back. Maybe the only way to stop this from happening would be the immediate, wholesale elimination of all machines that produce carbon, which would equate to the immediate obliteration of all industry, which would generate the same level of chaos we're desperately trying to avoid. Maybe this is how humankind is supposed to end, and maybe the downside to our species' unparalleled cerebral evolution is an ingrained propensity for self-destruction. If a problem is irreversible, is there still an ethical obligation to try to reverse it?

Such a nihilistic question is hard and hopeless, but not without meaning. It needs to be asked. Yet in the modern culture of certitude, such ambivalence has no place in a public conversation. The third rail is the enemy of both poles. Accepting the existence of climate change while questioning its consequence is seen as both an unsophisticated denial of the scientific community and a blind acceptance of the non-scientific status quo. Nobody on either side wants to hear this, because this is something people really, really need to feel right about, often for reasons that have nothing to do with the weather.[1]

---

1 This was validated by several people who read an early draft of this book and advised me to cut the section on climate change entirely, contradicting the advice of my editor (who wanted me to retain it and write even more about the psychology behind people's need to feel right about this particular issue). I ultimately ignored everyone.

[2] There's a phrase I constantly notice on the Internet, particularly after my wife pointed out how incessant it has become. The phrase is, "You're doing it wrong." It started as a meme for photo captions but evolved into something different; it evolved into a journalistic device that immediately became a cliché. A headline about eyewear states, "Hey Contact Wearer, You're Doing It Wrong!" A story about how many people are watching streaming TV shows gets titled "Netflix Ratings: You're Doing It Wrong." *Newsweek* runs a story with the headline "You're 100 Percent Wrong About Showering." *Time* opens a banking story about disgust over ATM fees by stating, "You're doing it wrong: most Americans aren't paying them at all." These random examples all come from the same month, and none are individually egregious. It could be argued that this is simply an expository shortcut, and maybe you think I should appreciate this phrase, since it appears to recognize the possibility that some widely accepted assumption is being dutifully reconsidered. But that's not really what's happening here. Whenever you see something defining itself with the "You're doing it wrong" conceit, it's inevitably arguing for a different approach that is just as specific and limited. When you see the phrase "You're doing it wrong," the unwritten sentence that follows is: *And I'm doing it right.* Which has become the pervasive way to argue about just about everything, particularly in a Web culture where discourse is dominated by the reaction to (and the rejection of) other people's ideas, as opposed to generating one's own.

For a time, *GQ* magazine ran a monthly film column called

"Canon Fodder," where a writer would examine a relatively contemporary movie and assert that it deserves to be considered a classic. Now, this was not exactly a groundbreaking approach to criticism. It's been attempted forever. But the concept still bothered people, mostly for the way the writer, Natasha Vargas-Cooper, framed her mission in the debut essay about *Terminator 2*: "It's an obligation that every generation must take upon itself in order for art to thrive: tear down what's come before and hail our own accomplishments as good enough . . . Let's be untethered from history, ignore the tug of the familiar, and resolve that any movie made before, say, 1986 has received its due respect and move on . . . History does not inform the value of a film; you need never see a stylized Godard flick or Cary Grant comedy to understand the enthralling power of *Fargo* or *Independence Day*. Movies are a mass art and everyone should have opinions on them regardless of if they've seen *The Deer Hunter* or not."

As a premise for a magazine column, this is fine, outside of the suggestion that *Independence Day* isn't complete dog shit. It has been pointed out to me (on two separate occasions) that it seems like something a younger version of myself might have written and believed. But the reason it annoyed certain serious (and self-serious) film consumers was the militancy of the tone, which might have been accidental (although I doubt it). It projects a heavy "You're doing it wrong" vibe. The proposal is not that some modern movies are *also* as good as those defined by prehistoric criteria, but that there is an "obligation" to reinvent the way cinematic greatness is considered. On the surface, it might seem like deliberately ignoring history and focusing on the merit of newer movies would increase our ability to think about the art form. But it actually does the opposite. It multiplies the avenues for small thoughts while annihilating the possibility for big ones. The easiest, most obvious example is (once again) *Citizen Kane*. Could it be argued that *Citizen Kane* has been praised and pondered enough, and that maybe it's time to move on to other concerns? Totally. But doing so eliminates a bunch of debates that will never stop being necessary. Much of the staid lionization of *Citizen Kane* revolves around structural techniques that had never been done before 1941. It is, somewhat famously, the first major movie where the ceilings of rooms are visible to the audience. This might seem like an insignificant detail, but—because no one prior to *Kane* cinematographer Gregg Toland had figured out a reasonable way to get ceilings into the frame—there's an intangible, organic realism to *Citizen Kane* that advances it beyond its time period. Those visible ceilings are a meaningful modernization that twenty-first-century audiences barely notice. It's an advance that raises a whole series of questions: Was it simply a matter of time before this innovation was invented, or did it have to come specifically from Toland (and would it have happened without the specific visual vision of Orson Welles)? And in either case, does the artist who invents something deserve a different level of credit from those who employ that invention later, even if they do so in a more interesting way? Is originality more or less important than we pretend?

Certainly, movies can be critically considered without worrying about these abstractions, just as they can be critically considered without any consideration over the visibility of ceilings. A writer can design whatever obstructions or limitations she desires. But when you do that, you're not really writing about canonical ideas (which wouldn't be a problem, except that this was the premise of the column).

I don't want to pop this too hard, because—having written for glossy magazines (including thousands of words for *GQ*)—I know how this process works. I assume the goal here was to create a film column that immersed itself in movies the mag's audience had directly experienced, so a high-minded reason was constructed to explain why this was being done (and the explanation for that reason was amplified to create a sense of authority). In a completely honest world, the column would have been titled "Here Are Movies We Arbitrarily Want to Write About." But I note it because this particular attempt illustrates a specific mode of progressive wisdom: the conscious decision to replace one style of thinking with a new style of thinking, despite the fact that both styles could easily coexist. I realize certain modes of thinking can become outdated. But outdated modes are essential to understanding outdated times, which are the only times that exist.

[**3**] My DVR automatically records *The McLaughlin Group* every weekend. It airs on Sunday morning in New York, but I tend to watch it on Tuesday or Wednesday night, depending on my desire for escapism. I started watching *The McLaughlin Group* in 1986, as a high school freshman. I've never really stopped. This is a syndicated public affairs program hosted by John McLaughlin, a man who's currently eighty-nine years old and may not be alive by the time this book is published. But I certainly hope he's still around. I want him in my life. There are few things that give me as

much low-stakes pleasure as his weekly TV show. The program bills itself as a political roundtable featuring the "sharpest minds," the "best sources," and the "hardest talk." All three of these statements are patently false, though it's hard to isolate which detail is the most untrue, particularly since "best sources" is willfully unclear[2] and "hardest talk" is wholly ambiguous in any non-pornographic context. The content is ostensibly about Beltway gossip, but it's much closer to wide-angle political science for semi-informed lunatics. My wife refers to *The McLaughlin Group* as *The Yelling Hour*, which is technically incorrect twice—the show is only thirty minutes. But it probably feels like an hour to her.

I cannot overstate the degree to which I love *The McLaughlin Group*. It's not merely older and weirder than the other political shows it inadvertently spawned—it's culturally (and structurally) ancient, and at least three times more entertaining than every show on Fox, MSNBC, and CNN combined. I love it so much that I convinced *Esquire* magazine to let me write a reported column about the production of the show in 2008, the only time in my journalistic career I pitched a story solely to meet the personalities involved. In theory, *The McLaughlin Group* is supposed to be a panel of two conservatives and two liberals, with McLaughlin as the clearheaded moderator. But this doesn't translate, since (a) clearheaded McLaughlin was a speechwriter for Nixon, (b) one of the alleged liberals is often billionaire media mogul Mort Zuckerman, and (c) Pat Buchanan is on almost every single episode (and it

---

2 Are *these particular pundits* the best sources, or do these pundits *know* the best sources? This has never been explained and probably should have been fixed the week after the show first debuted, but they've elected to just stick with the ambiguity for thirty-four years.

would be impossible to find a public figure who's as liberal as Buchanan is conservative, unless they suddenly hired Lena Dunham or Jello Biafra). To say *The McLaughlin Group* sometimes traffics in "outdated modes of thinking" is a little like saying Elon Musk sometimes "expresses interest in the future." But this roundtable forces me to think about things I normally ignore—and not so much about politics, but about the human relationship to time.

The McLaughlin Group pre-tapes its episodes on Friday afternoon. But they tape the show that runs during Thanksgiving weekend much further in advance, which means they have to ignore pressing current events (since something critical or catastrophic could transpire in the days between the taping and the broadcast). Holiday episodes focus on conceptual issues that move slow. In 2015, one of the evergreen Thanksgiving topics was the future of space exploration, specifically as it pertains to the discovery of water on Mars and what that means for NASA. Listening to McLaughlin and Buchanan (who was seventy-seven at the time) debate the conditions of outer space made me feel like my TV had transmogrified into a time machine. My living room became a South Boston dive bar from 1952. It wasn't that they were necessarily wrong about the things they were saying; it was more that even the things they were correct about seemed like points no modern adult would possibly employ in a televised argument. Buchanan kept stressing how all the distant celestial stars are actually alien versions of our own sun, as if this realization was some controversial, game-changing theory. McLaughlin briefly conducted a semantic argument with himself about the correlation between the word "universe" and the word "universal." They could have just as easily debated the future of centaurs. And what I thought while I watched was this: At some point, if you live long enough, it's probably impossible to avoid seeming crazy.

I mean, disregard however you feel about McLaughlin's and Buchanan's politics—it's not like these guys have spent the last sixty years in a cave. McLaughlin has a PhD in philosophy. Buchanan has a master's degree in journalism and once received 450,000 votes for president. Moreover, they've both spent decades mainlining the news and talking about it on TV. They are part of the world, and they are well-paid to be engaged with it. But maybe the world simply changes too much for everyone. I sometimes suspect that—just after the Industrial Revolution—the ongoing evolution of society accelerated beyond the speed human consciousness could evolve alongside it. We superficially accept things that can't be understood or internalized. My grandmother was born before the Wright Brothers' virgin 852-foot flight and died after we'd gone to the moon so many times the public had lost interest. Everything in between happened within her lifetime. It might be unreasonable to expect any normal person to experience this level of constant change without feeling—and maybe without literally *being*—irrefutably nutzo. Consciously trying to keep up with what's happening might actually make things worse.

We spend our lives learning many things, only to discover (again and again) that most of what we've learned is either wrong or irrelevant. A big part of our mind can handle this; a smaller, deeper part cannot. And it's that smaller part that matters more, because that part of our mind is who we really are (whether we like it or not).

[4] Like many little boys, I was maniacally obsessed with sports statistics, perhaps because I was a maniac. I collected copies of *Sports Illustrated*, but I cared about *The Sporting News* way more. I didn't need pictures. I wanted numbers. I wanted to memorize those numbers and recalculate them, despite my palpable disinterest in actual math class. This, I now realize, was a product of my geography and caste. There was no local pro basketball team for most of my childhood, and we did not have cable television. The first nationally televised NBA game of the year would be the All-Star game, and the handful of games that came after always involved at least one of three teams (the Celtics, Lakers, or 76ers). I was able to see only two and a half pro football games a week: whoever the Vikings played at noon, whoever was nationally broadcast at three p.m. (usually the Cowboys), and the first half of the Monday-night contest (because I went to bed at ten p.m.). My relationship to pro sports was mostly built through reading the newspaper, particularly by staring at statistics and imaging how those numbers must have been complied, often by players I would see only once or twice a year. Throughout childhood, I believed statistics were underappreciated by other people. I was obsessed with athletes who I believed deserved to be more famous, based on their statistical production (James Wilder of the Tampa Bay Buccaneers, Lafayette "Fat" Lever of the Denver Nuggets, Eddie Murray of the Baltimore Orioles). When you're a little kid, you feel an almost ethical obligation to root for whoever is best at whatever it is they happen to do; all little kids are

bandwagon front-runners. I felt the adult world was wrong about how they gauged athletic greatness, and that many complicated questions regarding the relative value of various superstars could be easily answered by looking at the Tuesday edition of *USA Today* and comparing one column of digits against another column of digits, even though every announcer on TV seemed to incessantly suggest the opposite. Statistics, my father and Dick Stockton often reminded me, do not tell the real story (and players obsessed with statistics lack integrity).

It has been bizarre—and a little depressing—to see how the culture has inverted itself on this particular issue. There is now a limitless volunteer army of adults who resemble vitriolic versions of my twelve-year-old self. The explosion of analytics has reinvented the way people are supposed to think about sports, even if they don't have any desire to think differently about anything at all. It's way beyond "You're Doing It Wrong." It's more like "How the Fuck Can You Not See That Tobias Harris Is More Efficient Than Carmelo Anthony You Illiterate Fucking Moron Who Is So Obviously Doing It Wrong." There's simply no prick like a math prick in a sports bar. But those sophisticated pricks are, of course, almost[3] always right, at least about measurable events that (a) have

----

3 I insert the word "almost" because there's at least one thing analytics always get wrong: They refuse to acknowledge the existence of "clutch shooting" or "clutch hitting." Math tells us that being "clutch" is a myth, and that the performance of athletes placed in identical "clutch" scenarios will roughly equate with however they'd perform in any normal scenario. This is wrong. For one thing, every "clutch" situation is unique and distinct, so there's no way to compare any two real-life scenarios, even if all the technical details are identical. But the larger reason is that *absolutely everyone* who has played sports *at any level* knows that clutchness is real, to a depth that would make it *become* real (even if it wasn't) for purely psychological reasons. I am not the type who would ever argue

happened in the past or (b) will happen repeatedly ten thousand times in the future. The numeric nature of sports makes it especially well suited for precise, practical analytics. I fully understand why this would be of interest to people who own teams, to coaches looking for an edge, to team executives in charge of balancing a franchise's payroll, and (particularly) to gamblers. It's less clear why this is of interest to normal fans, assuming they watch sports for entertainment.

My adolescent obsession with statistics came from *not* being able to see enough sports, in the same way so many sci-fi writers began as kids who longed to be astronauts. Statistics were a way to imagine games that weren't there. But now there is no game that isn't there. Sometimes there are four televised college football games on a random Thursday evening. I can watch them all, and I watch them to be surprised. Sports are among the increasingly rare moments of totally unscripted television. The human element informs everything, in confounding and inconsistent ways. And since these are *only* games, and since all games are ultimately exhibitions, the stakes are always low. Any opinion is viable. Any argument can be made. It's a free, unreal reality. Yet everything about the trajectory of analytics pushes us away from this. The goal of analytics is to quantify the non-negotiable value of every player and to mathematically dictate which strategic decisions present the highest likelihood of success; the ultimate goal, it seems, would

----

that you can't understand pro basketball if you haven't played pro basketball. That argument is dumb. But you probably do need to have competed in a physical sport somewhere, at some level (even if it was just an especially serious summer of Little League). The recognition that certain people respond better under pressure will happen instantly, and you'll never try to convince yourself otherwise.

be to predict the exact score of every game before it happens and to never be surprised by anything. I don't see this as an improvement. The problem with sports analytics is not that they are flawed; the problem is that they are accurate, to the benefit of almost no one. It's being right for the sake of being right, in a context where there was never any downside to being wrong.

The fact that my twelve-year-old self would have loved this only strengthens my point.

[5] "But isn't that the whole point of this exercise?" you might ask yourself, almost as if I have temporarily rented an apartment inside your skull. "If we won't be alive in a hundred or three hundred or a thousand years, what difference will it make if we're unknowingly wrong about everything, much less anything? Isn't *being right for the sake of being right* pretty much the only possible motive for any attempt at thinking about today from the imagined vantage point of tomorrow? If it turns out that the citizens of 2216 have forgotten the Beatles while remembering the Butthole Surfers, what difference will that make to all the dead people from the twentieth century who never saw it coming? If someone eventually confirms that gravity is only an entropic force, it's not like concrete blocks from the 1920s would retroactively float. The only reason to speculate about the details of a distant future is for the unprovable pleasure of being potentially correct about it now."

Here again, my twelve-year-old self would likely agree. There is, however, more than one way to view this. There is not, in a material sense, any benefit to being right about a future you will

not experience. But there are intrinsic benefits to constantly prob-
ing the possibility that our assumptions about the future might be
wrong: humility and wonder. It's good to view reality as beyond
our understanding, because it is. And it's exciting to imagine the
prospect of a reality that cannot be imagined, because that's as
close to pansophical omniscience as we will ever come. If you
aspire to be truly open-minded, you can't just try to see the other
side of an argument. That's not enough. You have to go all the way.

Over the past ten years, there's been a collective reassessment
of the octopus (this has been happening in the science community
since the 1950s, but it didn't become something civilians adopted
until much more recently). We now realize that octopi can do
amazing things, despite a limited three-year life span that doesn't
provide much time for learning. They can open jars and latches.
They can consider the practicality of foreign objects and test how
such objects could be used to their benefit. At the Seattle Aquarium in 2015, it was reported that an octopus tried to systemati-
cally escape from its own aquarium, prompting a (subsequently
debunked)[4] clickbait story headlined "Shocking Claim: Scientists
Think Octopuses Might Be Aliens After Studying Their DNA."
There's growing evidence that the octopus is far more intelligent
than most people ever imagined, partially because most people
always assumed they were gross, delicious morons. Yet this new
evaluation is still conducted through a myopically human lens.
We classify the octopus as intelligent because of its ability to do
human things, based on the accepted position that we are the most

---

4 A follow-up story on the website Evolution News clarified the rumor with
the story "The Octopus Genome: Not 'Alien,' but Still a Big Problem for
Darwinism."

intelligent species on Earth. What's harder to comprehend is the intelligence of an octopus in a world where they are more intelligent than we are.

This is an old problem, best answered (and maybe even solved) by the philosopher Thomas Nagel in his 1974 essay "What Is It Like to Be a Bat?" For philosophy students, the essay is about the conflict between objectivity and subjectivity, and Nagel's exploration of a bat's consciousness was simply the example he happened to use. But the specifics of "What Is It Like to Be a Bat?" are pertinent to the problem of personification. Nagel asks if it's possible for people to conceive what it's like to be a bat, and his conclusion is that it (probably) is not; we can only conceive what it would be like to be a human who was a bat.[5] For example, bats use echolocation sonar to know what's in front of them (they emit a sound and listen for the returning echo). It's not difficult to imagine humans having echolocation sonar and how that would help us walk through a pitch-black room. That experience can be visualized. But what we can't understand is how that experience informs the consciousness of a bat. We can't even assess what level of consciousness a bat possesses, since the only available barometer for "consciousness" is our own. The interior life of a bat (or an octopus, or any nonhuman creature) is beyond our capacity. And as a society, we are comfortable with not knowing these things— although less comfortable than we were in (say) the nineteenth

----

5 I am, to a degree, reducing (and extrapolating) the complexity and nuance of Nagel's concept. In a note, he writes: "My point, however, is not that we cannot *know* what it is like to be a bat. I am not raising that epistemological problem. My point is rather that even to form a *conception* of what it is like to be a bat, one must take up the bat's point of view. If one can take it up roughly, or partially, then one's conception will also be rough or partial."

century and much less comfortable than we were in (say) the fifteenth century. So imagine that this evolution continues. What would happen if we eventually concluded—for whatever collection of reasons—that our human definition of logic is an inferior variety of intelligence? Humans would still be the Earth's dominant life form, but for reasons that would validate our worst fears about humanity.

For a little under three years, I wrote an advice column called "The Ethicist" for *The New York Times Magazine*. It was a job that was easy to do poorly but difficult to do well. The risks were greater than the rewards. But I always enjoyed fielding the questions, and my favorite came late in my tenure. It involved Koko, a gorilla living in the San Francisco Zoo who was renowned for her use of sign language and the intimate relationship she shares with her handlers. The reader's query focused on the suicide of comedic actor Robin Williams. Koko had met Williams, once, in 2001, and they evidently had an excellent rapport. According to press reports, Koko cried when informed of Williams's 2014 death. The writer of the question wanted to know if there was any moral purpose in making a gorilla depressed over the suicide of a person she met only once, fifteen years prior.

The ethical ramifications of this act certainly matter. But they don't matter nearly as much as the scenario itself, were we somehow able to prove that it was real.

From the perspective of a human, the whole story seems a tad specious. At worst, it looks like an exploitative publicity stunt by the zoo; at best, it seems like a smart gorilla might adopt the characteristics of sadness anytime her handlers suggested that she had something to be sad about. Moreover, the alternative possibilities in-between are fucking bananas. Since Koko is a gorilla, there is no way she can comprehend the concept of "celebrity" (which would mean either she deduced something about Williams that's alien to her own species or she remembers every person she's ever met, even if they met only once). Would this mean that apes empathize with all other animals equally? How would a gorilla know what death is, or what suicide is, or that death is sad, or that she, too, will die? These are unthinkable abstractions to apply to a creature with the cognitive faculties of a three-year-old human toddler. But when I said that to veterinarian Vint Virga, the respected pro-animal author of *The Souls of All Living Creatures*, he told me my view was too locked into a simplistic conception of intellect (and that it would be unethical *not* to tell Koko about the passing of Williams).

"I would set aside the issue of the animal's cognitive intelligence and focus on the concept of an animal's emotional intelligence, which studies continue to show is much greater than we ever previously imagined," says Virga. "Animals and humans both experience joy and sadness throughout their life. Why would you want to shelter a gorilla from that experience? I believe a gorilla absolutely has the ability to understand the loss of someone who was important to her, and animals are often able to deal with grieving and loss much more effectively than humans."

Let's assume that Virga is not only correct, but underselling his correctness. Let's imagine deeper neurological research shows an inherent inverse relationship between logical intelligence and emotional intelligence, and that mammalian species strong in the former category (i.e., people) tend to be weak in the latter category. Let's also assume that the standard perception of what makes any given person *intelligent* continues to shift. As recently as the 1980s, the idea of "emotional intelligence" was not taken seriously, particularly by men; today, most professions regard it as important as any scholastic achievement. In a hundred years, qualitative intelligence might be unilaterally prioritized over quantitative aptitude. So if humankind decides that emotional intelligence is really what matters while simultaneously concluding that nonhuman species are superior to humans in this specific regard . . . society would adopt a highly uncomfortable imbalance. I mean, the relationship between man and beast wouldn't really change. Humans would remain the dominant species. But that dominance would (suddenly) appear to derive exclusively from brute force. It would essentially derive from the combination of opposable thumbs and a self-defined "inferior" brand of intellect that places us in a better position to kill and control our rivals.[6] This actuality would swap the polarity of existence. The current belief (among the animal rights community) is that humans are responsible for the welfare of animals and that we must protect them. Our apex slot in the intellectual hierarchy forces us to think on behalf of animals, since they cannot think for themselves. Their innocence is childlike. But if animals are actually more intelligent than humans—and if we were all to *agree* that they are, based on our own criteria for what constitutes an intelligent being—it would mean that our sovereignty was founded on mental weakness and empathetic failure. It would mean the undeniable success of humankind is just a manifestation of our own self-defined stupidity.

Would this change the world? It would not. This is not a

---

6 I suppose some might argue this is already true.

relationship that can be switched. The world would continue as it is. We would not elect a cat as president, or even as comptroller. But this would be a helluva thing to be wrong about, and maybe a good thing to pretend we're wrong about (just in case).

[**6**] In the early pages of this book (that you are about to finish), I refer to the writer and critic Kathryn Schulz, based on her publication of *Being Wrong* and her role as a book critic for *New York* magazine. In the gap between my interviewing her and writing this sentence, Schulz published an article for *The New Yorker* that received roughly as much attention as everything else she'd done in her entire career. The article, headlined "The Really Big One," was about the Cascadia Subduction Zone, a fault line running through the Pacific Northwest. The story's takeaway was that it's merely a matter of time before the tectonic plates abutting along this fault line will rupture, generating an earthquake with a magnitude in the vicinity of 9.0, followed by a massive tsunami that will annihilate the entire region. According to multiple researchers, the likelihood of a significant Pacific Northwest earthquake happening in the next fifty years is one in three. The likelihood that it will be "the really big one" is one in ten. FEMA projects that such an event would kill thirteen thousand people. The story's most memorable quote came from the region's FEMA director, Kenneth Murphy: "Our operating assumption is that everything west of I-5 will be toast."

The timing of this story was not ideal. I realize there's no "ideal time" for information about a killer earthquake, but this one was problematic for personal reasons. Over the past two years, my wife and I have been talking about moving to Portland, Oregon, where my wife was born and raised. Her childhood home sits twenty-five miles west of I-5 (although I doubt the earthquake would actually use a road atlas when deciding which areas to devastate). Whenever we mention the possibility of relocating to Portland to anyone who reads magazines or listens to NPR or lives in New York, we are now asked, "But aren't you worried about the earthquake?" My standard response equates to some rambling version of "Kind of, but not really." It's not something I think about, except when I'm writing this book. Then I think about it a lot.

This is, at its core, a question about the security of our informed imagination. In one sense, thinking about this earthquake is like thinking about climate change. It's not really speculative: Tectonic plates shift, and—eventually—these plates will, too. The part that's unknown is the timing and the specific consequence. In another sense, our move (and the thinking behind that move) becomes a You're Doing It Wrong proposition: The existence of an article about an event doesn't increase the chance that the event will happen; the seismic danger of living in Portland right now is the same as it was five years ago. The article could likewise be seen as another example of unhelpful analytics: Though I'm confident the mathematical odds of this earthquake's transpiring in my lifetime are roughly one in three (or, for the worst-case scenario, one in ten), the validity of those calculations has no practical or instructional application, outside of my knowing what they supposedly are.[7] Most significant, it's also an illustration of the limits

----

7 If there's a 10 percent chance an event that might kill 13,000 people will occur in a region with a population of 8 million residents, am I really in that much

of my mind and the tenacity of my own naïve realism: Perhaps I'm just not able to intellectually accept the inevitability of an event I can't comprehend, so I'm fixating on a geographic risk I know about without considering all the rival risks that have yet to be discovered or written about in periodicals.

The future is always impossible.

But, you know, at least we're used to it.

In 2005, Indiana senator Richard Lugar surveyed eighty-five national security experts about the possibility of a nuclear detonation "somewhere in the world." They placed the odds of an attack within the next ten years at around 29 percent. Ten years have now elapsed, and it doesn't seem like such a scenario was ever particularly close to coming to fruition. Yet as we continue to look forward, it *always* seems plausible. In 2010, CBS did a story on the possibility of nuclear terrorism. Martin Hellman, a professor emeritus at Stanford (specializing in engineering and cryptography), estimated that the odds of this event increase about 1 percent every year and will approach 40 percent in five decades. Certainly, there's a logic ladder here that's hard to refute. An organization like ISIS would love to possess a nuclear weapon, and the potential availability of nuclear technology is proliferating. Everything we know about the group's ethos suggests that if ISIS were to acquire such a weapon, they would want to use it immediately. If the target wasn't Israel or France, the target would be the United States. Based on common sense and recent history, the two cities most likely to be attacked would be New York and Washington, D.C. So

----

danger? Is anyone? Are those odds better or worse than the possibility that I'll have a heart attack?

if I believe that a nuclear weapon will be detonated in my lifetime (which seems probable), and I believe it will happen on US soil (which seems possible), and I live in New York (which I do), I'm consciously raising my family in one of the few cities where I suspect a nuclear weapon is likely to be utilized. Based on this rationale, it would make way more sense for me to move to Portland, where there's only a 10 percent chance we'll drown in a tsunami.

But I don't think like this, except when I'm trying to make a point about how this is not the way I usually think. Instead, I think about whether Jon Franzen will get over, or how people who no longer watch television will remember what television was, or if I'll still be able to follow the Dallas Cowboys as I deteriorate in an assisted living facility. I think about a future that is totally different, yet unambiguously familiar; people are still walking around and arguing about art and politics and generating the same recycled realizations that every emerging demographic inevitably consumes as new. Do I believe our current assumption about how the present will eventually be viewed is, in all probability, acutely incorrect? Yes. And yet I imagine this coming wrongness to resemble the way society has always been wrong about itself, since the beginning of time. It's almost like I'm showing up at the Kentucky Derby and insisting the two-to-one favorite won't win, but refusing to make any prediction beyond "The winner will probably be a different horse."

Somebody once told me a joke about meteorology. (It's the kind of joke that somebody's dad would put on Facebook.) The premise is that we've been trying to predict the weather since 3000 BC. The yearly budget for the National Weather Service is $1 billion, which doesn't even include all the costs incurred by privately funded meteorological institutions and the military and local TV stations and every other organization with a vested interest in predicting what the unexperienced world will be like. Even a conservative estimate places the annual amount of money spent on meteorology at somewhere around $5 billion. And as a result of this investment, our weather can be correctly predicted around 66 percent[8] of the time. As a society, we can go two out of three. Yet if some random dude simply says, "I think the weather tomorrow will be the same as the weather today," he will be right 33 percent of the time. He can go one for three. So we've invested hundreds of billions of dollars and countless hours into meteorological research, with the net effect of becoming twice as accurate as some bozo who looks out a window and points at the sky. (And that's the joke.) I assume this joke is supposed to be a commentary on governmental waste, or an anti-intellectual criticism of science, or proof that nobody knows anything. It might be all of those things. But I don't care about any of that jazz. I just want the bozo to get lucky. I want the weather to stay the same. I'm ready for a new tomorrow, but only if it's pretty much like yesterday.

----

8 I have no idea where that specific figure comes from, or what constitutes a "correct" weather prediction. Based on my own unscientific sense of the world, I feel like weather forecasters are roughly correct a little more often, even in Ohio. But remember, this is allegedly a joke. Do not cite this in your term paper.

Acknowledgments

The first person I must thank is Melissa Maerz, without whom nothing else is possible.

The second person is researcher Dmitry Kiper, the person who helps me find things I need to find.

Next on the list is affable Brant Rumble, followed by dogged Daniel Greenberg. I'd also like to express appreciation to everyone at Blue Rider Press (particularly David Rosenthal, Aileen Boyle, and Anna Jardine) for making this book exist, along with all the folks back at Scribner who put me in this position to begin with.

I sincerely appreciate everyone I've interviewed over the past eighteen months for providing their time and intelligence. I'd like to acknowledge everyone whose work is specifically cited in this book (for having conceived of ideas I could merely replicate). I must also express gratitude to all the interesting people who helped me without even knowing it, particularly James Burke (creator of the documentary series *The Day the Universe Changed*), Jim Holt (author of *Why Does the*

World Exist?), and George Harrison (for *All Things Must Pass* and *Living in the Material World*).

The following fine people read versions of this manuscript and provided feedback directly reflected in the text: Jon Dolan, Jennifer Raftery, Mat Sletten, Bob Ethington, Sean Howe, David Giffels, Rex Sorgatz, Ben Heller, Rob Sheffield, Brian Raftery, Greg Milner, Michael Weinreb, Willy Staley, Phoebe Reilly, Aja Pollock.

I would also like to thank my mom, because I can never thank her enough.

A final note about hedgehogs: In "The Case Against Freedom," I spend a few pages describing a period of my life when I watched a hedgehog from the balcony of my Akron apartment. It turns out there is a problem with this memory—hedgehogs are not native to North America. Whatever was chomping apples outside my window must have been either a groundhog or a woodchuck (although it was definitely *something*). I have to assume this is not a well-known fact, since I've been telling this anecdote for almost two decades and not one person has ever remarked, "Hey idiot—don't you realize there are no hedgehogs in Ohio?" That said, I've never dated an Erinaceidae zoologist. I'm (very slightly) embarrassed by all this, since I based an entire chapter around a metaphor I did not technically experience. But there was no practical solution to this contradiction, outside of re-naming this book *But What If We're Wrong? Thinking About Woodchucks As If They Were Hedgehogs*. Chuck Klosterman regrets the error.

Index

Index

Index

Index

Index

Lennon, John, 60*n*, 67*n*, 86
Lethem, Jonathan, 86–87
Lewis, Jerry Lee, 60*n*, 79
Lewis, Sinclair, 92
lies and untruths, 154–57
life after death, 11–12
Limbaugh, Rush, 185
Lincoln, Abraham, 24, 96, 173*n*, 218
Linklater, Richard, 139–44, 150–51
literature, criticism of, 7–8, 10
London Review of Books, 151
lucid dreaming, 137, 141
Lugar, Richard, 260

MacCambridge, Michael, 181
machines, and attempts to kill people, 227
Mad Men (TV show), 164–65
Madison, James, 207, 210
Mahler, Jonathan, 152
Man Without a Country, A (Vonnegut), 43
Manhattan, attack on police in, 150–51
marching music, 64–65
marginalization, 41–42, 81
Marley, Bob, 65
Marlowe, Christopher, 94
"Mathematics of the Past" (Kasparov), 136
Mathog, Mike, 109*n*
Matrix, The (film), 28–30, 122*n*, 227
Maugham, W. Somerset, 31
Mayweather–Pacquiao fight (2015), 187
McCarley, Robert, 138
McCartney, Paul, 67
McLaughlin, John, 245–48
McLaughlin Group, The (TV show), 245–47
media alienation, 47–48
Meltzer, Richard, 61
Melville, Herman, 7–9, 21–22, 31–32
memory, 150–51, 230
Mencken, H. L., 233
merit, 89–94
Metamorphosis, The (Kafka), 36
Miami Herald, The, 234*n*
Millay, Edna St. Vincent, 93
Moby-Dick (Melville), 7–10, 21–22
modern verification process, 154–55
Mondale, Walter, 204
monomyth (hero's journey), 74
Moore, Michael, 197
morality, 126–28
Moravec, Hans, 121
Morozov, Nikolai, 135
movies. *See* film industry
Mozart, Wolfgang Amadeus, 72, 73
multiverse hypothesis, 103–5, 119–20

music
  author's qualifications as a critic, 95–96
  blues, 81
  classical, 72, 73
  critics' role, 78–79
  decline in interest, 63–64
  dominance of single artist, 64–66
  electronic dance music (EDM), 79
  for extraterrestrials, 83–84
  finding the best example of a genre,
    85–87
  industry, 14*n*
  marching, 64–65
  1920s, 77
  punk-vs.-disco divide of the 1970s,
    79–80
  records and LPs, 19–20, 81, 83–84
  repurposing rock songs, 62–63
  rock, 14, 60–87, 92*n*, 95, 161
  rock and roll, 59–60, 68, 74, 82, 86.
    See also rock music
  rock 'n' roll, 59–60, 72, 78, 82, 85, 159.
    See also rock music
  skiffle, 161
My Struggle: Book 2 (Knausgaard), 213
myth of universal timeliness, 44–45

Nagel, Thomas, 254
naïve realism, 10–11, 34, 116, 239
NASA, 83–84, 118–19
Nashville (TV show), 170, 171*n*
National Football League (NFL), 180–81,
    182–83
Native American population, 41–42
Navy SEALs, and assassination of bin
    Laden, 151
near-death experiences, 141–42
Neptune, discovery of, 109
Never Mind the Bollocks (album), 79–80
Nevermind (album), 92*n*
New Musical Express (*NME*), 79
New Republic, The, 154*n*, 235
New York magazine, 217
New York Times, The, 25, 26, 150–51, 154*n*
New York Times Magazine, The, 22–23,
    152, 255
New Yorker, The, 177, 189, 258
Newton, Isaac, 3–4, 5–6, 105, 108–9, 110,
    112, 149
Newton's Third Law, 119
Niemitz, Hans-Ulrich, 134
9/11 attacks, 11, 18*n*, 199
Nirvana, 70, 92*n*
Nixon, Richard, 186

Index

"normal science," 115–16
"now," perpetual sense of, 232
nuclear weapons, 260–61
numerical constants, 124–25, 130
Nussbaum, Emily, 164

Obama, Barack, 1, 217–18
objective ranking, 94
Occam's Razor, 17
octopuses, 253–54
Odd Clauses, The (Wexler), 208
Ohio, 196–97
"On Colors" (Aristotle), 111
On the Genealogy of Color (Adams), 148
"100 Notable Books" (*The New York Times*, 2014), 25–27
"100 Notable Books" (*The New York Times*, 2015), 26n
Oswald, Lee Harvey, 17
outdated thinking, 247
overthinking, 39

Page, Jimmy, 85
Pakistan, and assassination of bin Laden, 151
paradigm shifts in science, 114–15, 117–18, 120–21
Particle Fever (film), 130–31
patriotism, 219
persecution, cultural, 187–88
Pet Rocks, 182
Petrusich, Amanda, 80–82
Phantom Time Hypothesis, 134–37
    Dark Ages, 145
    evidence against, 135–36
    "major theory," 135
    "minor theory," 134
    New Chronology, 135
    role of historical figures, 135
    Russia, centrality of, 136
physics, 108, 110–11, 113–14, 130–31
Physics (Aristotle), 5
Piper, "Rowdy" Roddy, 234
Plato, 215, 219
poetry, 93–94
political polarization, 198–99
Polybius of Megalopolis, 157n
popular, how things become, 182
Portland, Oregon, 259, 261
predictions
    author's, 1–2, 182
    making, 49
presidencies
    color or religion as non-issue, 217–18

judging and ranking, 203–6, 218–19
    Obama's legacy, 217–18
presidential election (2000), 197–98
Presley, Elvis, 74–77
pressure, responding to, 250n
Pride and Prejudice (Austen), 45
probability, 109–10
proof, scientific, 120, 135–36
public opinion
    on football, 184
    influenced by name recognition, 90–92
    on unfamiliar subject, 90–91
punk music, 79–80

quantum mechanics, 4, 105, 107, 120

radio, and incomparability to television, 160n
Radiohead, 66, 73
Radiolab (radio show), 190–91
Rage Against the Machine, 197–98
Reagan, Ronald, 79, 203–5, 235
Real Sports (TV show), 185
Real World, The (TV show), 170
reality TV, 169–70
realization of a simulated world, 126–28
"Really Big One, The" (Schulz), 258–59
relevance of written work, 45–47
Republic, The (Plato), 215
respect for past classic works, 243–45
Rest Is Noise, The (Ross), 73
retrospective insight, 14–17
reversals of scientific opinions, 3–7, 97–98
Revolution Was Televised, The (Sepinwall), 164
Revolver (album), 67
Rhodes, Dusty, 234–35
Richards, Keith, 85
Riddle, Nelson, 78
risks, calculating, 258–61
Road, The (McCarthy), 47–48
rock music, 14, 60–87, 92n, 95, 161
    "Albums of the Year" list (*SPIN*), 92
    authority of youth over age, 69
    Chuck Berry as the epitome of, 85–86
    limitations and demise of, 63, 68–69
    monomyth of, 74–77
    "Rock is dead" assertion, 61–64
    "Southern rock," 85n
    style vs. substance, 75–76
    subgenres, 60–61, 66–67
    subjectivity of appreciation, 72–73
rock music vs. rock 'n' roll music, 60–61

Index